The Economic Payoff
from the Internet Revolution

BROOKINGS TASK FORCE ON THE INTERNET

The Economic Payoff from the Internet Revolution

ROBERT E. LITAN

ALICE M. RIVLIN

Editors

INTERNET POLICY INSTITUTE

BROOKINGS INSTITUTION PRESS

Washington, D.C.

ABOUT BROOKINGS

The Brookings Institution is a private nonprofit organization devoted to research, education, and publication on important issues of domestic and foreign policy. Its principal purpose is to bring knowledge to bear on current and emerging policy problems. The Institution maintains a position of neutrality on issues of public policy. Interpretations or conclusions in Brookings publications should be understood to be solely those of the authors.

Library of Congress Cataloging-in-Publication data
The economic payoff from the internet revolution / Robert E. Litan and
    Alice M. Rivlin, editors.
        p.   cm.
Brookings Task Force on the Internet.
Includes bibliographical references and index.
    ISBN 0-8157-0065-2 (pbk. : alk. paper)
        1. Technological innovations—Economic aspects.   2. Business
enterprises—Computer network resources.   3. Internet.   4. Evolutionary
economics.   I. Litan, Robert E., 1950–   II. Rivlin, Alice M.   III. Brookings Task
Force on the Internet.
    HC79.T4 E25283 2001   2001002503
    330.9—dc21   CIP

9 8 7 6 5 4 3 2 1

The paper used in this publication meets minimum requirements of the
American National Standard for Information Sciences—Permanence of Paper for
Printed Library Materials, ANSI Z39.48-1992.

Typeset in Adobe Garamond

Composition by R. Lynn Rivenbark
Macon, Georgia

Printed by R. R. Donnelley and Sons
Harrisonburg, Virginia

Foreword

THE INTERNET REVOLUTION has been one of the most remarked-on events of recent times. In a short period, the Internet has blossomed from an infrastructure used primarily by university and government scientists and other academic scholars into a nearly ubiquitous presence in the lives of more than half of all Americans and hundreds of millions more users around the world. Although constantly revised, virtually all projections indicate continued rapid growth in the penetration of the "Net" throughout the rest of the world's population and in the way it is used by businesses and individuals alike.

Given its relatively young age, it is not surprising that there has been little quantitative study of the economic impact of the Internet. This book is one of the first comprehensive efforts at changing that situation. Led by Robert Litan and Alice Rivlin, the Brookings Institution convened scholars from various distinguished universities in the United States to apply their analytical tools, experience, and insights to form their best judgments about the likely economic impact of the Internet in eight sectors of the U.S. economy through the year 2005. Collectively, these sectors account for about 70 percent of the value added of the U.S. economy and thus provide a broad sample on which to make reasoned projections.

The members of the Brookings Internet Task Force, as the convened group came to be called, were asked for their informed judgment because the Internet is too new to be subject to traditional statistical analysis. The analysts also were asked to limit their time horizons to five years—the study was launched in the year 2000—because the way in which the Internet is used, as well as the economic and legal landscape in which it is situated, change too rapidly to permit defensible projections even further into the future. The authors projected economic impact in terms of estimated cost reductions and hence improvements in productivity growth. However, as they point out, the Internet is expected to deliver significant nonquantifiable benefits, including enhanced convenience and wider opportunities for product and service customization that are not captured by the quantitative estimates provided in the book.

The preliminary findings reported in this book were presented at a conference held at the U.S. Department of Commerce in September 2000 and jointly sponsored by Commerce, the Berkeley Roundtable on the International Economy, and the Organization for Economic Cooperation and Development. The various chapters were revised thereafter, taking into consideration comments at the conference and suggestions by the task force leaders.

Robert Litan is the vice president and director of Economic Studies and Alice Rivlin is a senior fellow at Brookings. Both are grateful to all of the other members of the task force (listed on a subsequent page) for their willingness to tackle the difficult assignments that made up this project and for their diligence and hard work in completing them. They also wish to thank the Internet Policy Institute for its advice and financial support of the project. The project could not have been completed without the superb research assistance of Steve Baron and Samara Potter; the editing of Marty Gottron, Tanjam Jacobson, and Janet Walker; the organizational assistance provided by Alicia Jones; and the verification services of Debra Hevenstone. In addition, Carlotta Ribar proofread the final pages and Shirley Kessel provided an index.

The views expressed in this book are those of the authors and should not be ascribed anyone whose assistance is acknowledged here or later in the volume, to the organizations that supported the project, or to the trustees, officers, staff members of the Brookings Institution or the Internet Policy Institute.

MICHAEL H. ARMACOST   KIMBERLY JENKINS
President, Brookings Institution   *President, Internet Policy Institute*

Washington, D.C.
June 2001

Contents

The Economic Payoff
from the Internet Revolution

1

ROBERT E. LITAN
ALICE M. RIVLIN

The Economy and the Internet: What Lies Ahead?

USE OF THE INTERNET has exploded in a very few years. Tens of millions of Americans e-mail each other daily at home and at work. Businesses use the net to transmit information to employees, find suppliers, contact customers, and file taxes. Individuals of all ages use the net to stay in touch with friends and relatives, do homework, express their opinions, pay bills, or just explore the infinite varieties of information and entertainment that can be found there.

In short, the Internet has had an unquestionable and pervasive impact on the way Americans communicate and spend time—an impact that is certain to grow. But the effect of the Internet on the performance of the economy and the future standard of living of average Americans is far more uncertain and controversial.

—Is the net just a new way to communicate—an alternative to phone or fax or airmail—and thus not likely to have a fundamental impact on the functioning of the economy?

—What does it mean for the importance of the Internet that investors were willing to pour billions into Internet companies with dubious earnings in the late 1990s only to find many of them virtually worthless by the end of 2000?

—Or will the Internet prove to be a major economic phenomenon, significantly increasing productivity and enhancing the prosperity of average wage earners?

—Similarly, will the net alter the structure of industries and the size of companies, while enriching the variety of products and services available to consumers and their ease in obtaining them?

This volume has been written to help answer these questions. It contains detailed analyses of how the Internet is likely to affect the economic performance of eight sectors of the U.S. economy during at least the next five years. These eight sectors collectively account for more than 70 percent of gross domestic product (GDP). Initial drafts of the chapters that follow were presented at a two-day conference held in Washington, D.C., in late September 2000, jointly sponsored by the Internet Policy Institute, the Brookings Institution, the Berkeley Roundtable for the International Economy, the U.S. Department of Commerce, and the Organization for Economic Cooperation and Development. The authors have since revised their analyses to take account of the discussion at this conference, and the final results are reflected here.

The eight papers in this volume focus primarily on the impact of the Internet on productivity growth, which is the engine of improvement in living standards. In particular, the authors ask whether the Internet will contribute significantly to the chances that U.S. productivity growth will continue to outperform—as it has for the past five years—the relatively disappointing performance of the 1973–95 period, when productivity grew by roughly 1.5 percent a year. If the answer is yes, the papers then ask how much productivity enhancement reasonably can be expected from the net. A companion volume of papers, sponsored by the Berkeley Roundtable for the International Economy and published by Brookings, explores the impact of the Internet on the structure of American industries.[1]

Adding up the projections of the authors in this study yields the conclusion that the Internet does have the potential to add significantly to productivity growth in the United States over the next few years—as much as 0.25 to 0.50 percent a year. These may not look like large numbers, but to productivity specialists, they are significant figures. If continued over a decade, they imply that average living standards will be 2.5–5 percent

1. BRIE Task Force (2001).

higher than they otherwise might be. In monetary terms, that would translate into additional income per person of roughly $1,250–$2,500 by 2010.

We cannot emphasize too strongly that the productivity enhancements attributable to the net, however large they turn out to be, do not depend on a resurgence of companies devoted to e-commerce—the so-called "dot.coms." The improvements identified here result from the application of networked computing—both from "intranets" and the Internet itself—to business activities carried out in companies devoted to such "old economy" activities as manufacturing, transportation, financial services, and conventional retailing. Major cost savings resulting from Internet use in the government and health sectors are also likely to contribute to productivity growth, although positive impacts of the Internet on productivity in education will probably be felt further in the future.

Some of the effects of the Internet on productivity will flow from cost reductions in standard products and will be relatively easy to measure. Others will come in the form of new products and services and a wider variety of consumer choices—benefits that are difficult to measure with conventional economic statistics.

In this introductory chapter we try to identify some of the common themes that cut across the sectors, briefly summarize the findings of the authors, and offer our own interpretation of what it all adds up to—some very tentative conclusions about the impact of the Internet on the productivity of the economy as a whole over the next few years. We begin by explaining why these projections, uncertain as they are, matter to all Americans, whether they are employed in the "new" or "old" economic sectors, and to policymakers who are charged with the responsibility for managing the economy.

Why Projections of Productivity Growth Matter

Asking experts of any type to project the future is always hazardous. It is especially tricky when the subject is changing as rapidly as the Internet, which as a commercial proposition is less than a decade old (dating from the invention of the browser).

Nonetheless, peering into the future is a job that individuals in both the public and private sectors must do, because they have no other basis on which to make needed decisions. The Federal Reserve, for example, is charged with setting monetary policy that will keep the economy growing at its highest sustainable rate. To determine what monetary policy is appropriate (in practice, what short-term interest rates ought to be), the Fed must estimate, among other things, the *potential* growth rate of the economy— how fast the economy can grow at full employment without serious risk of accelerating inflation. When the economy is close to or at full employment and growing faster than its potential growth rate, the Fed is likely to feel compelled to raise interest rates, as it did several times between 1999 and 2000 (and before that, in 1994). The aim is to slow the growth down to a sustainable rate (the potential rate) and thereby reduce the risk that tightness in labor markets will push up wages faster than productivity and thus ignite an acceleration of inflation. Conversely, if economic growth falls short of potential, the Fed is likely to lower interest rates in order to stimulate faster growth (as it began to do in early 2001, when indicators pointed to a more rapid slowdown than had been expected in the fall of 2000).

The president and Congress also need estimates of the potential growth rate of the economy when formulating both near-term and long-term budget policy. In the near term a particular change in the budget deficit or surplus may be appropriate or inappropriate depending on whether the economy is expected to be growing above its potential or lagging below it. For example, if the economy is at full employment and growing faster than its potential, additional stimulation from a growing budget deficit (or declining surplus) will increase the risk of inflation. If, however, the economy has underutilized resources and is growing below its potential, the additional stimulation will likely produce additional jobs and income but little additional inflation.

There is controversy among economists and policymakers over whether budget policy can be used effectively to offset the ups and downs of the business cycle, since the length of time required to enact and implement tax and spending changes may result in their having unintended and perverse effects. In general, monetary policy is a more flexible tool for stabilizing the economy.

There is no doubt, however, that the president and Congress should consider the impact of their tax and spending actions on the structural deficit or surplus in the federal budget over the longer run. It makes a lot of difference to the future vitality of the economy whether the government runs sustained deficits and piles up debt for the future, or, alternatively, whether it runs surpluses, reduces the national debt, and releases savings to be invested in private sector growth. Calculations of the impact of current budget actions on future deficits or surpluses in the federal budget depend heavily on estimates of the potential growth rate of the economy.

What determines the economy's potential growth rate? The answer to that question is simpler to state than to estimate: the anticipated growth in the labor force plus the projected growth in labor productivity, or the efficiency of workers. Because population growth and the proportion of the population that is in the labor force are reasonably stable, future labor force growth is relatively easy to project; in the United States it is generally projected to be about 1 percent a year for the next decade or more. The much harder, but more important, challenge is to project the growth rate of labor productivity.

Productivity growth forecasts are important not only to policymakers, but also to individuals and firms. For individuals, faster productivity growth means faster growth in compensation and thus living standards. Firms making long-term investment plans need to project productivity growth because that will determine the economy's purchasing power in the years ahead. For the public sector, meanwhile, faster growth in productivity means a larger tax base and more resources available to improve public services or to cut taxes or both. As noted earlier, the size of future federal budget surpluses, whose use was a major issue in the 2000 presidential campaign, is greatly influenced by the magnitude of future productivity growth.

Unfortunately, economists understand less than they would like about how to project the growth in productivity. Productivity growth depends, in part, on the rate at which firms invest in new plant and equipment—and, in recent times, in information technology (IT). Even more important, productivity growth is determined by the pace at which new ideas are commercialized in new products and services, a trend that is affected by accumulated past investments in research and development, both by the private and public sectors, but that is inherently unpredictable.

Productivity growth trends have fluctuated widely since World War II, and these variations have been neither anticipated nor well explained. From 1945 until 1973 labor productivity grew at roughly 2.5 percent annually, a pace that enabled the standard of living of the average American to double about every thirty years. From 1973 to 1995 annual productivity growth slowed dramatically, to 1.4 percent. Analysts pointed to various culprits that might have accounted for the slowdown—higher energy prices (but this explanation became less convincing when oil prices fell sharply after the early 1980s yet productivity growth stayed low), the influx

of untrained baby boomers into the work force (but this became less per-
suasive as they gained experience), variable rates of inflation that allegedly
deterred investment, increases in regulation, and so on. No definitive case,
however, has been made for any combination of these explanations.

The slow growth of productivity—and associated slow growth in average incomes—persisted for more than two decades. Then, in the mid-
1990s, just when most economists were resigned to enduring a permanent
"Age of Diminished Expectations"—the title of one of Princeton economist Paul Krugman's many books—productivity growth soared, averaging
close to 3 percent a year in 1996–2000, an outcome virtually no one anticipated, either inside or outside government.

Although no one fully understands why productivity growth slowed
down after 1973, several studies have shed a lot of light on the reasons for
the dramatic pickup in productivity growth since 1995. One source is
clear: dramatic improvement in the speed and thus the quality of computer chips, which has driven significant improvements in the computer
hardware industry in particular.[2] Until recently economists were more
divided over whether the information technology revolution has significantly enhanced productivity growth *outside* the computer industry. But
recent evidence reported by the President's Council of Economic Advisers
indicates a fairly strong correlation between industry productivity growth
since the mid-1990s and the IT intensity of investments, suggesting that
IT has been helping to improve productivity throughout the economy.[3] In
fact, it would be a surprise if this were not the case. Spending on IT equipment and software accounted for almost half of equipment investment by
the end of the 1990s (up from 42 percent in 1992).[4] Although the computer and telecommunications revolutions began earlier, they apparently
did not have enough impact on business processes, practices, and organization to show up in aggregate productivity growth until the second half of
the 1990s. The macroeconomic conditions of the late 1990s—tight labor
markets, low inflation, and fierce global competition—also encouraged
firms to use the new technologies as a way of economizing on labor while
surviving in an increasingly competitive marketplace.

The big question is whether the recent rapid pace of productivity
growth will continue. Official government forecasts suggest it will, but not

2. Gordon (2000); Oliner and Sichel (2000); Jorgenson and Stiroh (2000).
3. Council of Economic Advisers (2001).
4. U.S. Department of Commerce (2000).

quite. The latest long-term budget projections of the Congressional Budget Office—the official budget scorekeeper for congressional expenditure and tax policies—show labor productivity growing at about 2.5 percent through 2010, somewhat slower than the torrid 3 percent pace during the 1995–2000 period, but faster than the earlier projections of just 2 percent growth. The recent estimates implicitly reflect some optimism that the Internet will contribute to strong productivity performance in the years ahead. This volume examines the potential for realizing those hopes.

What We Asked the Authors to Do

If the objective is to understand how and to what extent the Internet will affect productivity growth, then examining aggregate economic statistics will not provide meaningful answers. That is because the Internet is too new and too small a part of the total economy. The volume of e-commerce is currently only about $100 billion–$200 billion. There just is not enough historical aggregate data yet to allow economists to use conventional statistical techniques to explain how the Internet has affected the economy in the past—let alone enough to serve as a basis for making projections into the future.

We therefore decided that the best way to gather clues about the future impact of the Internet was to ask experts on particular sectors of the economy to examine how the Internet was being used in leading-edge firms or institutions in these sectors; what its impact on cost, prices, and productivity appeared to be; and how rapidly it might spread to other parts of the sector. The authors were asked to present enough background on the recent history and structure of their sector to give the reader a context for understanding their projections. In the most daunting part of the assignment, the authors were asked to provide their best estimates as to how the Internet might alter productivity in their sector over the next five years or so.

These tasks were extremely challenging, and all of the authors protested that the Internet was such a new tool and its use evolving so rapidly that their estimates should not be construed as more than tentative guesses. Nevertheless, taken together, their work clearly indicates that the Internet has the *potential* to increase productivity growth in a variety of distinct, but mutually reinforcing ways:

—by significantly reducing the cost of many transactions necessary to produce and distribute goods and services;

—by increasing the efficiency of management, especially by enabling firms to manage their supply chains more effectively and to communicate more easily both within the firm and with customers and partners;

—by increasing competition, making prices more transparent, and broadening markets for both buyers and sellers; and

—by increasing consumer choice, convenience, and satisfaction in a variety of ways that may not be reflected in standard economic statistics.

In the balance of this introduction, we summarize some of the examples, drawn from the papers, of how these claims might prove true. We then do our best to add up the potential impacts suggested by the authors and offer some tentative views on the factors we believe will influence the amount of benefits and the pace with which these benefits are likely to be realized.

Reducing the Cost of Transactions

The most important attribute of the Internet also may be the most obvious: it provides a cheap way of transmitting a lot of information quickly and conveniently. Many routine transactions—making payments; processing and transmitting financial information; record-keeping; search and analysis; ordering, invoicing, and recruiting; getting information to suppliers, employees, and customers—can simply be handled less expensively with web-based technology than on paper or in other electronic ways. Many firms, especially those in data-intensive industries, such as financial services and medical care, can reduce their cost of production without doing anything new or different—just by doing the same things cheaper using Internet technology.

Within manufacturing firms, intranets (closed communications systems within organizations) and other web-based technology allow management to share information easily and cheaply across the organization and to cut the cost and improve the accuracy of accounting, ordering, tracking, invoicing, recruiting, and other routine functions. Net-based communications also enable employees in different parts of the firm to work together on product development, marketing, and other projects. Firms such as Cisco Systems and Oracle, which rely heavily on web-based technology for their internal communications and management, claim significant savings from this source.

Andrew McAfee of the Harvard Business School, who examined the manufacturing sector, projects that additional reductions in cost should materialize as more and more firms shift to web-based technologies for information flow and back-office functions, such as purchasing, invoicing, and payments. "While these activities are mundane and only rarely considered possible sources of competitive advantage, they still are time consuming and expensive to carry out in the absence of automation. In the Internet era, this automation is becoming readily available."

Patricia Danzon and Michael Furukawa from the Wharton School at the University of Pennsylvania note that the potential for transactions cost savings from transition to the Internet is especially high in the health care sector, because it is so large (14 percent of gross domestic product, or GDP), so information-intensive, and still so dependent on paper-based records. Moving processing of health insurance claims from the current mix of paper and electronic data interchange (EDI) onto the Internet would require aggressive efforts to standardize claims formats, but savings could be large. EDI providers allege that they can reduce the cost of claims processing from $10–$15 for a paper claim to $2–$4 for an EDI claim. Web-based processors may be able to deliver the same service for less than $1 a claim. Perhaps as much as $27 billion a year could be saved if health insurance claims processing were shifted to the web, with improved speed and convenience thrown into the bargain.

Medical record management is another area in which the Internet offers great potential not only for cutting costs, but for improving the quality and effectiveness of care. In January 2001 the Department of Health and Human Services issued comprehensive rules protecting the privacy of individuals' medical records. It is still too early to know if these regulations will constitute a significant barrier to the development of databases that can be accessed by a wide range of providers with appropriate authorization. But if such databases can be built and maintained, patients and providers would benefit enormously from conversion of current, mostly paper, medical records, into an electronic medical record (EMR) in standard format. Health care providers would then be able to access the patient's full medical history quickly and enter their own observations and treatments. The instant availability of the EMR would save time for the patient as well as for the various providers, reduce the costs of sending records, and avoid duplicative or medically inconsistent treatment. The EMR would also be enormously valuable to individuals who require medical attention when they are away from home. Prescriptions also could be entered on the EMR and simultaneously sent directly to the pharmacy, reducing both cost and error rates in filling prescriptions. Of course, full utilization of the EMR by physicians requires standardization of formats and development of convenient handheld devices for entering treatment information and prescriptions easily as doctors walk around the hospital or office. These standards are now being developed, and investments in computerized personal assistants continue to grow.

In the financial services arena, Eric Clemons and Lorin Hitt, also from the Wharton School, argue that most of the savings from automating internal transactions already may have been realized in the pre-Internet era. Nonetheless, the net should enable financial institutions to lower their processing costs further, while customers will enjoy reduced waiting and travel time as well as mailing costs.

The economy as a whole could also realize substantial savings if online banking were to replace not only face-to-face transactions with bank tellers, but also the whole system of payment by check. Checks have to be sorted and transported back to their original writers—an archaic and expensive process compared to sending payments over the Internet (some estimates put the difference in cost at 10 to 1 or even higher). The transition to online small-value payments, however, may be slow. Many customers like interacting with a real person and continue writing checks not only out of habit, but also because the true costs of check use are not visible to them, or because they regard a cancelled check as a tangible proof of payment not reliably replaceable by anything electronic. Hence, the need to maintain dual technologies for retail banking may limit the realization of the potential savings from online banking for some time.

Retail banking is an example of a major tension exhibited across the financial services industry. This tension is between financial services based on customer-provider relationships tied to geography and the provider's knowledge of the customer, on the one hand, and the savings offered by online markets for standard financial products that bypass traditional intermediaries, on the other. The tension is perhaps most evident in brokerage services, where the advent of the Internet has precipitated a split between the relationship-dependent services of investment advising and portfolio management and the standardized service of stock trading. Customers benefit from the lower transactions cost of online trading, if they are willing to do their own research and forgo advice, as well as from their ability to shop for lower commissions by searching the web. Some of the cost reduction is offset by increased advertising and marketing costs as online brokers compete with other brokers.

In the mortgage lending industry customers are using the Internet to shop for information and compare rates, although only a tiny fraction of mortgages now originate online. A substantial portion of mortgage originations may shift online over the next few years, however, as consumers grow more comfortable using the newly authorized "digital signatures." If this occurs, consumers will save through lower margins in this part of the business, plus lower costs in processing mortgage applications.[5]

Another source of potentially significant savings in transactions costs, perhaps surprising to some, is found in the government sector. As Jane Fountain, of Harvard's Kennedy School of Government, notes in her study, governments at all levels spend substantial resources answering questions—where to get services, who is eligible for benefits, what laws and regulations apply—or gathering information from citizens who want to report a pothole, apply for a permit, renew a license, or give their views on a public issue. The Internet has enormous potential, only beginning to be realized, for dispensing information to citizens less expensively and more accurately than telephone inquiries. A website can be updated more easily and cheaply than a paper publication, and can be designed for quick, user-friendly retrieval of the information needed for a wide variety of purposes. In particular, filing tax returns online cuts costs both to the government and to the taxpayer, and the same can be said for filing many kinds of applications for benefits, permits, licenses, and the like. Building contractors can file architectural drawings online in many jurisdictions and avoid walking around from one government office to another with huge rolls of blueprints. Students can apply for scholarships and loans online; workers who lose jobs, for unemployment benefits; seniors, for retirement benefits and other services.

Fountain stresses that the e-government revolution nonetheless has a long way to go. Some state governments, such as Washington and Georgia, offer significant services on the Internet; others are only beginning to move into the digital age. Most federal agencies and local governments have just started to explore the Internet's potential usefulness to them. Realization of savings will be hampered—as it will in financial services—by the need to maintain alternative systems for those unable or unwilling to use the Internet. Moreover, ease of access to government information and services may generate more inquiries and more demands for service. To the extent that the Internet reduces the cost of interaction between government and

5. Insurance sales offer another potential area for online sales of standardized financial products, although the insurance market has so far been relatively unaffected by the Internet primarily because insurance is typically bought infrequently, many insurance products are complex, and the regulation of them is fragmented by a state-based system.

the private sector, part of the benefit will show up in private sector productivity. Part will also be reflected in lower government expenditures and greater citizen satisfaction, neither of which enters explicitly into productivity statistics.

Education is also a large information-intensive sector of the economy, where the long-run impact of information technology and the Internet may turn out to be considerable. Austan Goolsbee of the University of Chicago, however, expects that the impact of the Internet on education productivity in the next few years is likely to be slight. Distance-learning opportunities are growing at the postsecondary level and have the potential for saving students travel time and giving them a chance to learn at their convenience and at their own pace. But the Internet is only one tool of distance learning and so far has not been used very effectively. The greatest potential appears to be in developing interactive course material in subjects where drill and individual pacing pay off. These learning tools are expensive to develop, but once they are, they can be replicated and distributed on the net at close to zero marginal cost. Integration of such opportunities with other teaching methods could increase the productivity of education at several levels, but these developments are not likely to occur soon.

The Internet and Efficient Management

So far we have been focusing on examples of the Internet's potential for cutting the cost of information-intensive activities without necessarily reorganizing those activities to make them work better as well as cost less. The Internet may have even greater potential as a management tool, however. It may make possible changes in operations that enhance efficiency within firms and across partnerships and alliances in many sectors of the economy and may cause significant restructuring of those sectors in the process.

Many of the potential efficiency gains come from use of web-based technology to manage supply chains more effectively and reduce inventory. These savings may show up within the firm, from better scheduling or information sharing across the company, or in more efficient interaction with other firms in the supply chain. As McAfee documents, Cisco Systems has been a leader in dealing with suppliers on the web to enhance the efficiency of its procurement. Indeed, Cisco has changed the definition of what it means to be a "manufacturer," since it outsources most of its manufacturing operations to other companies in its net-based supplier community. Some of the savings to Cisco comes from competitive bidding by suppliers, which reduces the price to the buyer (but whose ultimate effects we view cautiously, as discussed later). The company also realizes savings from improved information flow throughout the value chain. Cisco attempted to quantify the savings it derived from intensive use of the Internet as a management tool in the period 1995–99 and concluded that the cumulative savings amounted to more than 5 percent of its revenue in 1999—perhaps an upper bound for such savings, especially in light of Cisco's subsequent misjudgment of demand in late 2000. As discussed later, McAfee uses this cost savings estimate to develop a range of projections for how effective the Internet will be more generally in reducing costs throughout the entire manufacturing sector.

The Internet is also being used effectively in other industries to link partners in joint enterprises across large distances, enabling partners to share production schedules and integrate their operations. One of the benefits of the closer linkage is speeding up decisionmaking when problems arise. The net-based information flow can reduce the phenomenon known as the "bullwhip effect," which arises when small changes in consumer demand are magnified by poor information flow and cause delays and inventory accumulation up the supply chain.

Charles Fine of MIT and Daniel Raff of the University of Pennsylvania examine the automobile industry—an important segment of manufacturing—and find multiple potential opportunities for Internet-aided increases in efficiency in this highly visible industry. They project productivity improvements in product development, procurement, and supply and in various aspects of the manufacturing process itself. They also explore the applicability to automobiles of the "Dell model," under which customers specify exactly what features they want and the product is then built to their order and shipped directly from the factory. Fine and Raff also suggest that the automobile sector of the future will involve far fewer dealers and sales personnel than it does now.

Internet retailing has attracted a great deal of attention in the last few years. Much of the attention has focused on a few "pure play" retailers, such as Amazon.com and eBay, which sell only on the net. Joseph Bailey, of the University of Maryland, examined the retail sector, which constitutes about 9 percent of the economy. He concludes that although Internet sales are now only about 1 percent of total retail sales and are unlikely to account for more that 10 percent of retail revenues in five years, there is considerable potential for retailers using the Internet to increase efficiency. He does not expect, however, that much of the Internet's impact on retail efficiency will come from the "pure play" retailers. Rather, he expects that conventional retailers will increasingly use the net to manage their supply operations more effectively, bypass intermediaries, and reduce inventories. Conventional retailers, such as department stores, will also grow their Internet sales, using the Internet as an alternative way of reaching customers, along with catalogues and in-store sales. At the same time, the pure net retailers will add brick-and-mortar warehouses (Amazon.com has already taken this step) and become more like conventional retailers. A hybrid model will come to dominate retailing, in which almost all retail establishments use the net to communicate with and sell to customers, but few depend solely on Internet sales.

Addressing a less visible sector of the economy, Anuradha Nagarajan and a team of researchers at the University of Michigan point out that the Internet is also in the process of radically transforming the trucking industry—or as it more accurately should be called, the *logistics industry*—which depends heavily on timely information for efficient operation. Customers need a low-cost way of finding the truck capacity that they need when they need it and of comparing rates to get the best deal. Truckers need to find customers that will use their capacity fully, so that they can avoid costly downtime and empty backhauls. The Internet is proving to be an inexpensive tool for matching these needs, and use of the Internet by both large and small trucking companies has risen rapidly since the mid-1990s. Traditional freight brokers are rapidly being replaced by electronic brokers, some set up by groups of carriers in search of the greater efficiencies made possible by integrating their fleets and schedules on the net.

Moreover, the Internet has made it possible for truckers to offer additional services to their customers, such as tracking shipments, rerouting them if necessary, and providing quick access to all relevant documentation. As a result, some trucking companies have been evolving into *transportation managers* offering a wide range of services customized to their users' particular needs. This transformation of traditional truckers into firms offering more comprehensive services makes it hard to identify the potential contributions of the Internet to productivity growth in the trucking sector narrowly defined. Greater efficiencies in transportation management will ultimately enhance the productivity of the many industries that use trucking services, and that is where the Michigan research team sees the greatest potential for Internet-related transportation savings.

Making Markets More Competitive

One of the major features of the Internet revolution is its potential to broaden the reach of markets and make the whole economic system more competitive nationally and internationally. If prices of well-specified goods and services are posted on the net, buyers can shop for the best deal over a wide geographic area, even across international borders, and sellers can reach a larger group of potential buyers. The Internet has the potential to bring many markets closer to the economists' textbook model of perfect competition, characterized by large numbers of buyers and sellers bidding in a frictionless market with perfect information. Moving markets in this direction should mean more efficient production, lower profit margins, and lower prices for consumers.

Part of the benefit of online procurement to a firm or hospital or government agency comes from increasing the pool of bidders, often across a wider geographic area, and finding the most efficient suppliers. Firms and groups of firms are increasingly organizing e-markets in hopes of lowering their costs, although as McAfee points out, many of these markets are still not very sophisticated. Some e-markets are organized to encourage firms to pool their purchasing power to get the best deal from suppliers. The major automobile companies, as Raff and Fine note, are among the highest-profile examples of such joint efforts. Governments, as Fountain observes, are also beginning to use the Internet to pool their purchasing power.

Broadening markets and making them more transparent and competitive clearly benefits consumers, but not all of the benefits flow from greater efficiency. Efficiency benefits occur when the Internet lowers barriers to competition by increasing the chances that a firm that develops a better product or a more efficient process or organizational structure can find its way into broader markets, win bids, sell its product, and exert pressure on its competitors to improve their efficiency. If, however, greater competition in a wider online marketplace simply cuts profit margins, consumers will benefit, but no productivity increase will have occurred, as we explain shortly.

Some of the high claims for productivity increase attributable to the Internet are suspect because they fail to distinguish between these two effects. A well-known study by two Goldman Sachs analysts projects large Internet-induced productivity gains in the manufacturing sector.[6] The two analysts believe that Internet markets will lower costs by eliminating various intermediaries. They also suggest that the profit squeeze among suppliers, induced by more intense competition in business-to-business, or B2B, Internet commerce, will lower procurement costs significantly during the next decade and that the combined effects will increase the annual rate of productivity growth by 0.25 percent over what it might be otherwise.

We are dubious that there is that much imperfect competition among supplier firms to be "corrected" by the Internet. Moreover, we believe the Goldman Sachs estimate suffers from a more fundamental conceptual flaw. Although the Internet may reduce profit margins among suppliers somewhat, any resulting reduction in prices that they charge will not directly reduce the quantity of inputs required to generate the same level of output—that is, they will not increase productivity. Instead, any cost savings from lower supplier profit margins will represent a *transfer of income* from suppliers to producers. Moreover, if the markets in which the final goods and services are sold are competitive—and this is likely to be the case for the vast majority of those markets—the benefits of reduced supplier margins will then be passed on to *consumers*. The same result should occur to the extent the Internet also causes profit margins among final producers to fall, as it should for standardized "plain vanilla" products and services for which price is the most important factor in a purchaser's decision (such as books and common financial instruments, mortgages, and most lines of personal insurance). In short, to the extent the Internet compresses profit margins throughout the economy, the benefits will show up in the form of lower prices to consumers—perhaps in a series of one-time gains—but not in added productivity.

Nonetheless, a compression of profit margins throughout the supply chain is quite likely to enhance true productivity in another fashion. With less room for error, firms should be more focused on adopting the kinds of cost-savings measures already described that should reduce the quantity of inputs required to generate any given level of output. Moreover, in a competitive environment, it is likely that inefficient firms will be weeded out more quickly so that at any given time, there should be more firms in each market operating at cutting-edge levels of efficiency. This effect should

6. Brookes and Wahhaj (2000).

raise the average level of productivity in each sector, and in turn, in the entire economy. Our sector studies have not attempted to isolate these types of effects—indeed, it is not clear that such impacts can be quantified—and for this reason (among others) the total quantifiable estimates of the Internet on productivity that we present later may well be conservative.

Benefits That May Not Show Up in Measured GDP

The Internet—and e-commerce in particular—is also generating and will continue to generate benefits to users that are not easily measured and, in any event, not likely to be counted as increased GDP and thus enhanced productivity. The ability to purchase products and services, or to obtain advice and information, from the comfort of one's home or office offers convenience that is implicitly reflected in the price, but so far not counted as an added measure of quality by government statisticians. The same is true of added choice and customization. The computer that this introductory chapter has been written on, a Dell with various customized features, was ordered over the Internet. To be sure, the same thing might have been accomplished had one of us gone to a store and purchased another personal computer (Dell only sells direct, over the telephone or the Internet). But it would have been far more time consuming to do so, and there is no guarantee that the store would have precisely the configuration that one of us wanted—and got—by filling out a brief order form on the net.

Danzon and Furukawa make a strong case in chapter 7 that the Internet will even help save lives. Some patients have suffered needlessly, and in some cases, died because of mistakes that nurses and pharmacies have made in reading a physician's hand-written notes. That will change as more physicians use handheld computers to record their observations and order prescriptions, through built-in wireless connections, directly from pharmacies. Furthermore, assuming that privacy hurdles can be overcome, the Internet should enable physicians to reduce diagnostic errors when they are able to access from anywhere databases holding patients' medical histories.[7]

To be sure, it may be possible to quantify and even express in monetary terms certain of the foregoing benefits. For example, the benefits of convenience could be estimated by applying a wage rate to the savings in time

---

7. Of course, it is possible that the same benefits could be realized without the Internet if it turns out that patients record their histories on smart cards they carry with them rather than on centralized databases that could be less secure and thus less private.

earned by consumers when ordering over the net rather than traveling to
the store. Similarly, it might be possible to estimate the numbers of patients
whose lives will be saved by the application of Internet technologies and
then to multiply the result by an average value per life to arrive at a dollar-
ized estimate of medical benefits. Yet so far, estimates of this type have not
been counted as part of GDP, and we do not anticipate they will be any
time soon.

Other quality improvements encouraged by the Internet may show up
in the official output statistics, however, but not necessarily in the sectors
in which they are generated. In their chapter on the trucking industry
(chapter 5), Anuradha Nagarajan and his colleagues demonstrate how
modern logistics firms, hooked up by the Internet to fleets of trucks, help
manage increasingly complex order delivery patterns for their business customers, combining all means of transportation—truck, rail, and air—to
produce the most efficient means of moving merchandise among various
locations. Because the firms have fundamentally altered the nature of the
services they offer, the savings generated by this process do not primarily
show up in the transportation sector. Instead, the improved transportation
management reduces costs incurred by the customers themselves—perhaps
by as much as $71 billion on an annual basis within the next five years, as
discussed later. These savings *will* show up in the GDP statistics in lower
costs for the many sectors that use transportation services and thus will add
to productivity growth as they materialize.

Similarly, the additional choice and convenience afforded by the
Internet may generate costs savings in other ways that also find their way
into the official output data. The Dell model, which allows customers to
pick the characteristics of the product they want and have it shipped
directly to them from the factory, may eventually reduce distribution costs
for automobiles and other big-ticket items.[8] This "build-to-order" process
would reduce the need for extensive inventories by manufacturers and
dealers (cost savings that would be reflected in the productivity data), while

8. This could happen in automobiles even if the current state franchise laws that protect auto dealers are not changed. Faced with continued pressure to cut costs and serve the interests of consumers,
automobile manufacturers and their dealers may *voluntarily* agree to a system whereby customers order
direct from manufacturers' websites and then pick up their cars and have them serviced by local dealers. As more business takes this form, either dealers might then charge customers for test driving cars,
or be subsidized by the manufacturers to offer test driving services.

saving shopping time for the consumers who insist on specific features of the product they purchase (benefits that probably would not be counted).

Adding It All Up

The evidence discussed in the following chapters, when cumulated, leads to the following broad conclusions:

—The *potential* of the Internet to enhance productivity growth over the next few years is real.

—Much of the impact of the Internet may not be felt in e-commerce per se, but in lower costs for quite mundane transactions that involve information flows—ordering, invoicing, filing claims, and making payments—across a wide range of existing "old economy" sectors, including health care and government.

—The Internet produces considerable scope for management efficiencies in product development, supply chain management, and a variety of other aspects of business performance.

—The Internet will enhance competition, both increasing efficiency and reducing profit margins throughout the economy, but the profit squeeze itself should not be counted as a productivity enhancement.

—The Internet is improving consumer convenience, increasing choices, and leading to other benefits that may not be readily measured, or if they are, may show up as productivity gains in industries or sectors other than those in which the savings may be initially generated.

But what of the benefits that *can* be measured? How significant are they likely to be? Table 1-1 tabulates the projected cost savings that the authors of each of the sector chapters have estimated. All estimates refer to the potential annual cost reductions that the authors believe to be achievable within the next five years.

In sum, table 1-1 suggests that the total cost savings for sectors that collectively account for about 70 percent of GDP range roughly between $125 billion and $251 billion. In an economy with annual output of roughly $10 trillion (in 2000 dollars), these savings represent 1.2–2.5 percent of GDP. This range reflects the cumulative savings of primarily "one-time" cost reductions. In reality, the savings are likely to be spread out over time, as cutting edge techniques spread from first movers to later adopters. If spread out over the five-year period, therefore, the foregoing savings

Table 1-1. *Estimates of Potential Internet-Related Cost Savings*
Billions of 2000 dollars

Sector	Annual cost savings in five years
Education	Not clear
Financial services	19
Government	At least 12
Health care	41
Manufacturing	50–100
Retailing	Not clear
Trucking	3–79
Total	125–251

Source: Authors' calculations.

estimates imply annualized gains in productivity—relative to a "baseline" in which the Internet is not present—of 0.25–0.50 percent.[9]

Several points about what the table does and does not include should be kept in mind. First, the Internet is not projected to generate measured cost savings in all of the sectors. Education and retailing, in particular, stand out as exceptions to the general pattern. This is not because the authors of the chapters on these sectors expect the Internet to have no impact. To the contrary, as Austan Goolsbee documents in chapter 9, the Internet is expected to make it easier for many students to take advantage of distance learning, as it already has at a number of colleges and business schools and within corporations (especially for the teaching of IT-related subjects). Similarly, Joseph Bailey in chapter 6 demonstrates how e-tailing has enhanced customer convenience while compressing profit margins of all retailers, thus lowering prices.

Second, table 1-1 does not indicate the importance of the cost-reducing impact of the Internet in one particular subsector—automobile manufacturing and sales. Based on what they believe to be the most reliable reports from Wall Street analysts, Charles Fine and Daniel Raff in chapter 3 estimate that the Internet could shave as much as 13 percent of the cost of producing the average automobile. Like the estimates for the other sectors,

9. Economists frequently distinguish between labor productivity (output divided by labor input) and total factor productivity, or TFP (output divided by a weighted average of capital and labor inputs). The productivity estimates reported above do not distinguish between these two concepts but can be viewed as rough approximations of both, except to the extent that additional investment spending is required to generate the cost savings, an amount that may not be that large for reasons we discuss shortly.

Fine and Raff believe these savings are likely to be realized in "one shot" rather than in continued improvements. Even so, as long as they do not occur all at one time in all firms, the gradual one-time improvements should improve measured productivity growth in the automobile industry during the period of adjustment.

Third, the estimates for some of the sectors are expressed in ranges rather than point estimates, and in some cases—notably, for the trucking industry—that range is rather wide, reflecting the considerable uncertainty about the Internet's likely economic impact. For example, the savings estimates for the manufacturing sector are based on the assumption that firms within the sector, on average, are less successful than industry leader Cisco has been in using the Internet to cut production costs. Even so, the range for savings estimates reported in the table reflects considerable conservatism about other firms' relative success; the upper-bound figure, for example, assumes that the average firm is able to reduce its costs by just 2 percent, well below the 5 percent cost reduction estimated by Cisco. Meanwhile, a major reason for the large range in the case of trucking is that the lion's share of the estimated cost saving is in sectors that *use* trucking services rather than in trucking itself. Given the diversity of customers and the industries in which they compete, this provides another complication that is not present in the case of the other sector studies.

Fourth, table 1-1 does not include nor do the sector chapters provide estimates of the investment spending that may be required to generate the cost savings. In fact, there is some evidence that companies need only spend relatively small sums for software and added hardware to make their business operations more Internet ready.[10] Most of the required spending is for personnel who must reengineer the companies' internal processes. Such spending for what Erik Brynjolfsson has called "organizational capital" is expensed and consists of a reallocation of employees that firms already have on board plus perhaps some fees for consultants.[11] In any event, a fully accurate accounting for the impact of the Internet on productivity should take account of the additional expenditures for both physical and human capital that are required to generate the savings just summarized.

However large the productivity savings turn out to be—and the accumulated preliminary estimates reported here suggest the annual economy-wide cost savings, once fully realized, could exceed $200 billion annually—

10. Frances Cairncross, "E-Management," *The Economist*, November 11, 2000, pp. 1–2.
11. Bresnahan, Brynjolfsson, and Hitt (1999).

there should be no mistake about who the ultimate beneficiaries will be: consumers, not businesses. In our highly and increasingly competitive market, most temporary market advantages—reflected in high profit margins—get competed away (unless firms accumulate and then abuse their monopoly positions). Perhaps the best evidence for this is that relative shares of national income going to labor, on the one hand, and capital (interest payments, dividends, and retained profits), on the other, have been remarkably stable for several decades. Why then will firms invest and make increasing use of the Internet if they cannot permanently enjoy the extra profits? Very simply, because they will have no other choice. If they do not stay at the cutting edge, then someone else will. Andrew Grove of Intel could not have put it any better than in his famous book title *Only the Paranoid Survive.*

The productivity gains from the Internet will not necessarily increase the already high productivity growth rate of the past few years. All we have attempted to do in this project is to isolate the portion of any future productivity growth that may reasonably be attributed to the Internet, or more precisely, to networked communications (which would also include intranets). The actual productivity growth rate will be some combination of Internet-specific contributions plus the continued contribution of other technologies, improvements in workplace practices, and capital deepening— the same processes that have contributed to productivity growth in the past.

Finally, the estimates produced for this project more or less assume the continuing use and penetration of existing Internet-related technologies, including the extended rollout of broadband as a vehicle for transmitting data (more on this shortly). It is entirely possible, however, that within the next five or ten years, there will be another "disruptive" technological advance associated with the Internet—fiber optic cable connected to many, if not most, businesses and homes—that could be just as transformative in its impacts as the current Internet is projected to be. Should this be the case, then our estimates understate the ultimate impact of the Internet. At the other extreme, it is possible that the nightmare scenario envisioned by some experts—a major hacker attack that brings the entire Internet down for some time—unfolds, thereby not only severely disrupting commerce and perhaps financial markets, but over the longer run causing a loss of confidence in the security and reliability of the Internet. Should this dark scenario come to life, then our estimates may prove to be too optimistic.

Realizing the Internet's Potential

Putting aside the draconian and hopefully remote possibility that the Internet can be severely disrupted, what will determine the extent to which the potential benefits of the Internet—both the quantifiable improvements to productivity and the less quantifiable benefits of convenience and quality improvement—will in fact materialize, and at what pace? One way to think about the answer is to distinguish between the effects that are likely to grow out of the increased penetration of the Internet throughout the rest of the population (the "width" of the Internet revolution) and those effects likely to stem from the benefits realized within individual sectors and activities (the "depth" of the Internet revolution). Mindful of the difficulty of projecting anything about the Internet, we offer the following impressionistic judgments about the differences between these two types of effects.

We suspect that the growing width of the Internet revolution will have more effect on the distribution of the benefits of the Internet than on the total amount of those benefits for the whole economy. When we speak of the width of the revolution, we are concentrating primarily on individuals rather than businesses, most of whom may be hooked up to the Internet but have only begun to scratch the surface when it comes to integrating it into the full range of business operations.

For individuals the Internet is still very much at the marker of a "digital divide," one that runs primarily along income (and to a lesser extent racial) lines. As tools to access the Internet, including cellular phones and personal computers, become cheaper, the divide will gradually close. As it does, nonquantifiable benefits such as convenience will surely rise, but how much, if any, of these benefits will affect the productivity statistics is not clear.

Of course, the impact of the Internet on businesses has a width dimension as well. The more pervasive e-commerce becomes, the greater will be the pressure on firms to adopt cutting-edge cost savings techniques that can be passed on to consumers. At this point, however, we have no way of estimating how significant this impact may be.

For many businesses the impact of the Internet may be just beginning. As one of our authors, Andrew McAfee, pointed out in another context in November 2000, "Whenever I visit software companies, I get them to complete the sentence: 'The business-to-business revolution is X% complete.'

The biggest number I have heard is 5%. Many say 1%."[12] We have no way of knowing whether these estimates are right or how fast the revolution will spread, but we suspect that a key to realizing the potential productivity gains identified by our authors will be whether the Internet turns out to be as "deep" as they project. That is, will each of the sectors actually use the Internet more intensively and, in the process, change business practices?

The answers will depend heavily on the extent and pace of adjustment of individuals within these organizations, that is, on changes in corporate or organizational culture. If past experience with IT investments is any guide, this may be a serious qualification. The business and government landscapes are littered with examples of poorly planned IT projects. Fortunately, competition should supply a positive countervailing force, provided that markets are not unduly constrained by anticompetitive practices and that the antitrust laws are enforced. Firms that are now realizing the projected benefits will gain market share at the expense of those who are not and thereby speed up the diffusion process. But the improvements will still take time, and we cannot be confident at this point of the pace at which the process will play out.

What about the impact of broadband—faster cable, telephone (DSL), wireless, and perhaps one day, direct fiber optic—hookups to the Internet? Shouldn't the increase in speed accelerate the projected productivity impacts? Surely, broadband has already made life easier for the approximately 3 percent of the population who have it. But to the extent that the benefits of B2C (business-to-consumer) already consist largely of non-quantifiable gains that are not reflected in the national income accounts, the benefits of broadband will be no different in character.

One possible exception will be for the millions of Americans who telecommute or will in the future. To the extent that workers are more productive at home than in the office, business-quality speed in the home could help improve measured productivity. As for businesses themselves, most already have or will soon have faster connections to the Internet. Thus, the diffusion of broadband access to residential customers should not affect the gains they realize through B2B transactions, except indirectly: through the added competitive retail pressure that increased use of the Internet should make possible.

Does policy have a role in helping to realize the projected benefits of the Internet? In theory, if more people had confidence in the security and pri-

---

12. Quoted in Frances Cairncross, "E-Management," *The Economist,* November 11, 2000, p. 6.

vacy of their e-transactions, then e-commerce would grow faster, thereby increasing the benefits from its use. Again, however, much of the benefit of more intensive retail use of the Internet is likely to be nonquantifiable and thus not evident in the productivity statistics. At the same time, if the current controversy surrounding Internet taxes resulted in forced collection on such transactions, the growth rate of e-commerce would slow. But taxation of the Internet would also help rectify an imbalance between the treatment of off- and online commerce and thus probably would not have a significant material impact on overall productivity.

A different story might emerge if new laws, or even better, enhanced technology to secure intellectual property rights for music, videos, books, and software, encouraged more Internet-based distribution of content. This would reduce distribution costs of entertainment and software products, in particular, and would improve productivity in this sector (one that we do not examine in detail in this book) because the outcomes would show up in the national income account data.

Beyond the Dot.Coms

The conclusions advanced in this study rest on a far firmer foundation than—and extend much further beyond—the many (now defunct) dot.com firms that so populated the business landscape and garnered so much attention from the media only a short time ago. The Internet is a new technology, much as the railroad and the automobile were in their day. And at the launch of these two latter technologies, hundreds of firms initially rushed into the business. Now, each has only a few competitors left, the rest having been merged or forced by competition—and economies of scale—out of business. But would any serious observer claim that the demise of so many enterprises somehow "proved" that the technologies they attempted to exploit and market were not important? Of course not. In a competitive economy, the benefits of new technologies ultimately flow through to consumers, with firms as the intermediaries.

This study has concentrated on how the economy outside the dot.coms—the sectors that are using the Internet and the various tools that have been developed around it—is changing and is likely to change because of various ways the Internet enables firms to produce and deliver goods and services at less cost, and often with more convenience and choice, to consumers. In the process, the "new economy" is very rapidly blending with, and ultimately will become indistinguishable from, the "old economy." For example, Bailey describes in chapter 6 how traditional retailers, prompted by the initial apparent success of the pure e-tailers, now have websites or Internet divisions of their own, while conversely the e-tailers have had to build the back-end infrastructure (warehouses and distribution facilities) that the offline retailers have always had. The same blending of the Internet with traditional "bricks-and-mortar" offices is occurring in the financial services sector as well. As this melding process continues, new economy techniques will gradually become absorbed into the old economy, and soon the distinctions between the two will be gone, in fact and in common discourse.

The Internet is also leading to changes in the structure of particular markets, the subject of a companion volume to this one.[13] Without repeating that analysis set forth in detail there, it is simply worth noting here that the impacts of the net on market structure are likely to be diverse and almost certainly unpredictable.

For example, the Internet makes it far easier and cheaper for smaller firms to reach national, even global, markets. This tends to lower barriers to entry, leaves room for more niche players in any industry, promotes outsourcing, and generally intensifies competition. At the same time, firms are finding that they have just as much trouble getting noticed in cyberspace as they do in the real world. In part because e-commerce is still relatively new and the trustworthiness of vendors on the net cannot be verified, consumers are still as attracted to brand names online as they are offline. It is not an accident, for example, that in late December 2000, one survey reported that seven of the ten most popular web sites in the United States were those of traditional offline retailers.[14] This finding indicates that the Internet may not, after all, be lowering barriers to entry as much as enthusiasts might have originally hoped. Nonetheless, for all firms, the competitive pressure is greater because the net reduces the costs of search and makes it far easier for purchasers to comparison shop than ever before.

One other effect of the Internet much remarked upon is its tendency to put severe pressure on, if not eliminate, certain kinds of traditional "intermediaries"—stock brokers, insurance agents, travel agents, and so forth. After all, if individuals can purchase their goods and services direct from

13. BRIE Task Force (2001).
14. David Streitfeld, "Old-Line Retail Sense Humbles Dot-Coms," *Washington Post,* January 1, 2001, p. A5.

the provider, why bother with an intermediary at all? In some cases—automobile dealers are the best example—the law may require it. But in others, the impact of the Internet already is being felt. As Clemons and Hitt discuss in chapter 4, a substantial portion of stock purchases already are made through online brokers. Although the online market share in insurance and mortgages is much lower now, it should grow. Trends like these portend ill for traditional financial agents.

Still, there should continue to be a place, albeit a much smaller one, for some traditional agents who will continue to serve customers who refuse to conduct business online and who want and *are willing to pay for* the personal service of those agents. In addition, the Internet already has spawned a new type of "cyber" intermediary—some call them "infomediaries"—who help guide users to the best deals on the Internet. Yet because consumers also expect so much on the net to be free, the financial viability of some of these new intermediaries is also as much open to question as it is for the traditional intermediaries they are trying to displace.

The economic impact of the Internet will likely not be as insignificant as some pessimists claim and not as overwhelming as many cyber-enthusiasts suggest. Still, there are reasons for believing that its effect on the economy will be important. The Internet will produce significant cost savings in many sectors of the economy, resulting in faster productivity growth for some (unknowable) period of time. The Internet also will lead to lower prices for consumers, resulting in faster growth in living standards.

The Internet should also generate a variety of benefits to users, in their capacities as consumers and citizens, which are not easily quantified but nonetheless real: savings in time, added convenience, and products and services tailored specifically for them. In an era when consumers are aware more than ever that "time is money," these benefits to many may be far more noticeable and appreciated than the numbers that economists often like to count.

References

Bresnahan, Timothy F., Erik Brynjolfsson, and Lorin M. Hitt. 1999. "Information Technology, Workplace Organization, and the Demand for Skilled Labor: Firm-Level Evidence." NBER Working Paper 7136. National Bureau of Economic Research, Cambridge, Mass. May.

BRIE-IGCC E-conomy Project Task Force on the Internet. 2001. *Tracking a Transformation: E-commerce and the Terms of Competition in Industries.* Brookings.

Brynjolfsson, Erik. 2001. "Investment in Organizational Capital." Paper presented at the Conference on Advances in the Measure of Intangible (Intellectual) Capital, sponsored by the Stern Business School, New York University, May 17.

Brookes, Martin, and Zaki Wahhaj. 2000. "The Shocking Economic Impact of B2B." Global Economic Paper 37. Goldman Sachs, New York. February 3.

Council of Economic Advisers. 2001. *Economic Report of the President, 2001.* Washington, D.C.

Gordon, Robert J. 2000. "Does the 'New Economy' Measure Up to the Great Inventions of the Past?" *Journal of Economic Perspectives* 14 (4): 49–74.

Grove, Andrew. 1998. *Only the Paranoid Survive.* Harper Collins.

Jorgenson, Dale W., and Kevin J. Stiroh. 2000. "Raising the Speed Limit: U.S. Economic Growth in the Information Age." *Brookings Papers on Economic Activity* 1:125–211.

Krugman, Paul. 1997. *Age of Diminished Expectations.* MIT Press.

Oliner, Stephen D., and Daniel E. Sichel. 2000. "The Resurgence of Growth in the Late 1990s: Is Information Technology the Story?" *Journal of Economic Perspectives* 14 (4): 3–22.

U.S. Department of Commerce. Economics and Statistics Administration. 2000. *Digital Economy 2000.*

2

ANDREW McAFEE

Manufacturing: Lowering Boundaries, Improving Productivity

MANUFACTURING—the procurement, transformation, and commitment to customers of physical goods—accounted for 18.5 percent of U.S. GDP, employed 18.6 million people, and shipped $3.7 trillion worth of goods in 1996, the most recent year for which data are available.[1]

While manufacturing commands a large portion of the economic pie, it often is not perceived as exciting or full of promise by communities, such as investors and pundits, who look for the "new new thing."[2] Recently, however, this historically prosaic sector of the economy has become a focal point for Internet-era excitement.

Beginning in 1999 companies involved in Internet-based business-to-business (B2B) activities were the beneficiaries of the kind of media and investor attention that had previously been reserved for "e-tailers," portals, content providers, and other business-to-consumer (B2C) companies. Although the stock market correction of March and April 2000 dampened some of this enthusiasm, interest in B2B remained comparatively high.[3]

The author gratefully acknowledges the research support of Greg Bounds on this project.

1. U.S. Bureau of Economic Analysis (1998), p. 460; U.S. Census Bureau (2000) and Slater and Strauser (1998).

2. This phrase was the title of a book by Lewis (1999) about the search for new entrepreneurial opportunities in Silicon Valley by Silicon Graphics founder Jim Clark.

3. For an overview of the efforts of B2C firms to transform themselves into B2B providers, see Shore (2000).

According to one estimate, B2B e-commerce will hit $2.7 trillion in 2004, accounting for 17 percent of total trade, with 93 percent of firms surveyed expecting to conduct some B2B trade by 2002.[4]

Not all of this interest is devoted to manufacturers—Internet-based provision of logistics and financial services, for example, is also commonly included in the B2B category—but in the opinion of many observers the workaday world of production is in the early stages of large-scale change, at least comparable to the revolution brought on by the forced introduction about twenty years ago of "Japanese manufacturing" techniques— largely around quality and process management.[5] For example, a study by the research firm IDC predicts that spending on web development infrastructure within the manufacturing sector will reach $24 billion by 2002, while spending within financial services will be only $16.6 billion, despite the fact that both manufacturing and financial services are comparably large sectors of the economy.[6] And some manufacturing industries appear poised for hyperfast adoption of Internet-based trade: B2B e-commerce in industrial supplies, for example, is projected to grow from $17.6 billion in 2000 to $287.3 billion in 2004.[7]

This chapter explores the transformation under way within U.S. manufacturing as a result of the Internet's explosive growth over the past five years.[8] It reviews the magnitude and dimensions of the transformation to date, offers a framework for understanding how and why the observed changes are occurring, and finishes with speculation about how the journey toward Internet-enabled manufacturing might continue in the near future with suggestions for the federal government's data collectors. A taxonomy of the mechanisms by which the Internet is currently affecting manufac-

4. Kafka (2000). This study's definition of trade encompasses all B2B commerce and is not confined to the manufacturing sector. Most other estimates do not wildly diverge from this, varying by less than a factor of two. See Lawrence (2000) for a comparison of these estimates.

5. For managerial overviews of these approaches, see Schonberger (1996); Hayes and Wheelwright (1984); Hayes, Wheelwright, and Clark (1988). For a review of the impact of these approaches on the U.S. auto industry, see Womack, Jones, and Roos (1990).

6. Elizabeth Clampet, "Corporate Internet Spending Poised to Triple Soon," *InternetNews*, February 23, 1999. According to the U.S. Bureau of Economic Analysis (1998, p. 460), manufacturing in 1997 contributed $1.57 trillion to GDP, while finance, insurance, and real estate contributed $1.29 trillion.

7. Bill Roberts, "B2B Commerce in 2000: The Spigot Opens," *Internet World*, January 1, 2000, p. 36.

8. Throughout this chapter, the "Internet" refers to data carried using the TCP/IP protocols. This definition includes virtually all World Wide Web traffic.

turing is the main goal here, but this categorization, of course, cannot be comprehensive in terms of firms, tools, and approaches covered, nor can it guarantee a complete articulation of the mechanisms at work. The phenomenon of interest is simply too new, and too dynamic, to be captured at this point in time by a review of any length, let alone a book chapter. The taxonomy is based on research, primarily field based, conducted by the author over the previous four years with the objective of understanding the general mechanisms of the impact of information technology, or IT, on operational performance. In recent years, this work has naturally become more focused on the Internet and has continued to use manufacturing firms to study phenomena of interest.

Before offering this framework, the chapter first presents data on the extent and type of influence exerted by the Internet on manufacturing. Instead of presenting the results of original research, this section is primarily a review and a synthesis of relevant work, including academic studies, case studies, and articles in the popular and trade press. Some of this work is the author's, but the great majority of it is not. Furthermore, most of the nonacademic work has not been subjected to peer review. While the author has attempted to use and cite only high-quality work, regardless of its source, it is important to keep in mind that the body of rigorous academic research on the Internet's impact is still quite small; and it is therefore necessary to accept research, thinking, and insights from a variety of sources.[9]

Information Technology and Productivity

Figure 2-1 below provides clear evidence that labor productivity growth in the United States has in recent years dramatically increased and that the manufacturing sector is improving even faster along this dimension than the rest of the economy. This trend was almost totally unanticipated; in the early and mid-1990s observers highlighted the fact that productivity

9. It is worth repeating the cautions offered in the first footnote of chapter 2 (the ninth footnote overall) of Buckley and others (2000): "Specific estimates from private sources and company-specific examples are included in this report to be illustrative of developing trends and their inclusion does not signify . . . validation or approval. Disparities among private estimates can result from differences in definitions, methods, data, model and sampling error, and product coverage. Variations also reflect the research needs of customers. While data used for estimates and forecasts are based on a combination of surveys and interviews, the survey questions and answers are not made public, sample sizes vary considerably across surveys, and little information is available on the respondents."

Figure 2-1. *Productivity Growth Rates, 1990–99*

Percent change vs. previous quarter, annualized

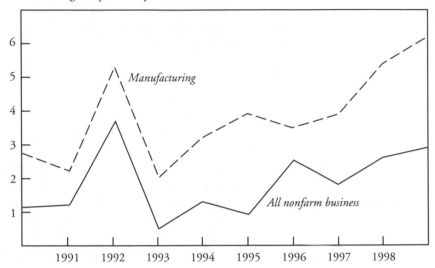

growth was largely stagnant, with unpleasant consequences for the economy as a whole.[10] The many efforts to explain this sharp reversal have largely arrived at a common conclusion—that much of the increase in productivity growth can be attributed to sustained heavy investments in information technology and the resulting increase in the nation's IT capital stock.

In 1996 Brynjolfsson and Hitt offered the first cross-sectional firm level evidence to contradict Solow's long-standing observation, "You can see evidence of the computer age everywhere except the productivity statistics."[11] A number of recent studies have found clear evidence that the production and use of computers are having a substantial and positive impact on U.S. productivity and output growth.[12] Five recent studies, for example, compared productivity growth rates in the latter half of the 1990s with those of an earlier time period and calculated how much of the difference was

10. See, for example, Krugman (1994, 1998).

11. See Brynjolfsson and Hitt (1996); also Robert M. Solow, "We'd Better Watch Out," *New York Times Book Review,* July 12, 1987, p. 36.

12. See, for example, Dewan and Min (1997); Whelan (2000); Sichel (1999); and Oliner and Sichel (2000).

attributable to IT; their estimates ranged from 48 to 74 percent.[13] All of these studies agreed that extremely rapid productivity growth rates within the IT manufacturing sector were significant contributors to the economy's overall growth rate, but they also confirmed that information technology added value primarily through capital deepening, or changing the relative balance of capital and labor inputs, in the non-IT manufacturing sectors of the economy. In other words, these studies concurred that IT products, not IT producers, primarily are driving productivity increases.[14]

Observers have offered two chief reasons for the productivity acceleration of the late 1990s. The first is that before this the total accumulated capital stock of IT was simply not large enough to have made a visible difference across the economy, especially given the very high obsolescence rates of information technology products.[15] According to Oliner and Sichel, in 1994 "many observers were wondering why productivity growth had failed to revive despite the billions of dollars U.S. companies had poured into information technology over the previous decade. We concluded that, in fact, there was no puzzle—just unrealistic expectations . . . computing equipment still represented a small fraction of the total capital stock [in the early 1990s]."[16]

The second reason given for increased U.S. productivity gains—and without contradicting Oliner and Sichel's conclusions—has more to do with a specific information technology, namely the Internet. After 1995 computers became increasingly interconnected using the Internet. Users had access to each other's data and other resources, making work both more efficient and productive. According to economist Alan Blinder, "One theory is that all these high-speed computers required greater interconnectivity before they could really boost productivity on a national scale—and the Net has now provided the missing link."[17]

A brief review of the Internet's recent history buttresses this contention by revealing that Internet usage began to explode in the United States at the same time that productivity growth began to increase. In the mid-1990s, the IT investments of many U.S. firms began to acquire an Internet component, due largely to the invention over the previous few years of a

13. These studies are reviewed and compared in Buckley and others (2000), p. 38, table 4.1.
14. As discussed in Oliner and Sichel (2000), this conclusion differs from that reached by Gordon (1999).
15. For a discussion of rapid IT obsolescence, see Sichel (1997).
16. Oliner and Sichel (2000), p. 1-2.
17. Blinder (2000), p. 5.

suite of technologies, including the HTTP protocols, the HTML programming language, and the first Internet browser applications. Together
these components created the multimedia, easy-to-navigate World Wide
Web on top of the pre-existing Internet data transmission protocols.[18] In
the few years since its birth, usage of the web has exploded, and the Internet now almost completely dominates other networking technologies. As
a result, IT investment in the United States has become increasingly
skewed toward hardware, software, and networks that are Internet enabled.

One consequence of this trend is that it is becoming increasingly difficult to discern which portion of a company's IT investments are Internet
based and which are based on other information technologies. This chapter will attempt to make this distinction wherever possible and to concentrate on the impact of the Internet on manufacturing rather than the
impact of information technology in general.

The Internet and Manufacturing

Goldman Sachs has conducted one of the most comprehensive analyses to
date of the economic impact of the Internet alone by considering seventeen
U.S. manufacturing and extraction industries.[19] It found that the Internet's
impact would be strongly felt in the output and equity markets but not in
bond prices or inflation rates. The Internet would reduce the purchase cost
of raw and intermediate materials across the industries studied, from an
almost 40 percent reduction in electronic components to only 2 percent in
coal.[20] These lower costs will allow producers to increase output without
raising prices and thus shift downward along an aggregate demand curve.
Demand may also rise, however, due to consumers' increased wealth from
stock market gains or due to lower interest rates. The net effect of these
supply and demand shifts is likely to be an economy with increased output
and unchanged prices. According to this study, output from the economy
as a whole could be up to 5 percent higher, with the bulk of this increase
coming within the first ten years. This implies an increase in GDP growth

18. For a review of the early history of the Internet, see Hafner (1996) and Leiner and others
(2000). For an account of the birth of the web by one of its primary architects, see Berners-Lee and
Fischetti (1999).

19. Brookes and Wahhaj (2000).

20. Brookes and Wahhaj (2000), p. 12.

rate of at least 0.25 percent a year over this period.[21] Some observers have urged caution in accepting the study's conclusions, pointing out that the analysis makes highly optimistic assumptions about the Internet's ability to reduce component prices in industries, such as computer manufacturing, that are already highly competitive and that have been facing intense cost reduction pressure for some time.

Interestingly, studies have found that productivity gains from IT (whether Internet based or not) within manufacturing have in some cases *not* been matched within the service sector of the economy. A study by the U.S. Department of Commerce's Economics and Statistics Administration found that a labor productivity-like measure was higher in IT-using industries that produced goods than in their non IT-using counterparts. However, a similar pattern was not apparent among producers of services; in fact, service producers who were heavy users of IT experienced a decline in productivity growth over the period under investigation.[22]

Internal Cost Reduction

One of the most direct results of a firm's investment in information technology is a reduction in internal costs. This gain can yield profit increases as well as increased output and enhanced consumer welfare in the form of lower prices, and it is difficult to determine ex ante which of these will dominate in a given context or industry. It is also difficult to assess the value of other IT benefits, such as increased reliability, flexibility, and customer service. Consequently, straightforward estimates of the internal cost reductions brought to U.S. manufacturing by the Internet are a useful starting point; they are both informative and tractable. Later I discuss the mechanisms by which these gains are achieved; this section's goal is to provide an initial estimate of their magnitude.

This exercise is helped by a U.S. manufacturer that has, for the previous five years, been engaged in a highly successful Internet-based transformation of both its external and internal practices. This company, Cisco Systems, is the leading maker of routers and other Internet networking equipment. Beginning in 1994 Cisco undertook a series of initiatives to

21. Brookes and Wahhaj (2000), p. 2. See also *Economist*, "Internet Economics: A Thinker's Guide," April 1, 2000, pp. 64–66.
22. Prakken (1999). The authors caution, however, that measurement problems related to service producers greatly decrease confidence in this finding.

Table 2-1. *Cisco Cost Savings from Internet-Based Efforts, 1994–99*
Millions of dollars unless otherwise indicated

Category	Cumulative savings
Customer care	269
Internet commerce	57
Supply chain management	269
Work force optimization	55
Total cost savings	650
Cisco 1999 revenue	12,200
Cost savings as percent of revenue	5.3

Source: Internal Cisco estimates, published on a CD-ROM entitled *Internet 101: Roadmaps for Success in the Internet Economy.*

fully leverage the potential of the Internet, both for its internal business processes and for its dealings with external firms. By many accounts, these initiatives were great successes, and Cisco is often held up as an example of what embracing the Internet can do for a company.

In late 1999 Cisco conducted an internal review of these efforts and attempted to quantify their benefits in reducing costs.[23] Table 2-1 shows these cumulative benefits over a 4.5-year period, compared to a zero Internet investment baseline. Cisco realized cumulative cost reduction benefits during this time amounting to 5.33 percent of its end period revenues. These data provide an interesting benchmark; they represent something close to an upper bound on what other companies can hope to achieve over a comparable period of sustained Internet-based IT investment. They are an upper bound because of the wide perception that Cisco's successes will be quite difficult to emulate; even if other firms make comparable heavy Internet-based IT investments, many of them will be unable to emulate the managerial and organizational context that has allowed Cisco to benefit so heavily from them.[24]

The distribution for which this is the upper bound can be imputed and then used to calculate a first estimate of the cumulative impact of the

---

23. It is important to stress that this estimate has not been validated by the author or external reviewers.

24. The author has found support for this statement in sessions with executives from many firms. Almost uniformly, they consider themselves to be unable, for a variety of reasons, to emulate Cisco's demonstrated success.

Internet on U.S. manufacturers' internal costs over five years. It seems appropriate to begin this five-year period in 1999, because, as discussed above in the introduction, this is when many manufacturers began making the kinds of investments Cisco started making five years previously.

Cisco between 1995 and 1999 could not take advantage of e-marketplaces, which are discussed below, because these novel organizational forms did not yet exist. Many observers feel that e-marketplaces will have a large positive impact on manufacturing firms' performance, so an argument could be made that many manufacturers will be able to outstrip Cisco's performance because of their participation in e-marketplaces. However, by virtue of its market dominance, Cisco was able to compel many, if not all, of its suppliers to join the digital communities that it established, thereby creating the equivalent of an e-marketplace. Because of this, Cisco is still considered to represent an upper bound on observed performance; Internet-based marketplaces that have sprung up since 1999 are, essentially, only mimicking what Cisco had in place earlier.

The distribution for which Cisco's results are an upper bound is chosen here to be log normal, with a lower bound at zero.[25] A log normal form was chosen because this distribution is extensively used to characterize the returns from many kinds of investments.

Table 2-2 below shows the results of this estimate for five different scenarios—one where Cisco's demonstrated performance is at the 67th percentile of what manufacturing firms in general will achieve between 1999 and 2004 (in other words, one in three of these firms will have greater success than Cisco), and ones where Cisco is at the 75th, 90th, 95th, and 99th percentile. The mean of each of the resulting derived distributions was then multiplied by an estimate of U.S. manufacturing value added for 2004 to yield a total estimated internal cost reduction figure.

As this table shows, if Cisco's demonstrated results are at the 90th percentile of projected results throughout manufacturing in the coming years, there will be an estimated cumulative cost reduction of approximately $114 billion throughout this sector of the economy. If Cisco's results are at the 95th percentile, this estimate is reduced to approximately $89 billion. Of course, these results should be interpreted with great caution; they are intended to serve only as indications of the magnitude of efficiency gains brought by Internet usage within manufacturing.

25. This initial estimate ignores the possibility that IT investment increases a firm's cumulative internal costs over a five-year period.

Table 2-2. *Estimates of Cumulative Internal Savings from Internet-Based Efforts across U.S. Manufacturing Firms, 1999–2004*

Year	A Cisco savings (percent)	B Cisco anchor (percent)	C Projected 2004 manufacturing value of shipments (billions of dollars)	D Mean savings across all U.S. manufacturing (percent)	E Total projected savings (billions of dollars)
1999	5.3	50	5,221.83	5.3	278.22
2000	5.3	67	5,221.83	3.9	206.29
2001	5.3	75	5,221.83	3.3	174.34
2002	5.3	90	5,221.83	2.1	114.47
2003	5.3	95	5,221.83	1.7	88.99
2004	5.3	99	5,221.83	1.0	55.49

A = Percentage of Cisco's 1999 revenue saved by the company; 1994–99. Source: Internal Cisco estimates published on a CD-ROM, *Internet 101: Roadmaps for Success in the Internet Economy.*

B = Estimated percentage of firms that will, from 1999 to 2004, save a lower percentage of revenue than Cisco from 1994 to 1999.

C = In 1999 dollars, using 1996 value of shipments and actual GDP growth for 1997–99 and assuming 4.33 percent yearly GDP growth from 1999 to 2004. The 4.33 percent figure is the average real U.S. GDP growth from 1997 to 1999.

D = Mean savings with Cisco percentage as noted and sigma of 2, assuming log-normal distribution of returns.

E = C*D/100.

Unfortunately, Cisco cannot serve as a straightforward harbinger of coming productivity gains as well as cost reductions. Cisco's labor productivity, as measured by revenue per employee, actually decreased substantially between 1995 and 1999.[26] This is because Cisco needed to hire a great many employees, in addition to investing heavily in IT, to manage its hypergrowth. However, the new employees were, in all likelihood, working in less productive environments before joining the company, and so their individual productivity improved. Each move, therefore, led to an increase in overall worker productivity, but it is not possible to estimate this increase's magnitude with Cisco data alone, let alone to extrapolate from it to the economy as a whole.

New Organizational Forms

The Internet lowers the costs of finding, connecting to, and sharing information with other organizations. With all of these transaction costs lowered, there is increased freedom to choose among markets, alliances, and firms as coordination mechanisms. A number of authors have predicted that the Internet and other information technologies will lead to smaller firms, greater levels of decentralization and freelancing, increased fluidity in the number and types of partnerships explored by the average firm, and the rise of the "virtual factory."[27]

In the short history of Internet usage within manufacturing, many of these predictions have already been borne out. For example, Cisco has become the most valuable corporation in the world in terms of market capitalization.[28] It has done this in part through what, to the outside world, looks like "world-class manufacturing"—efficiently producing a family of high-quality products and reliably fulfilling customer demands for them. However, Cisco does little manufacturing internally, and the majority of its products reach the customer without ever having been seen or touched by a Cisco employee.[29] The company has accomplished this remarkable feat in

26. Cisco's revenue per employee was over $900,000 in 1995 and less than $600,000 in 1999 (Sources: Cisco annual reports and Compustat).

27. Brynjolfsson and others (1994); Malone and Laubacher (1998); Gurbaxani and Whang (1991); Malone (1997); Upton and McAfee (1996).

28. As of August 29, 2000, Cisco's market capitalization was $466 billion. Microsoft's was $373 billion, and GM's was $395 billion. Source: Bloomberg.

29. Ansley (2000).

large part by heavily leveraging the Internet to integrate closely with its suppliers. Information about forecasts, production schedules, shipments, manufacturing activity, and quality is available to Cisco and its suppliers at the same time. The end result is that ownership of the physical assets used in production has become unnecessary for Cisco and irrelevant to its customers.[30]

Many other manufacturers are trying to emulate this success and to build "virtual supply chains."[31] A salient feature of these networks is that information is not designed to flow sequentially from partner to partner, but rather to be continuously available to all qualified viewers. To date, very few of these are as advanced as Cisco's, but this may change rapidly. A recent manufacturing industry analysis flatly states: "Five years down the road, today's linear manufacturing chains will have broken down. In their place will be networks of manufacturing specialists, all cooperating at Internet speed to deliver products."[32]

This great thirst on the part of manufacturers to find new partners and work very closely with them has given rise to a novel Internet-based organization—the e-marketplace. Also called e-hubs, net marketplaces, and B2B exchanges, e-marketplaces are purely digital meeting places that provide to their participants two broad categories of service: aggregation and facilitation. Aggregation refers to making available large numbers of potential partners—both buyers and suppliers—along with, in many cases, listings of the goods they want to buy or sell. In many cases, aggregation of suppliers entails creating a comprehensive online catalog of their wares.[33] Aggregation provides the obvious benefit of liquidity, an important consideration for all traders. Facilitation refers to helping e-marketplace participants interact with each other, before, during, and after their decisions to do business together. Before making these decisions, e-marketplaces facilitate by providing information about potential partners, including certification as to their demonstrated qualities (credit, fulfillment reliability, and so on). E-marketplaces often assist contracting and partnership deci-

---

30. For more information on Cisco's IT and Internet efforts, see Nolan and Porter (2000).

31. See, for example, David Joachim, "Dell Links Virtual Supply Chain," *InternetWeek*, November 2, 1998, p. 1.

32. Radjou (2000).

33. The largest acquisition in the history of the software industry—i2 Technology's $9.3 billion purchase of Aspect Development—was driven by i2's desire to incorporate Aspect's catalog database of 17 million parts and 7,000 manufacturers into its e-marketplace products. For a discussion of the deal, see Mary Mosquera, "i2, Aspect in Biggest Software Merger," *InternetWeek*, March 13, 2000.

sions by conducting auctions, reverse auctions, and other dynamic pricing events. Finally, many e-marketplaces also offer postpartnership facilitation services such as arranging credit and logistics services and, in some cases, taking responsibility for order fulfillment.

E-marketplaces have, perhaps fittingly, proliferated with Internet-like speed. Estimates for the total number of e-marketplaces in existence range from 750 to over 1,400.[34] E-marketplaces now play a role in every sector of the economy, from utilities to surplus goods, and they have deeply penetrated manufacturing, perhaps because markets for many manufactured goods are characterized by high numbers of geographically dispersed buyers, suppliers, or both. In addition, many manufacturing firms, especially smaller ones, did not have sophisticated digital interconnection capabilities before the Internet. This combination of fragmentation and heterogeneity in IT capability across firms in manufacturing industries makes them attractive sites for an e-marketplace.

Within e-marketplaces themselves, new organizational forms have already begun to appear. The first wave of e-marketplaces was dominated by independent start-up firms without direct ties to incumbent firms in a specific industry and often backed by venture capital. More recently, established manufacturers in many industries have jointly formed their own e-marketplace, called a consortium, to compete with or preempt independent start-ups. Because these consortia start with large firms, typically on the buyer side, as both participants and backers, they enjoy a substantial advantage over start-ups that must convince initial members to join when benefits are lower. In large industries such as automotive and aerospace manufacturing, the emergence of consortia has significantly dampened enthusiasm for start-up e-marketplaces.[35]

Summary

Economy- and industry-level investigations of the general impact of information technology largely reach consensus that in recent years these technologies, and the industries that produce them, have been important contributors to the observed sharp increases in labor productivity. According

34. The lower number comes from "Seller Beware," *Economist*, March 4, 2000, pp. 61–62. The larger is the total number of e-marketplaces identified by a Deloitte Consulting effort as of mid-August 2000. Information about this effort is available from Shaun Greene, sgreene@dttus.com.
35. For a discussion of consolidation in e-marketplaces, see Kafka and others (2000).

to some observers, the Internet may have played a specific role in these increases by allowing previously isolated computers to interconnect cheaply and efficiently. There is also agreement that, in a broad sense, the good times seem likely to continue.[36] IT will continue to positively influence productivity growth, and the Internet alone will be responsible for increases in supply, and perhaps demand, throughout the economy, leading to higher GDP growth rates.

The Internet has also contributed to the creation of new configurations for efficient manufacturing, such as Cisco's, and novel e-marketplace organizations. Of course, there are many other ways in which the Internet could have, now or in the future, an impact on producers and production. It could, for example, lead to increased rates of failure among firms that do not embrace it; this possibility will be considered below. The Internet could also affect competitive dynamics and industry structure in many other ways, a discussion of which is well beyond the present scope.[37] Instead, this section has concentrated on identifying the most concrete ways that the Internet has affected manufacturing. The next section identifies the *mechanisms* by which the Internet is achieving this impact.

Framework: Transformation at Three Levels

For manufacturers, the Internet is already having a substantial impact at three levels: within *companies* themselves, among *alliances* formed across partners with an ongoing relationship, and within *markets* created to help companies find partners and trade with them. Boundaries between these levels are not firm. Free markets, for example, help companies conduct Internet-based auctions (a net market), but the result of these auctions is often a relatively long-term contract between a customer and a supplier (an alliance). In many cases, in fact, the customer's existing supplier is encouraged to participate in the auction; if its bid is accepted, the alliance will continue (although probably with new prices). The boundary between the company and the alliance is also becoming blurry, with many software vendors offering Internet-based tools to enable an "extended enterprise" where information flows efficiently within and among collaborators.

36. See, for example, Oliner and Sichel (2000) and Buckley and others (2000), ch. 3.
37. For discussions of the Internet's impact on firms and strategy, see, for example Downes and Mui (1998); Evans (1999); Cash and Kosynski (1985); and Porter and Millar (1985).

Company Level

A manager interviewed for a recent Forrester Research survey stated, "We are doing business e-commerce to be more efficient, offer better customer service, reduce processing costs, create savings, and utilize volume discounts through negotiated price deals."[38] An important question is how do Internet technologies help firms become more efficient *internally*, in addition to helping them interact better with external partners and markets? There are three main avenues by which the Internet delivers internal efficiency gains.

INTRANETS. The Internet benefits companies most directly by providing them with a wide and useful channel for internal information sharing. Intranets, or private, within-company networks that use Internet and web technologies, can ensure that all employees have access to the same information. This information can include messages from management, online phone books and maps, benefits data, and other amenities.

Intranets can also be easily used for collaboration, especially among employees who are in different functions or at various sites or other countries. Product development activities in many large corporations, for example, typically involve many different functions (research and development, product and process engineering, manufacturing), which must coordinate both their parallel and sequential activities across labs, offices, and factories in many different places. Simple Internet-based tools like websites, e-mail, and groupware can greatly facilitate these tasks, reducing both expense and time.[39] As another manager in the Forrester study explained, "This shift to the Net is absolutely necessary if we are to meet our price targets. Right now there is too much manual work, and the cost to support our sales is prohibitive."[40]

Finally, intranets are also used to provide a web-based "front end" to corporate applications. Instead of using proprietary desktop software to access mainframe or client-server applications and their data, companies can instead web-enable these applications so that they can be accessed by

---

38. Kafka (2000).

39. According to the online dictionary *Webopaedia*, groupware is a "class of software that helps groups of colleagues (work groups) attached to a local area network organize their activities. Typically, groupware supports the following operations: scheduling meetings and allocating resources, e-mail, password protection for documents, telephone utilities, electronic newsletters, [and] file distribution." For an overview of groupware, see Chaffey (1998). For a case study of its adoption, see Orlikowski (1993).

40. Kafka (2000).

an employee using an Internet browser. This not only has the advantage of making applications and data much more widely available, but also greatly reduces IT support costs, a large part of which consists of maintaining desktops.[41]

Heavy reliance on intranets can yield impressive benefits. Cisco Systems, for example, estimates that it saves more than $300 million a year over a previous baseline because of web enablement of applications for customer care and "work force optimization."[42] Similarly, Oracle Corporation believes that its internal IT alignment efforts, which are largely based around web-enablement, will save the company a total of $1 billion.[43]

ENTERPRISE INFORMATION TECHNOLOGY. Internet-based technologies benefit corporations not only because they provide a convenient channel to get data out of applications, but also because they help get data into them. In general, most firms do not have IT infrastructures that allow all of their enterprise applications to share data internally, much less with the applications of external firms.[44] In a survey of fifty global manufacturing companies, for example, the most commonly cited "biggest problem" was "poor visibility into plant operations" with 38 percent. "Poor communication" was third, with 24 percent.[45] One respondent stated, "In our experience, the biggest coordination problems come from interfacing with the legacy systems that our remote locations still use. We don't have an enterprise-wide standard for integrating these systems; this makes communication very difficult."[46]

Internet technologies like file transfer protocol (FTP) and especially eXtensible markup language (XML) provide convenient, highly functional, and relatively inexpensive (due to the zero incremental cost pricing structure of most Internet usage plans) means to share data between applications and to format it so that it is machine comprehensible.[47] Previous

41. The expense of maintaining desktops is often captured in a metric called "total cost of ownership," or TCO. See Jacqueline Emigh, "Total Cost of Ownership," *ComputerWorld*, December 20, 1999.

42. These figures come from a presentation given by Cisco manager Amir Hartman and included on a CD-ROM entitled "Internet 101: Roadmaps for Success in the Internet Economy," jointly produced by Cisco Systems and KPMG.

43. Jeff Sweat, "Oracle Is Talking. Should You Be Listening?" *InformationWeek*, February 7, 2000, p. 54.

44. For academic work on IT heterogeneity within firms, see Goodhue, Wybo, and Kirsch (1992).

45. Radjou (2000), p. 3.

46. Radjou (2000), p. 5.

47. For a discussion of the benefits of XML, see Jon Bosak and Tim Bray, "XML and the Second-Generation Web," *Scientific American*, May 1999.

technologies such as value added networks (VANs) and electronic data interchange (EDI) were typically more expensive, less flexible, and less functional than their Internet-era counterparts.[48] Most modern enterprise information technologies (EITs) now have the capability to automatically accept XML-formatted data and to output data in this format.

PROCUREMENT SAVINGS. The Goldman Sachs study of the macroeconomic impact of the Internet cited above considered only the improvements in manufacturers' procurement activities. Some of these improvements arise from enhanced ability to find trading partners and are discussed below, but other benefits come from the Internet's help in streamlining the routine activities of procurement for both raw materials and indirect materials such as office supplies and maintenance, repair, and operations (MRO) goods.

Many of these supplies can now be purchased from integrated and fairly comprehensive online catalogs, maintained by companies such as Ariba and CommerceOne, which are integrated into a company's IT infrastructure and made available via a browser.[49] These services also automate many steps of the procurement process, from authorization through generation and transmission of a purchase order to invoicing and payment. While these activities are mundane and are rarely considered possible sources of competitive advantage, they still are time consuming and expensive to carry out in the absence of automation. In the Internet era, this automation is becoming readily available.

Alliance Level

Once two or more companies agree to do business with each other on activities beyond simple procurement, they again face a challenge in executing many joint processes as efficiently as possible. In addition, these processes are typically less well defined in advance than those of the procurement cycle; there is, therefore, the added challenge of process definition before automation can take place. At present, Internet technologies are being widely deployed to meet these twin challenges—to build rich point-to-point links between alliance partners and to enable communities of manufacturers to work in harmony.

---

48. For a discussion of the advantages of Internet Technologies over EDI, see Upton and McAfee (1996) and Emily Kay, "From EDI to XML," *ComputerWorld*, June 19, 2000.

49. Edward Robinson, "Battle to the Bitter End," *Business 2.0*, July 25, 2000, pp. 135–49.

POINT-TO-POINT LINKS. The most obvious intercompany use of the Internet is probably construction of a point-to-point link between two alliance partners. These are companies that have agreed to do a substantial amount of business together and so are willing to invest resources in building a highly functional link, especially one that allows their information systems to interact on routine tasks without human intervention. This intervention is costly and can slow down necessary activities. However, it is also currently widespread; in a survey of 50 global manufacturing companies, 62 percent reported that they used primarily manual methods to share production schedules with their partners, with one respondent stating, "Our biggest coordination headaches come from a lack of visibility into our suppliers' systems. That translates into long and inconsistent lead times."[50]

A number of technology providers are offering Internet-based products that address exactly this problem. Some of them concentrate on integrating information systems across companies, while others focus on defining and automating processes that cut across companies and may involve multiple systems.[51] Both of these approaches have proved productive for manufacturing firms.

MULTIPARTNER INTEGRATION. In addition to enabling rich point-to-point links, the Internet is also being used to integrate groups of alliance partners, just as it is being employed to unite dispersed functional or geographic groups within a firm. While automatic process execution continues to be valuable for these networks, the greater goal of integration often appears to be better and faster decisionmaking. For example, current versions of supply chain management and advanced planning and scheduling software embed more advanced algorithms than their predecessors and offer the possibility of optimizing decisions across an entire supply chain, as opposed to within single firms.[52] To do this effectively, this software obviously requires accurate concurrent data from all members of the supply chain, and the Internet-based technologies discussed above are rapidly proving to be the preferred channels for these data.

---

50. Radjou (2000), pp. 3, 5.

51. For a description of a company with the first focus, see Karen J. Bannan, "Staying on His Target: WebMethods' CEO Wants to Automate the World's Economy," *Internet World*, May 15, 2000. For a case study of the latter type of inter-company process automation, see Susan Scheck, "TSMC Builds Info Alliance," *Electronic Buyers' News*, October 26, 1998.

52. For a discussion of the shortcomings of the long-standing material requirements planning algorithm, see Hopp and Spearman (1996, ch. 3).

Better information sharing among alliance partners may have subtle yet important benefits. One of the most common and striking dysfunctions of manufacturing supply chains is the "bullwhip effect," where information gaps and delays cause small changes in customer demand to amplify as they move up the chain, leading to a counterproductive combination of spiky order patterns and inventory shortages and surpluses.[53] To the extent that the Internet can help reduce information gaps and delays, it can be expected to alleviate this situation.[54] Leading manufacturers like Dell and Cisco have, in fact, established extensive information sharing capabilities with their suppliers and appear to suffer less from the bullwhip effect as a result.[55]

PROCESS CONSORTIA. Manufacturers in many industries, realizing that their interactions are far from efficient, are exploring ways to improve. The U.S. high-tech manufacturing community is perhaps furthest along with this effort; it has created a consortium called RosettaNet to develop standards at all required levels—from XML data formats to interaction scripts (called "partner interaction processes")—to enable productive automatic interactions. To understand the goals of this effort, and the extent of current difficulties (even in this relatively IT-enabled industry), it is worth quoting extensively from the RosettaNet website's Executive Overview:

> The electronic components (EC) and information technology (IT) industries remain infinitely focused on creating and selling the next generation of our fast changing technologies, and thus we have not taken the time, effort, or collective resolve to develop a set of industry-wide electronic business interoperability standards. Given the deep changes exacted by the new digital economy, coupled with the growing size of the EC and IT sectors within the overall economy, we can no longer afford to further postpone attention to efficient business process interfaces between supply-chain trading partners.
>
> The lack of electronic business interfaces in the EC and IT supply chains puts a huge burden on manufacturers, distributors, resellers, and end-users, ultimately creating tremendous inefficiencies and

---

53. The bullwhip effect is explored in Sterman (1989) and Lee, Padmanabhan, and Whang (1997a and b).

54. For a case study of this process, see Hammond (1994).

55. For discussions of these companies' information sharing activities, see Magretta (1998) and Nolan and Porter (2000).

inhibiting our ability to leverage the Internet as a business-to-business commerce tool. Here are a few examples:

—Manufacturers today utilize complex processes to all but guess inventory levels and locations across the supply chain at any point in time. This is because there is no agreement on something as simple as how a part number is defined or how inventory queries can be made through a standard interface. This significantly impacts production planning, channel allocation, and the cost of returns.

—Distributors, who provide pre- and post-sale technical support to their resellers on tens of thousands of SKUs, must grapple with disparate forms of product information collected from hundreds of manufacturers with no common taxonomy. The lack of product information standards makes the current aggregation and dissemination of such content an expensive and inefficient proposition—an effort duplicated by each distributor in the channel. This problem is further compounded by content's explosive rate of change.

—Resellers must learn and maintain different ordering and return procedures and system interfaces to each distributor and direct manufacturer with whom they trade, causing them to spend valuable resources in back-office operations (50 percent by some estimates), which they could otherwise use to make new sales or service their customers.

—End-users have no mechanism enabling effective procurement through uniform templates, which can be contextually linked to government authorized schedules. This often causes a nonsensical lengthening of the purchasing cycle whereby most PC orders are old technology by the time they make it through this inefficient cycle and onto the desk of the requisitioner.[56]

Market

As discussed above, e-marketplaces are a novel organizational form of the Internet era that aggregate potential buyers and suppliers in a centralized online hub, often devoted to a particular industry, and facilitate interactions among these parties before, during, and after their agreement to trade. The Internet holds the promise of allowing manufacturers to par-

56. See www.rosettanet.org/general/index_general.html [August 2000].

ticipate in liquid, dynamic markets that go well beyond their own domain.[57]

GROWTH PROJECTIONS. A Forrester Research study concluded that e-marketplaces will account for 53 percent of all online business trade in five years; in other words, more online B2B trade will occur through e-marketplaces than through all other digital channels (TCP/IP links, EDI, and others) combined. A quarter of firms participating in this study anticipated that the majority of their trade would flow through e-marketplaces within this time.[58] The study's authors predict that in some industries, up to 74 percent of trade will occur through e-marketplaces.[59] An estimate by the Gartner Group is only somewhat more conservative, predicting that 37 percent of online trade will flow through e-marketplaces by 2004.[60]

CURRENT STATE. An interviewee at one surveyed company summarized the anticipated benefits: "Marketplaces will eventually save us time by freeing us from having to sift through hundreds of vendor catalogs anymore. We'll be able to prequalify vendors, analyze key variables, and support a matrix—anything you want at the touch of a button."[61] However, many current e-marketplaces do not yet support this level of sophistication and appear to be little more than listings of firms and (sometimes) their products. After surveying the primitive capabilities of many e-marketplaces, an executive from Dell computer commented, "Some of these exchanges are to B2B e-commerce what DOS 1.0 is to Windows 2000."[62]

Even advanced e-marketplaces currently providing valuable services to their customers are doing so in many cases by relieving them of the burden of executing manual processes. In other words, the process automation advances discussed above in the "Company Level" and "Alliance Level" sections have not yet pervaded e-marketplaces. This is at least partly because many e-marketplaces have rushed to achieve scale and provide initial liquidity to their members before devoting resources to process automation work.

57. A full discussion of e-marketplaces is well beyond the present scope; for deeper information, see Phillips and Meeker (2000); Blodget and McCabe (2000); Goldman Sachs (1999); and Kaplan and Sawhney (2000).

58. Kafka (2000).

59. Kafka (2000).

60. *Frontline Solutions* (2000).

61. Kafka (2000).

62. Tim Wilson, "B-to-B Traders Turn Up Heat on Vendors," *InternetWeek*, May 22, 2000.

Regardless of the reason, the contrast between the digital front end and highly manual back office of some e-marketplaces is striking. At one prominent e-marketplace, for example, paper catalogs from suppliers are manually re-entered into the central database by contract workers in a different country, with employees at the e-marketplace devoted to ensuring the work's accuracy. And while this marketplace has expended significant resources to integrate its IT platform with those of its partners (particularly large, relatively sophisticated customers), each of these customers' orders is followed up by the e-marketplace with phone calls to all involved suppliers to ensure receipt and monitor fulfillment. The company is presently working to automate these and other processes, but in the near term a great deal of manual intervention will continue to be required.[63]

A final important consideration for e-marketplaces is whether, over the longer term, they will continue to be valuable. Automated processes do not have to flow through a centralized hub; they can instead be executed by peer-to-peer interactions. Peers can also use the Internet to search for each other, as amply demonstrated by file sharing programs such as Napster and Gnutella, thereby reducing the value of e-marketplaces' aggregation services.[64] As indicated by the growth projections above, the current business-to-business (B2B) e-commerce model is dominated by e-marketplaces. It may be, however, that an alternate business-to-peer (B2P) model also becomes viable and widespread. The technical building blocks for such a model appear to be in place, and the success of Napster and Gnutella demonstrates the demand for Internet-based peer-to-peer interactions that circumvent central points.[65]

Future Developments

Even when confined to the manufacturing sector, speculation about the continued impact of the Internet can range widely across scenarios, technologies, competitive dynamics, predictions, and other aspects. This chapter concludes by attempting a much less ambitious program—the description of

63. Data on this e-marketplace's operations come from confidential interviews with the author. The e-marketplace has asked that its name not be used.

64. These programs, and their impact on industries that distribute digital goods, are discussed in Lee Gomes, "Gnutella, New Music-Sharing Software, Rattles the CD Industry," *Wall Street Journal*, May 4, 2000, p. B10, and Clay Shirky, "Content Shifts to the Edges," *Business 2.0*, April, 2000, p. 142.

65. For a short discussion of this possibility, see McAfee (2000).

two salient trends that seem very likely to continue into the future, a brief discussion of their implications, and presentation of one possible scenario for how Internet usage will continue to penetrate this segment of the economy. The two trends—realization of value from IT investments and great heterogeneity in these investments—are in opposition and raise the question of whether manufacturing firms must undertake significant IT investments in order to remain competitive. Large-scale outsourcing of information technology, with data and applications hosted remotely and delivered to firms via the Internet, is one possibility for resolving this dilemma. It appears that manufacturers will soon have the ability to get out of the business of running their own IT and use the Internet to hand this responsibility over to a partner. It remains to be seen whether they will take advantage of this possibility and whether there will be increasing pressure to do so.

Clear Demonstration of Benefit

Merrill Lynch chief economist Bruce Steinberg has a straightforward explanation for the salubrious economic statistics presented by the study described above and one that agrees with the study's authors: "It's the new economy triumphant. We're cranking out more output without that much more labor input. It reflects the technological revolution that's sweeping our economy."[66] Even Federal Reserve Board chairman Alan Greenspan, one of the most sober observers of the U.S. economy, has stated that "the remarkable, and partly fortuitous, coming together of the technologies that make up what we label IT—information technologies—has begun to alter, fundamentally, the manner in which we do business and create economic value, often in ways that were not readily foreseeable even a decade ago."[67] The case studies discussed above of leading Internet-era companies such as Cisco give some indication of how these benefits are accruing. While there are some clear examples of firms that have stumbled badly, and even failed, as a result of their IT initiatives, it is becoming increasingly clear that IT, in general, delivers benefits to its adopters and that the productivity paradox is a thing of the past.[68]

66. Stuart Silverstein, "US Productivity Growth in '99 is Best in 7 Years," *Los Angeles Times*, February 9, 2000, p. A1
67. Commencement address, Harvard University, June 10, 1999 (www.federalreserve.gov/boarddocs/speeches/1999/199906102.htm [February 2001].
68. Case studies of severe implementation difficulties include Emily Nelson, "Hershey's Biggest Dud Has Turned out to Be Its New Technology," *Wall Street Journal*, October 29, 1999, p. A6;

This consensus is not confined to academic observers of the IT phenomenon; managerial attitudes toward IT are also strongly positive. A survey of non-IT executives in North America, Europe, and Asia conducted
by IBM Global Services and the Economist Intelligence Unit revealed that
80 percent thought that information technology could increase product or
service quality, 70 percent believed that it could increase customer satisfaction, and over 60 percent were satisfied with IT's role in increasing revenue and reducing cost of goods sold.[69] Perhaps more tellingly, case studies of leading companies reveal that non-IT managers are willing to back
up this enthusiasm with discretionary investment. At Cisco, with hypergrowth, IT investment increased *faster* than revenue growth after IT decisions were devolved to line managers. Based on the Cisco model, the CFO
has to stay within the budget growth number the president gives him, but
he has the liberty to decide how those numbers will be spent. In a year
when the company grew 90 percent, he took all the incremental dollars
that he was given and invested them in IT. In one year he increased his rate
of investment in IT by 350 percent.[70]

Cisco chief information officer Pete Solvik described this process in
action: "Three years ago a new CFO joined Cisco. The previous CFO had
not been oriented towards investing in automation to make finance more
effective for the organization; the new CFO was."

Regardless of who is making the decision, IT investment in the era of
the Internet continues to expand dramatically, accounting for approximately 50 percent of total U.S. capital equipment spending in 1997.[71] This
level of expenditure indicates confidence that this investment is beneficial.

Heterogeneity

Despite increasingly clear evidence of the value of IT in the Internet era,
the U.S. manufacturing sector is still characterized by high levels of IT heterogeneity, both in rates of adoption of these technologies and in levels of

---

Elizabeth MacDonald, "Maker of Gore-Tex Sues PeopleSoft and Deloitte," *Wall Street Journal*,
November 2, 1999, p. B14; and Andrew Osterland, "Blaming ERP," *CFO*, January 2000, pp. 89–93,
provide some examples of firms that have stumbled. For failures, see Matthew Rose and Elizabeth
MacDonald, "FoxMeyer Trustee Sues SAP, Deloitte; $500 Million Is Sought from Each Firm," *Wall
Street Journal*, August 27, 1998, p. B8.

69. Telecomworldwire, "IBM Global Service," *Computer Weekly*, February 25, 1999.

70. Nolan and Porter (2000), p. 12.

71. U.S. Commerce Department figures cited in Champion and Carr (2000).

success from these investments. A full discussion of the reasons for both types of heterogeneity is not possible here, but these two phenomena are almost certainly linked; companies with a track record of successful implementation and use of IT are more likely to continue these projects in the Internet era, while those that have been disappointed, or worse, by previous IT investments may not be as eager to continue this kind of spending.

ADOPTION. By 2004, according to one estimate, 40 percent of total trade in the computing and electronics industry will be conducted via the Internet, compared to 26 percent in motor vehicles, only 7 percent in industrial supplies and equipment, and 3 percent in heavy industries trade.[72] This analysis also concluded that by that year 29 percent of total trade will occur specifically via e-marketplaces in the computing and electronics industry, and 15 percent in utilities, but only 3 percent in construction, and 0 percent in heavy industries.[73] These results indicate that within manufacturing different industries will adopt Internet technologies at very different speeds. If all firms within each industry adopt at the same rate, the Internet would not have a strong impact on competitive dynamics or the success and failure of individual firms (unless these firms are differentially successful adopters, a possibility discussed in the next section). There is evidence, however, that this will not be the case.

A Gartner Group study estimated that North American IT spending will average 10 percent of revenue by 2005, with aggressive "Type A" companies spending on average 16 percent of revenue. Participants reported that they were spending either well above or well below averages for their industry, as they either try to capitalize on new opportunities offered by the Internet and other modern IT or ignore these options and try to find other ways to compete. This study concluded, "Many brick-and-mortar enterprises will be marginalized in their industry because of the effects of e-business and because of their inability to reinvent themselves and their threatened business models."[74]

Support for this conclusion was provided by a survey of 250 National Association of Manufacturers (NAM) members, which found that while 80 percent reported having a website, 68 percent said that they were not yet using the Internet for business transactions. NAM president Jerry Jasinowski said that the survey "showed a wide disparity between the

72. Kafka (2000).
73. Kafka (2000).
74. Potter (2000).

recognition by business that the Internet is a vital new form of commerce and the actual application of that knowledge by American industry."[75]

OUTCOMES. Even if all U.S. manufacturers were to suddenly accept the necessity of investing in e-business IT up to the required level (and there is no clear consensus or theory on what that level should be), they would almost certainly not be equally successful at realizing value from these investments. The Gartner Group study referenced above predicted that before 2004, 30 percent of enterprises in mature industries would try to become "e-business hybrids," but that 75 percent of these enterprises would suffer poor financial performance because of over- or misinvestment in IT.[76] This study echoes conclusions from economist Erik Brynjolfsson that "despite what the statistics say about the 'average' return on IT investment, each manager must decide which projects are worthwhile. There is no bank where companies can deposit IT investments and withdraw an 'average' return."[77]

In fact, the default outcome from some kinds of large IT implementation projects seems to be marginal or negligible benefits, accompanied by dissatisfaction on the part of the project's sponsors. A recent study of 100 EIT projects by the Boston Consulting Group found that their sponsors considered them successful in only one-third of the cases and that tangible financial impact was achieved in only 37 percent of cases. The study's coauthor states, "Far too many CEOs and CIOs have rushed to embark on multimillion dollar enterprise efforts, only to discover halfway through that they've mired themselves in a sort of technological and operational quicksand."[78]

Midsize businesses could be particularly affected by an inability to effectively adopt modern IT; an estimate by Giga Information Group shows their percentage of total B2B online sales declining by 25 percent (from 16 to 12 percent) between 1998 and 2002, as they are squeezed by the greater resources of large companies and the greater nimbleness of small ones.[79] While it is early to look for examples of manufacturers driven out of business solely by their inability to incorporate the Internet, it is clear that difficulties in absorbing previous information technologies (such as

75. Vijayan Jaikumar, "Survey: Manufacturers Stalled by B2B's cost," *ComputerWorld*, February 28, 2000.

76. Potter (2000).

77. Erik Brynjolfsson, "Technology's True Payoff," *InformationWeek*, October 10, 1994 , p. 34.

78. Sirkin and Dickel (2000).

79. *InternetWeek*, "U.S. Ecommerce," May 31, 1999, p. 15.

enterprise resource planning [ERP]) have greatly harmed many producers and that the Internet has already proved destructive to longstanding businesses in other industries, such as publishing.[80]

Consolidation

The collision between the two trends discussed above is obvious: IT investments are delivering real value, but many manufacturing firms are not making them or are not making them successfully. The resulting question is: In the coming years, what will happen to the laggards and the unsuccessful adopters? If the studies cited above are accurate, and if more than half of recent productivity gains are attributable to IT, what happens to firms that, for whatever reason, do not have access to this benefit? Can they survive? Comparatively low productivity is a serious handicap for a manufacturing firm. While it is certainly true that there are other ways to increase productivity besides investment in IT, and that there are other sources of competitive advantage (the ability to generate a constant stream of innovative and desirable products, for example, or ownership of valuable intellectual property), manufacturers that survive and thrive do so, at least in part, by virtue of sufficiently high comparative productivity.[81]

Laggards should perhaps also be worried for reasons that go beyond productivity. IT can provide benefits in addition to increasing output per worker, including decreased cycle times and inventory levels, increased reliability of fulfillment commitments, improved customer service, and other capabilities of great value to a manufacturing firm's customers.[82] As Brynjolfsson states, "The number one benefit that managers of [surveyed] companies say they expect from their IT investments is improved customer service. Lowering costs is the next most important benefit . . . but [respondents] also stress timeliness of interactions with customers, high product and service quality, support for reengineering efforts, and better flexibility."[83] In total, then, firms that do not or cannot avail themselves of IT's benefits appear to be in jeopardy as they move deeper into the Internet era.

80. For a case study of IT-induced corporate failure, see McAfee (1999). In publishing, for example, the print version of the *Encyclopaedia Britannica* no longer exists; see Rayport and Gerace (1997).

81. The Toyota Production System (TPS), for example, achieves high productivity without heavy use of IT. For a discussion of TPS's mechanisms, see Spear and Bowen (1999).

82. For an investigation of the effects of EIT introduction on lead times and on-time delivery rates, see McAfee (1999).

83. Erik Brynjolfsson, "Technology's True Payoff," *InformationWeek*, October 10, 1994 , p. 35.

Outsourcing as a Way Forward?

Firms that want to avoid missing the rising tide of benefits offered by information technology may want someone else to build and operate their e-business vessels. Recently, a number of established and start-up IT providers made an intriguing proposition to firms in the manufacturing sector and elsewhere by offering to take over large amounts of IT management responsibility from their customers. Website hosting at a remote location has already become a common feature of Internet-era IT management, but many IT providers want to go much further than simply hosting their customers' web servers and providing "power, pipe, and ping" services.[84] In general, they want to be responsible for maintaining their customers' applications and data, in addition to hardware, thereby becoming an "application service provider" (ASP). Both start-ups and well-established companies such as Oracle and AT&T are entering this market.[85] Other companies want to go still further than this and are offering to design and implement customized (as opposed to packaged) IT solutions for their customers; then they host them at dedicated facilities and provide operations support.[86]

The ASP market is still quite young and in tremendous flux, with business models, products, and services evolving rapidly. It is already clear, though, that many IT providers, investors, and observers expect this market to be huge. IDC, a market research firm, projects that the market for ASP services will reach $2 billion by 2003.[87] Traditional corporate functions from customer support, bill processing, and accounting to engineering design, architectural design, and manufacturing have been "virtualized," and the market for these "remote services" is expected to expand dramatically in the coming years.[88] To date, however, few firms appear to be taking this route, and there have already been notable failures among ASPs: Pandesic, one of the first providers of e-business outsourcing ser-

---

84. "Pipe" in this context refers to bandwidth provision, and "ping" to basic monitoring that ensures a server is still functioning.

85. John Cox, "Larry's Latest: Oracle to Be Its Own ASP," *Network World*, October 11, 2000, p. 86. Marge Semilof, "AT&T Throws Its Hat into ASP Ring," *Computer Reseller News*, January 31, 2000, p. 10.

86. See, for example, Sarah Roberts-Witt, "Jam on It," *Business 2.0*, August 22, 2000, pp. 80–83.

87. Cox, "Larry's Latest."

88. Champion and Carr (2000), p. 96.

vices, recently announced its intention to wind down operations, apparently leaving its customers without a technology platform.[89] Despite this trend, e-business and IT outsourcing and ASP business models continue to attract a great deal of attention and entrepreneurial energy.

An extremely important question going forward, then, is whether firms will be able to conduct e-business without maintaining strong internal IT capabilities, and whether MIT media lab director Nicholas Negroponte is correct in his prediction that "being 'wired' does not mean becoming 'computer literate' any more than driving an automobile requires becoming 'combustion literate.'"[90] Cybernetics pioneer Norbert Wiener evidently disagreed with this view, stating, "The world of the future will be an ever more demanding struggle against the limitations of our intelligence, not a comfortable hammock in which we can lie down to be waited upon by our robot slaves."[91] For manufacturing firms, the coming years are likely to support one or the other of these viewpoints.

Data Needs

Some IT-related data collection and measurement issues, such as capturing improvements in labor productivity in the service industries[92] and accounting for investment in intangible assets, have been highlighted previously.[93] Of greater interest for the present purpose is that the U.S. Census Bureau has only begun to measure business-to-business e-commerce.[94] This effort should be supported as fully as possible. Without comprehensive and objective data on firms' e-business initiatives, it is difficult to paint a full picture of the digital economy and to test some of its important performance hypotheses (for instance, do firms that devote more resources to

89. Therese Poletti, "Intel's Joint Operation with German Peer to Shut Down Operations," *San Jose Mercury News*, July 29, 2000.

90. Nicholas Negroponte, "Toys of Tomorrow," *Wired*, March 1998.

91. As quoted in Sanjay Singhal, "Simple, Sensible Pricing," *Wired,* December 1995, pp. 135–40.

92. Buckley and others (2000), p. 68. This point is highlighted by Jorgenson and Stiroh (2000), who state, "The apparent combination of slow productivity growth and heavy computer-use [in specific service industries] remains an important obstacle for new economy proponents who argue that the use of information technology is fundamentally changing business practices and raising productivity throughout the U.S."

93. Buckley and others (2000), p. 67. See also Erik Brynjolfsson and Shinkyu Yang, "The Intangible Benefits and Costs of Computer Investments: Evidence from the Financial Markets," *Proceedings of the International Conference on Information Systems*, 1997.

94. Buckley and others (2000), n. 18, ch. 2.

e-business outperform their peers along important dimensions? If so, how quickly?).

A review of the Internet's impact on U.S. manufacturing indicates another potentially important data collection consideration. E-business cannot be considered in a vacuum; because the majority of firms are not pure-play Internet start-ups, they will have pre-existing EIT. The integration of *all* IT resources to deliver value is the phenomenon of interest, so it may be inappropriate to focus data gathering only on Internet-based efforts. One of the strongest conclusions from the present investigation is that boundaries within and among firms are being rapidly lowered, and that the Internet is being extensively used to integrate previously isolated IT resources. Specific requests of governmental data collection agencies in this regard include:

—Assessing information technology endowments, or capabilities, of U.S. manufacturers. These endowments include hardware, commercially available software, custom software (written either to provide specific end-user functionality, or to integrate disparate pieces of software), networking equipment, and Internet connectivity (that is, bandwidth). Salient aspects of these endowments include their age and cost to acquire.

—Calculating yearly investments made to increase, enhance, and replace existing endowments in each of these categories. Ideally, more than just the dollar value of these investments would be captured; respondents would also indicate what efforts these investments were serving as well as their firms' major IT initiatives for the year. At present, data in this and the previous category are largely captured by private institutions as opposed to the government, and it can be difficult and expensive for researchers to obtain them. If the public interest is served by giving to a large community of analysts data on how the infrastructure of the Internet economy is being assembled, the government may wish to collect these data.

—Establishing a standardized method of capturing those portions of endowments and investments that are purchased versus leased. If the progressive outsourcing of IT capability described above does in fact take place, it will become increasingly important to properly account for IT resources that are used but not owned by firms.

References

Ansley, Mike. 2000. "Virtual Manufacturing." *CMA Management* 74 (1) (February): 31–35.
Berners-Lee, Tim, and Mark Fischetti. 1999. *Weaving the Web: The Original Design and Ultimate Destiny of the World Wide Web by Its Inventor.* HarperSanFrancisco.

Blinder, Alan S. 2000. *The Internet and the New Economy*. Brookings Policy Brief 60. Brookings.

Blodget, Henry, and Edward McCabe. 2000. *The B2B Market Maker Book*. New York: Merrill Lynch.

Brookes, Martin, and Zaki Wahhaj. 2000. *The Shocking Economic Impact of B2B*. Global Economics Paper 37. New York: Goldman Sachs (February 3).

Brynjolfsson, Erik, and Lorin Hitt. 1996. "Paradox Lost? Firm-Level Evidence on the Returns to Information Systems Spending." *Management Science* 42 (April): 541–58.

Brynjolfsson, Erik, Thomas W. Malone, Vijay Gurbaxani, and others. 1994. "Does Information Technology Lead to Smaller Firms?" *Management Science* 40 (December): 1628–44.

Buckley, Patricia, Sabrina Montes, David Henry, and others. 2000. *Digital Economy 2000*. U.S. Department of Commerce, Economics and Statistics Administration (June), p. 38, table 4.1.

Cash, James I., Jr., and Benn R. Kosynski. 1985. "IS Redraws Competitive Boundaries." *Harvard Business Review* 63 (2): 134–42.

Chaffey, Dave. 1998. *Groupware, Workflow, and Intranets: Reengineering the Enterprise with Collaborative Software*. Digital Press.

Champion, David, and Nicholas G. Carr. 2000. "Starting up in High Gear: An Interview with Venture Capitalist Vinod Khosla." *Harvard Business Review* 78 (4): 93–100.

Dewan, Sanjeev, and Chung-ki Min. 1997. "The Substitution of Information Technology for Other Factors of Production: A Firm Level Analysis." *Management Science* 43 (12): 1660–75.

Downes, Larry, and Chunka Mui. 1998. *Unleashing the Killer App: Digital Strategies for Market Dominance*. Harvard Business School Press.

Evans, Philip. 1999. *Blown to Bits: How the New Economics of Information Transforms Strategy*. Harvard Business School Press.

Frontline Solutions. 2000. "B2B Market Set to Explode; Value to Exceed $7T by 2004." 1 (4): 14.

Goldman Sachs. 1999. *E-Commerce/Internet: B2B: 2B or Not 2B?* Goldman Sachs Investment Research (November).

Goodhue, Dale L., Michael D. Wybo, and Laurie J. Kirsch. 1992. "The Impact of Data Integration on the Costs and Benefits of Information Systems." *MIS Quarterly* 16 (3): 293–311.

Gordon, Robert J. 1999. *Has the "New Economy" Rendered the Productivity Slowdown Obsolete?* Working Paper. Northwestern University (June 14) (faculty-web.at.northwestern. edu/economics/gordon/334.pdf [February 2001]).

Gurbaxani, Vijay, and Seungjin Whang. 1991. "The Impact of Information Systems on Organizations and Markets." *Communications of the ACM* 34 (1): 59–73.

Hafner, Katie. 1996. *Where Wizards Stay Up Late: The Origins of the Internet*. Simon and Schuster.

Hammond, Janice H. 1994. *Barilla SpA (A)*. Case Study 9-694-046. Harvard Business School (June 14).

Hayes, Robert H., and Steven C. Wheelwright. 1984. *Restoring Our Competitive Edge: Competing through Manufacturing*. John Wiley.

Hayes, Robert H., Steven C. Wheelwright, and Kim B. Clark. 1988. *Dynamic Manufacturing: Creating the Learning Organization*. Free Press.

Hopp, Wallace J., and Mark L. Spearman. 1996. *Factory Physics: Foundations of Manu-facturing Management*. Burr Ridge, Ill.: Irwin.

Jorgenson, Dale W., and Kevin J. Stiroh. 2000. "Raising the Speed Limit: U.S. Economic Growth in the Information Age." *Brookings Papers in Economic Activity* 1:125.

Kafka, Steven J. 2000. *EMarketplaces Boost B2B Trade*. Forrester Report. Cambridge, Mass.: Forrester Research (February).

Kafka, Steven J., Bruce D. Temkin, Bill Doyle, and others. 2000. *The eMarketplace Shakeout*. Forrester Report. Cambridge, Mass.: Forrester Research (August).

Kaplan, Steven, and Mohanbir Sawhney. 2000. "E-Hubs: The New B2B Marketplaces." *Harvard Business Review* 78(3) (May): 97–106

Krugman, Paul. 1994. *Peddling Prosperity: Economic Sense and Nonsense in the Age of Diminished Expectations*. W. W. Norton.

———. 1998. *The Accidental Theorist and Other Dispatches from the Dismal Science*. W. W. Norton.

Lawrence, Stacy. 2000. "Behind the Numbers: The Mystery of B-to-B Forecasts Revealed." *The Industry Standard*, February 21, 2000.

Lee, Hau L., V. Padmanabhan, and Seungjin Whang. 1997a. "The Bullwhip Effect in Supply Chains." *Sloan Management Review* (spring): 93–102.

———. 1997b. "Information Distortion in a Supply Chain: The Bullwhip Effect." *Management Science* 43 (4): 546–58.

Leiner, Barry M., Vinton G. Cerf, David D. Clark, and others. *A Brief History of the Internet*. Internet Society website (www.isoc.org/internet/history/brief.html [February 2001]).

Lewis, Michael. 1999. *The New New Thing: A Silicon Valley Story*. W. W. Norton.

Magretta, Joan. 1998. "The Power of Virtual Integration: An Interview with Dell Computer's Michael Dell." *Harvard Business Review* 76 (2) (March–April): 72–84.

Malone, Thomas W. 1997. "Is Empowerment Just a Fad? Control, Decision Making, and IT." *Sloan Management Review* 38 (2): 23–35.

Malone, Thomas W., and Robert J. Laubacher. 1998. "The Dawn of the E-Lance Economy." *Harvard Business Review* 76 (5) (September–October): 145–52.

McAfee, Andrew. 1999. *Rich-Con Steel*. Case Study N9-699-133. Harvard Business School (January 27).

———. 1999. "The Impact of Enterprise Information Technology Adoption on Operational Performance: An Empirical Investigation." Working Paper. Harvard Business School.

———. 2000. "The Napsterization of B2B." *Harvard Business Review* 78 (6) (November–December): 18.

Nolan, Richard L., and Kelley A. Porter. 2000. *Cisco Systems, Inc.* Case Study 9-398-127. Harvard Business School (April 3).

Oliner, Stephen D., and Daniel E. Sichel. 2000. *The Resurgence of Growth in the Late 1990s: Is Information Technology the Story?* Federal Reserve Board (February) (www.sf.frb.org/conf2000/papers/resurgence.pdf [February 2001]).

Orlikowski, Wanda J. 1993. "Learning from Notes: Organizational Issues in Groupware Implementation." *Information Society* 9 (3): 237–50.

Phillips, Charles, and Mary Meeker. 2000. *The B2B Internet Report: Collaborative Commerce*. Morgan Stanley Dean Witter, Equity Research, North America (April) (www.msdw.com/mrchuck [February 2001]).

Porter, Michael E., and Victor E. Millar. 1985. "How Information Gives You Competitive Advantage." *Harvard Business Review* 63 (4): 149–60.

Potter, K. 2000. *E-business IT Spending: Type A, B, and C Enterprises.* Commentary. Stamford, Conn.: Gartner Group (May 18).

Prakken, Joel L. 1999. *Productivity and Potential GDP in the "New" US Economy.* Presented at Productivity Growth Workshop. Federal Reserve Bank of St. Louis, Macroeconomic Advisors (October 8, 1999).

Radjou, Navi. 2000. *Manufacturing Deconstructed.* Forrester Report. Cambridge, Mass.: Forrester Research (July).

Rayport, Jeffrey, and Thomas Gerace. 1997. *Encyclopaedia Britannica.* Case Study 396051. Harvard Business School.

Rebello, Joseph. 2000. "Fed Study Shows Computers Sparked Most US Productivity Gains in 1990s." Dow Jones Newswires. *Dow Jones Business News* (May 19).

Schonberger, Richard J. 1996. *World Class Manufacturing: The Next Decade, Building Power, Strength, and Value.* Free Press.

Shore, Melissa. 2000. *Beyond B-to-C.* Research Report. New York: Jupiter Research (April 26).

Sichel, Daniel E. 1997. *The Computer Revolution: An Economic Perspective.* Brookings.

——. 1999. "Computers and Aggregate Economic Growth: An Update." *Business Economics* 34 (2) (April): 18–24.

Sirkin, Harold, and Karl Dickel. 2000. *Getting Value from Enterprise Initiatives.* Boston Consulting Group (March 21) (www.bcg.com/media_center/media_press_release_subpage.asp [February 2001]).

Slater, Courtney, and Cornelia J. Strauser, eds. 1998. *Business Statistics of the United States* (Lanham, Md.: Bernan Press).

Spear, Steven, and H. Kent Bowen. 1999. "Decoding the DNA of the Toyota Production System." *Harvard Business Review* 77 (5) (September): 96–108.

Sterman, John D. 1989. "Modeling Mangerial Behavior: Misperceptions of Feedback in a Dynamic Decision Making Experiment." *Management Science* 35 (3): 321–39.

Telecomworldwire.1999. "Executives Starting to See IT Investment Value." *M2 Communications* (February 10).

Upton, David M., and Andrew McAfee. 1996. "The Real Virtual Factory." *Harvard Business Review* 74 (4) (July): 123–35.

U.S. Bureau of Economic Analysis. 1998. *Survey of Current Business.* November. National Data Book. U.S. Department of Commerce, Economics and Statistics Administration, p. 460.

U.S. Census Bureau. 2000. *Annual Survey of Manufactures* (May 22).

Whelan, Karl. 2000. *Computers, Obsolescence, and Productivity.* Financial Economics Discussion Series 2000-6 (January). Federal Reserve Board.

Womack, James P., Daniel T. Jones, and Daniel Roos. 1990. *The Machine That Changed the World.* Rawson Associates.

3

CHARLES H. FINE
DANIEL M. G. RAFF

Automotive Industry: Internet-Driven Innovation and Economic Performance

THE AUTOMOBILE INDUSTRY is among the largest industries in the American economy. Twice in the course of the twentieth century the industry led the world to a new paradigm for production, moving from craft to mass production between 1908 and roughly 1930 and on to lean production in the 1970s and 1980s. It has been a font of innovation in marketing methods as well. Automobile ownership quickly became widespread among U.S. households, and the car is generally the second-most expensive durable good (after only the home itself) that a household owns. No consumer product in history to date has had as profound an effect on life-styles and on landscapes (both for better and for worse) and on the physical locus of work and residence. Except for the city-states of Hong Kong and Singapore, no major economy in the world today is considered to have established itself without a significant automotive sector. Furthermore, the automobile industry has been a lightning rod for regulatory activity. From the safety regulations inspired by Ralph Nader and the pollution and electric vehicle regulations inspired by Los Angeles smog, to

We are grateful to the International Motor Vehicle Program, the Reginald Jones Center for Strategy Research at the Wharton School of Business, and the Wharton e-Business Initiative for financial support. We have had many long and fruitful discussions on related matters with our colleague John Paul MacDuffie. Participants at The E-Business Transformation conference gave helpful comments on an earlier version of this text.

the fuel economy regulations inspired by OPEC and the recycling initiatives inspired by German landfills, the auto industry has been every government's favorite target of regulatory opportunity. As industries go, it is naturally conspicuous.

Even more lies beneath the surface. The industry is remarkable for the complexity of the problems it poses for its managers. Its supply chains are broad and deep. Its technological challenges range across aerodynamics and fluid dynamics, as well as mechanical, electrical, materials, and civil engineering, to list only the most obvious fields. Automobile consumers demand excellence in both performance and aesthetics. Design costs are large and sunk, driving chronic industry overcapacity and price competition in all but the most fashionable of segments. The industry's relationships with growth-embracing but pollution-averse governments are anything but simple. Furthermore, the product has many parts and many, many options, so that the challenges in coordinating physical activities present extraordinary challenges in the planning and control of production and distribution. Network technologies (for example, the Internet, the World Wide Web, and so forth) promise major changes in the scope and cost of coordination by offering dramatic improvements in the ease and speed of communication. The automobile industry is thus a natural subject for this volume and a challenging environment for assessing the best use of these technologies.

Our paper proceeds in five steps. We first discuss briefly the historical evolution of the industry value chain and production processes (we give a much more detailed and critical account of this in a companion paper currently in preparation).[1] Present practices and possibilities are often partly determined and highly constrained by past choices and historical events, and this case may have lessons for other industries with similar histories as well as similar structural characteristics. Second, we discuss in this context recent web-related developments, future prospects, and implications. This discussion is qualitative but suggests an analytical structure (and the potential for radical change in the current order). Third, we discuss what we consider to be the key question of the paper: whether the performance improvements triggered by new networking technologies will emerge as a one-shot boost or as a series of continuous improvements to be accumulated over years and decades. We interpret Ford's moving assembly line as being in the first of these categories, but Taichi Ohno's lean production

1. See Nelson, Steil, and Victor (2001).

paradigm as being in the latter. Following this discussion, we turn to a systematic and, where possible, quantitative discussion of how the developments might affect practices in ways which could show up in the productivity statistics. Finally, we close with a discussion of the productivity statistics themselves and the industry's prospects.

Evolution of the American Automobile Industry

We find it helpful to think of the industry's history as proceeding in five stages: the artisanal age (1890–1908), the age of Ford (1908–30), the golden age of mass production (1930–73), the age of lean (1973–90), and the age of the extended enterprise (1990–2000). Post-2000, we expect the Internet to drive another transformation, the nature of which is the principal topic of this paper.

The artisanal age began with the product concept still in the hands of workshop tinkerers and dreamers. It proceeded from prototypes through the earliest genuinely commercial offerings. The first major auto show was in New York in 1901. The first model that ever sold in such volumes that it could not be manufactured by hand methods went into production only late in 1908. In this earliest period, most output was manufactured by single-establishment enterprises that were vertically very unintegrated. Just like the pioneer innovators and the first entrepreneurs, these firms bought most of their parts from upstream firms that also supplied, at least initially, other industries. This supply industry was horizontally fragmented. Some of its output was made to buyers' specifications, some produced for the general trade.

The automobile firms did not disdain customized orders. Total volumes, even of the standard models, were low. The physical organization of production was along job-shop or, at best, batch production lines. The system exhibited tremendous inefficiencies in such simple features of the production process as the distances parts traveled in the course of individual stages of production. The grouping of machine tools and other equipment by process flow rather than by equipment type still lay in the future. For the most part, the manufacturers employed relatively highly skilled work forces that carried out their tasks with general-purpose equipment. These tasks were partly assembly and partly construction, but both often involved fitting and other fine work. The fitting was often necessary because of the irregular tolerances of the incoming parts. Firms began to do better than making each car one-at-a-time during this period, but the old methods fell away slowly.

Firms had relatively modest product offerings; and both the trade journalism of the day and the surviving company records suggest that they did not plan much in the modern sense of the word. Cost accounting was primitive and apparently not widespread. Systematic forecasting of demand scarcely existed. Instead, production runs were short and prices high. The demand side of the market was almost entirely confined—perhaps not surprisingly—to the right-hand end of the income distribution.

Manufacturing firms came and went. Capital-intensive stages of production could be left to the supply industry, and it was often possible to contract for parts and components on 90-day trade credit, thus making it easier to establish a manufacturing entity. Many firms succeeded, at least for a time, in selling the cars before the bills for the parts came due. There was something of the air of a gold rush about all of this, and some failures were surely due to entrants proceeding without adequate managerial skills, financial resources, or strategic planning.

Another pattern to the shake-out was geographical. The industry was initially fairly dispersed, but it began clearly concentrating in the Upper Midwest as the first decade of the century progressed. Detroit soon became its unambiguous capital.

This period saw a tremendous amount of progress in the basic technology of the product. Early on, it was quite unclear if automobiles would be predominantly powered by steam, electricity, or internal combustion engines. By 1908 the answer was very clear. Many other basic elements of the mechanical systems and overall design were also taking shape, but it would be another twenty years before most were entirely in place.

The age of Ford really commenced in October 1908. Its centerpiece was the Model T. The Ford company had been in business for some years previously, but only with the Model T did it begin to make its fortunes. The basic approach was simple: "The way to make automobiles is to make one automobile like another . . . , to make them all alike, to make them come through the factory just alike—just like one pin is like another pin when it comes from the pin factory and one match is like another match when it comes from the match factory."[2] This sort of manufacturing could be done at a lower unit cost than more customized work. Offering these inexpensive vehicles for sale, Ford then in effect discovered (or perhaps created) the

2. Henry Ford quoted in Chandler (1964), p. 28.

mass market. His company became, by a very wide margin, the largest firm in the industry.

Once the company committed strategically to the Model T, Ford production methods and human resources were progressively optimized to this ideal of repetitive manufacturing. The changes included—crucially—the systematic deployment and exploitation of the so-called American System methods for producing truly interchangeable parts. (This had the incidental feature, which Ford found attractive, of lowering on average the typical employee's skill requirements.) None of this was, as a matter of implementation, straightforward. Ford machine design was highly innovative. The input tolerances required were unprecedented. The working conditions and demands were equally unusual in the industry of the day, and the institutions Ford developed to respond to this were distinctive and became quite famous. The coordination tasks were less glamorous but at least as challenging.

The idea behind this new production model was the imposition of process rigidity to produce uniformity in product at low cost. Designing into a machine the ability to carry out various tasks, or a single task on variously shaped pieces, has a cost. The same is true of production systems as a whole. The cost, which often appears substantial to decisionmakers, lay in an inability (or, at least, a more costly ability) to respond to shifts in customer preferences or design possibilities. But the low-end market facing Ford was vast and almost completely unaddressed. In the years during the teens when these decisions were being made, the cost must have seemed quite minor given the rewards.

Mass output required inputs on a similar scale. Flow coordination issues aside, where were the inputs to come from, particularly given the tolerance demands? Ford found many in the supply industry reluctant to invest in production capacity specific to his company. For this reason, as well as others, Ford's vertical integration was eventually substantial (but far from complete: many independent suppliers were still used). As the new system came into its own, Ford began to gather sales data to inform production planning; but the statistical evidence suggests the company was perfectly prepared to create inventories of finished goods if this smoothed production requirements or buffered small enough demand fluctuations.[3] The

3. On the transition, compare Sorensen (1956), pp. 40–41, with the discussion in O'Brien (1997). The statistical evidence is in O'Brien's paper, pp. 206–07.

buffer stocks of raw materials and work in process in the factory appear from contemporary photographs to have been substantial. Scale and continuous flow of production were paramount.

The effects of these innovations on productivity were dramatic, not least because some of the changes (in particular, large elements of the shop floor reorganization and moving assembly lines) were implemented quickly.[4] Diffusion across the industry was not immediate, but the Ford company itself saw double-digit total factor productivity growth on an annual basis for an extended period, starting with the Model T specialization.[5] With the development of the massive River Rouge manufacturing complex, however, current scholarship argues that productivity growth due to innovation essentially stopped.[6] In effect, we think it reasonable to conclude that the innovation introduced by the Ford production paradigm was an extreme type: it provided a one-shot (admittedly enormous) boost to economic performance, after which performance improvements tended to come from other domains.

Many elements of the initial approach to mass production persisted at Ford and elsewhere for many years. But starting in the mid-1920s, new developments took on increasing importance in the industry cross-section. The Ford Motor Company was essentially a single-product company, making a product that, famously, came in "any color the customer wants so long as it is black." In the early history of the industry, business combinations that did not follow this model tended to be small and not particularly prosperous. The General Motors Corporation was initially one such company. It grew significantly in size during the Model T era primarily by acquiring and (to a very limited extent) integrating many small players. But in this period, GM was never particularly profitable, and, in the years after World War I, it came close to financial crisis.[7] Organizational innovations developed by Alfred Sloan in the aftermath of its troubles brought on close to half a century of superior performance.[8] The innovations included a

4. Elements of the shop floor reorganization and many of the machine-based innovations occurred more slowly and sequentially, however, in part because they grew out of learning from new experiences rather than being part of a grand design thoroughly worked out from the start. The transition as a whole was very far from instantaneous.

5. Raff (1996).

6. Williams and others (1994).

7. Chandler and Salsbury (1971).

8. Sloan (1964).

broad product line with planned, fashion-based, obsolescence; systematic investment in brand planning and advertising; multidivisional structures for governance and control; and sophisticated systems for financial accounting, market surveillance, and forecasting. Still, some elements of the way business was done changed little. Life on the assembly line continued to be pressured and passive. There had once been a vibrant and innovative supply industry, but GM and the other principal U.S. car manufacturers brought and tended to keep in-house the assembly and, indeed, the product development work for components and subsystems, typically outsourcing only the low-level production of individual parts according to detailed specifications.[9] The automakers also worked to keep component prices down by demanding bidding competitions for each job.

For the period between 1930 and 1973, Ford, General Motors, and Chrysler (an entrant organized along GM-like lines) substantially dominated the American market. Unionization made no difference to this domination (though the first postwar United Auto Workers contracts enhanced whatever bias there had been toward hard automation and an inflexible division of labor on the shop floor), and there was little effective competition from imports. In the wake of the 1973 oil price rise, however, the product-market hegemony changed sharply. Detroit was at the time producing powerful but heavy and gas-guzzling cars, and the initial appeal of the Japanese products was their fuel economy. In addition, Toyota, Nissan, and Honda rapidly distinguished themselves with their manufacturing excellence and especially their quality levels. These had their roots in processes of continuous improvement and concurrent engineering. These manufacturers also offered more variety, more conveniently attainable, than could the Big Three. All these played well with consumers, and none proved easy to replicate rapidly.

The continuous improvement paradigm was a particular challenge for the Big Three. A key component of lean production, it originated at Toyota. As Toyota launched its postwar development, it faced a very different and very much smaller market than the one Ford had confronted in the teens. Toyota adopted appropriately different approaches to shop floor culture and human resource management practices, alternative mechanisms for coordination with suppliers, and different use of inventories, all directed at rooting out imperfection and inconsistency rather than used as a means to prevent shortages and shutdowns. Viewed as a system, it was

9. Helper (1991).

radically different. Through all its elements ran a red thread of investment in responsiveness to evolving demands and information and, in general, in flexibility. This led, in the end, to a production system with continuous flow attributes that seemed very similar to Ford's in many ways but which differed in basic orientation. It also had one consequence that is particularly salient in light of the discussion here: the so-called lean approach generated incremental improvement over long periods, in contrast to the "quick fix" regime generated by Ford's innovations.[10] The American firms eventually made significant headway in adapting this ongoing approach to productivity enhancement, but progress took several decades because the new system was so different.

The fully realized lean system of the Japanese is a collection of highly complementary complex procedures and routines. Employee relations, job design, division of labor, supplier relations, product development, outsourcing strategy, facilities design, shop floor culture, and management are all highly developed and subtly adapted and attuned to one another. It is difficult to discern what really drives overall performance, and it took the American firms many attempts to develop a working sense of how the policies and procedures operated and related to one another. Implementation also was both difficult and idiosyncratic. The process has been arduous as well as drawn out.

Chrysler was the leading firm in the most recent phase we see. By the 1980s the company had become cash poor and nearly bankrupt. As the smallest and weakest of the Big Three, it typically stood third in line with suppliers who were continuously at the beck and call of its much stronger and much larger cross-town rivals. At one of its darkest hours, Chrysler executives met with suppliers and, partly out of desperation, proposed a radical change in the way the company would deal with its value chain. Instead of dictating to suppliers and pitting them against one another— which the suppliers, of course, hated—Chrysler officials promised to commit to long-term relationships for developing entire subsystems and to share the benefits of any cost-saving ideas with suppliers. Long the norm in many Japanese companies, this mode of operation represented for Detroit a major departure from business as usual. Chrysler called the approach the Extended Enterprise and even trademarked the term.

10. Fine and Porteus (1989) discuss and model this feature of the system in some detail and provide a number of references to support the characterization.

At the same time, Chrysler accelerated the outsourcing of its components- and technology-development activities and, as a result, diminished the corporate overhead associated with them. The company began to design, assemble, and market vehicles to which it had contributed little of its own innovative component technology, instead relying on mutually beneficial partnerships. The results of this restructuring were sweet: Chrysler vehicles became Detroit's most profitable, their styles the most envied, their unit costs the lowest, and their time-to-market the swiftest. Chrysler's market share and market valuation soared. Ultimately, the turn-around led to Chrysler's shareholders receiving a premium price when the company was acquired by Daimler-Benz in 1998.

Chrysler's organizational innovation triggered important effects: its suppliers were strengthened by the systems design and integration work opportunities and invested in further development of the requisite skills. This, in turn, encouraged Ford and GM to increase outsourcing to their own supply bases and to divest their own components businesses to attain a cost structure more competitive with Chrysler's. The spin-offs of GM's and Ford's component-making arms, Delphi and Visteon, respectively, followed shortly thereafter.

Throughout this history, whatever the state of upstream organization, the downstream relationships were simple. In the earliest days, carmakers sold directly from the factory and also through dealers who maintained showrooms, sales staff, and product inventory. As the industry consolidated, direct sales effectively ended. For most of the next half of the century, a principal preoccupation of the dealers was establishing, primarily at the state level, legislation that protected the dealers against attempts by the carmakers to control them. If one wanted to buy a car, one had to go to a dealer with an exclusive local franchise. Virtually all purchases were made from that dealer's existing stock since lead times on custom orders ranged from many weeks to several months, depending on the make and model. The inefficiencies of this system included the high cost of finished goods cached in dealer lots across the country, the frequent mismatch of individual customer desires with the locally available inventory options, and the frequent discounting required to clear the dealer lots of models with unwanted configurations. Although many automobile dealers became quite prosperous in the postwar period, the system costs were high. The Big Three worked mightily during the age of lean to get their factory and supply chain inventories down to a few day's worth, but sixty or more days of inventory was typical in the distribution chain.

Possibilities and Implications of the Internet

The question at hand is how widespread access to Internet and web-based communication might alter practice and productivity in the automotive industry. Before homing in on details of current industry practice, it may be worth examining some available models and influences.

Developments in the computer industry provide a very striking example of how the automobile industry could move away from its costly make-to-stock tradition. Personal computer manufacturers once all worked in the traditional auto way. The Dell Computer Corporation wrought a radical change, with superior performance and profitability, with its "Dell Direct" model. Dell's approach eliminated links in the supply chain and generally reorganized the company's entire vertical structure. Downstream, the changes were relatively straightforward, at least in concept: Dell simply eliminated retailers and distribution channel inventories, selling only directly to final customers over the Internet on a make-to-order basis. Upstream, matters were more complex.

Dell's upstream innovation involved an end-to-end integration of the supply chain with the distribution (that is, demand) chain. In the mid-1980s Michael Dell began a business of assembling computers from his dormitory room at the University of Texas using parts ordered from catalogs. The basic process has changed little since that time. Dell Computer takes orders for customized PCs and workstations over the telephone and on its Internet site, begins building the machines almost immediately once the orders are complete, and ships the finished products as soon as they are built and tested. Dell thus assembles to order rather than to stock. The entire process now often takes less than 24 hours. The company carries no final goods inventories, nor, as stated above, does it employ any distributors or retailers who carry inventory: it ships all products directly from its factory to the customer. So there is no postproduction inventory risk. Capital tied up in parts inventory is minor, and parts inventory risk is more minor still.

Parts arrive on a short cycle, but orders typically must be placed somewhat further in advance. How does the company avoid getting stuck with commitments for parts the public no longer wants (at least at anticipated prices)? The company's buyers always opt for ordering components of latest technology when in doubt about customer preferences. These likely will have the longest shelf life and not need discounting in order to be sold in the near future. The range of parts options likely to be demanded at any one time in Dell's industry is relatively small, so the overall objective of minimizing inventories is not, as a practical matter, overwhelmed by mix-and-match possibilities. High-end users usually purchase machines with the latest components and have a relatively strong willingness to pay for the performance. Dell is careful to service this select group well. This too helps keep profit margins healthy.

Every other major PC maker still basically builds from stock and sells through resellers that carry inventory. The faster the pace of change in the underlying product technology, given this fact, the greater the advantage Dell has over its competitors. This is an industry in which inventory does not age gracefully.[11] In fact, aged inventory in the computer market is quite unattractive since the performance increments offered by new equipment are typically large. A few examples tell the tale. It was expensive to be caught holding a large inventory of PCs with built-in 28K modems when the new 56K modems hit the market. Who would have wanted to have on hand several thousand Pentium processors when Intel introduced the Pentium II, and the price of old Pentiums dropped through the floor? Such obsolescence is a major factor in the technologically dynamic PC industry. The more inventory in the chain, and the faster the pace of technical change, the higher the obsolescence costs. The leanest chain does best.

In summary, Dell reaps a number of advantages from its innovative organization. It ties up much less working capital in raw materials inventory and work in process, speculating only minimally on which particular configurations customers might want to buy (since it now makes only what they asked for). It is paid promptly—indeed, often before it has to pay for its own inputs. Its distribution channels require radically less management (though its supply chain probably requires significantly more). The advantages of this approach could be even more powerful in a less commoditized business. It might be that consumers place a high value on having very particular configurations of equipment and have a correspondingly high willingness to pay for them. If—unlike in Dell's business—these configurations are hard for other vendors to imitate—perhaps because brands matter—then the ability to give the customer precisely what he or she wants may be very profitable, even considering possibly substantial parts inventory requirements.

For better or worse, companies like Dell and the ever-conspicuous Amazon.com have created customer expectations that are beginning to affect the auto industry. Consumers are increasingly also Internet con-

11. Fine and Porteus (1989).

sumers, and Internet consumers have come to expect that the norm in retail commerce is at least converging towards custom-ordering products one day and expecting home delivery the next. The appeal of this model for automobiles is high for both customers and manufacturers, but achieving dramatic reduction in lead times with a build-to-order capability is far beyond the present-day capabilities for most auto manufacturers. Automotive supply chains are far broader and deeper that those of personal computers and incomparably more so than those of books. The ineradicable lead times in auto manufacturing are just much longer. These differences reflect the much greater complexity of an automobile and the much greater product variety demanded in the marketplace.

Build-to-order capabilities in the PC industry are also enhanced significantly by the modular structure of the dominant product platform. By the mid-1980s, a personal computer comprised such highly standardized modules that a college student like Dell could indeed launch a PC design-production-sales business by ordering standard components from a catalog and assembling these into a computer in a garage or a dormitory room. The automobile of the late twentieth century exhibits a highly integral product architecture, whereby each product takes many man-years to design and significant capital investments to assemble at efficient scale.

In addition, dealers with extensive legal rights to franchise exclusivity play a major role in car distribution. Automotive manufacturers are effectively prohibited from cutting out their established dealer; the resulting costs of distribution in the current system are often estimated as being as high as 30 percent of total vehicle price. Because such legal protections have never been present in the consumer electronics or book markets, Internet retailing was easily implemented by firms such as Dell and Amazon.

The pressures to reduce cycle times in the present-day automobile industry are nonetheless immense. One reason for this relates to the product itself. As the capabilities of small computers and chips steadily grow, the vehicle itself is becoming less mechanical and more electronic in its functioning. (It is becoming less a classically mechanical machine and more an information-and-electronics-intensive mode of transportation.) Many auto firms hope to exploit the promise of telematics (telecommunication capabilities in vehicles) to effectively use the vehicle as a portal to a wide range of new services that can be sold to the customer/driver. These might include offerings in the domains of enhanced safety, navigation, concierge services, telecommunications-based personal productivity, and entertainment. Whole new revenue streams might be available as well as mere new gadgets. But the development cycles in the auto industry are slow (four to six years) relative to those in the handheld device market (for example, six to twelve months for palm-sized computers and mobile phones). Unless the automotive industry can increase the clock speed for development and delivery, it may be relegated to merely offering the driver a place to rest a handheld device for mobile services.

One additional Internet-stimulated innovation still in its infancy is the business-to-business online marketplace. During 1999 and 2000 such marketplaces were announced in large numbers, covering many industries, and some were even launched. There was a great deal of fanfare and self-promotion about the value they would create. During this period, General Motors, Ford, and DaimlerChrysler (the OEMs, or original equipment manufacturers) formed an alliance to develop such a marketplace for sourcing automotive components and subsystems. The resulting organization ("Covisint") invested heavily in software and systems to ease the electronic integration of the automotive firms with the many tiers in their supply base. One result of this investment will surely be lower transaction costs across the entire automotive supply chain. Another may be an improved knowledge base about the entire supply chain, leading in turn to a deeper understanding of exactly what value is being added by first-tier suppliers who are often charged with developing and coordinating members of the lower tiers. Such an understanding may make it easier for OEMs to replace such first-tier coordinators once they see more clearly what and how the first tiers are contributing. Additionally, the resulting improved transparency of the supply chain may enable shorter supply lines and encourage product designers to attempt more modular vehicle designs in search of faster order-to-delivery cycle times.

In short, it is apparent even before any detailed examination of the process of making automobiles that networking technologies provide an array of opportunities and challenges for the processes of designing, manufacturing, and selling cars as well as for the bundle of services delivered by the product itself. In the former case, the challenges for traditional carmakers are to re-engineer their business processes from their supplier's supplier to their customer's customer and do so before a new entrant leapfrogs the existing dominant firms. In product space, the challenge is to enhance the vehicle with services offered through new networked technologies before other firms (for example, mobile phone providers) beat them to the punch.

Influence on Costs and Consumer Goods

This section is the analytical and evidentiary core of this chapter. We consider the whole of the value chain involved in automobile design, manufacturing, and distribution and identify the steps at which networked communications might conceivably have an impact. We summarize such literature as there is attributing numbers to these. The estimates derive from a suite of analyst reports recently circulated.[12] The reports are ultimately based on conversations with company experts, so they move our conceptual analysis in the direction of hard data. But they have two weaknesses as sources that we should clarify before the start.

The first weakness is structural. A social scientist might hope that such reports would have identical conceptual organization and focus but different sources and would represent, in effect, independent observations of common random variables. But there is little common organization and focus. Perhaps this is understandable. Analysts are paid in part for being well known authorities, and product differentiation is a far easier road to this status than head-to-head conflict. (It is also generally faster, and there can be no doubt that the institutional clients who are the principal audience for the reports wanted to hear something sooner rather than later.) Few of the reports in fact address the whole range of questions we have identified, even conceptually, and there is little overlap among the quantitative estimates. Collectively, however, they do offer numbers to fill in many of the cells.

The second weakness might be called procedural. Analysts are generally both intelligent and hardworking, and the best are very well informed and highly perceptive students of the firms and industry they cover. But the environment in which they work offers complex incentives geared to their employers' main services of investment banking and brokerage services. On a matter such as the significance of technical change for long-run growth—in which results are likely to emerge unambiguously only long after portfolio reallocation decisions will be made, and possibly even after analysts have retired to cultivate their gardens—a blue-sky bias is to be expected. We can at this point offer no remedy for this beyond a cautious attitude.

12. Lapidus (2000); Girsky and Quilty (2000); Blaschke and others (2000); Hynowitz and Hughes (2000); Hayes and Warburton (2000).

We begin our analysis by noting that it is easy to fall into the habit of thinking of this industry as pure manufacturing, but it does not represent the whole auto producing system. In that larger realm, we see four broad sets of activities worth detailed analysis, each with many subcategories. These broad categories are product development, procurement and supply, manufacturing systems, and the vehicle order-to-delivery cycle. To assess the potential economic impact of network technologies on the automobile industry requires a framework with which to categorize the effects. Figure 3-1 presents the framework we propose for this purpose.

Opportunities in Product Development

Product development in this industry is extremely expensive, with many projects costing between $1 billion and $3 billion over two to four years and consuming in excess of a million engineering man-hours.[13] The reason is not far to seek. Cars are complex mechanisms, and particular resolutions for many design problems have implications for the ways other problems can be resolved—the interaction effects are potentially quite intricate. This is the more so given that automotive product architectures are generally quite integral (dramatically so compared to the relatively modular personal computer). The costs will only rise as the product becomes more technologically sophisticated (for example, with the increasing integration of electronic control systems) and consumers increasingly notice and value the degree to which general design problems have been resolved in optimized ways (observing this either directly or through quality and durability records). Traditional methods for coping with innovation were slow. Yet both the technological possibilities and consumer tastes seem to be evolving rapidly. Thus fast new product development is increasingly seen as an important element of competitive advantage. Because the development process is information intensive, it is a natural target for network-based innovation.

Typical development processes have in fact changed significantly over the past decade. The days of Mercedes's twelve-year product cycles, for example, are past. Four areas of product development as it is currently organized and carried out offer significant network-based opportunities for speed and productivity enhancement.

13. See, for example, Clark and Fujimoto (1991).

Figure 3-1. *Framework to Assess Economic Effects of Networking Technologies*

PRODUCT DEVELOPMENT	PROCUREMENT AND SUPPLY
Engineering changes	*Reduce transaction purchasing costs*
Costs of making changes	Increase speed of existing processes
Threshold for quality	Redesign processes
improvement	*Consequences of aggregating orders*
Lower direct cost of communication	Bulk buying at firm's nth tier
Lower cost of n-way coordination	Bulk buy across OEMs
Increased speed in product	Bulk shipping
development cycle	*Consequences of price competition*
	Margin reduction
	Cost reduction
	Logistics
	Better information leading to fewer
	"rush" orders
MANUFACTURING SYSTEM	VEHICLE ORDER-TO-DELIVERY
Improved manufacturability	*Reduced order-to-delivery cycle times*
Faster setups	Lower inventory levels in pipeline
Smaller lot sizes, reduced	Better matching of supply to demand
inventory	Higher prices for higher customer
Higher capacity use	satisfaction
Easier assembly	Less discounting of undesired stock
More outsourcing	*Retail channel costs*
	Lower sales commissions
	Lower total overhead with fewer dealers
	Lower shipping costs to fewer stock points

The first of these concerns the ease of actually making engineering changes. Networked communication lowers the direct cost of implementing changes. Variant designs, created on CAD-CAM systems, can be circulated widely both rapidly and cheaply. Modification is also rapid and cheap. Even the cost of making a given list menu of changes declines.

There is more to the impact on making engineering changes than this, of course, since this list of desirable changes should not be taken as fixed. (In economists' language, there is a general equilibrium effect to the factor price change as well as the partial equilibrium change.) As change becomes cheaper, the threshold level of quality improvement large enough for change to appear worthwhile will fall. More of that which is possible will actually seem financially feasible: thus, more changes will actually take place.

As designs grow more complex and design interdependency increases, there will be more to the costs of making design changes than just the direct expenses of revising CAD-CAM calculations. The costs of new product development are principally the cost of human resources rather than of materials or equipment. Thousands of individuals and hundreds of specialties are involved. Direct and opportunity costs of communication decline as networked communications permit e-mail to replace face-to-face meetings and telephone calls. Increasing numbers of people become involved in making the decisions, but the decisionmaking takes less time collectively and no longer requires getting groups together into a common room at a specific time. "Meetings" become cheaper and more asynchronous.

The most important element, however, is likely to be a general equilibrium effect not yet touched on. With communication and coordination cheaper and implementation easier and more frequent, the fixed cost of new product development is lower, and the whole product development cycle is faster and can be carried out more frequently. This enables the manufacturers to get designs to market in a more timely and affordable fashion, permitting a better matching between products and customers.

Opportunities in Procurement and Supply

A second important element of the value chain is procurement and supply. The significance General Motors placed on the services of the Spaniard Ignacio Lopez, as well as the ferocity with which it fought his being hired away by Volkswagen in the mid-1990s, gives a crude measure of the importance the company saw in getting these activities, on the management of which in the old combative style he was the industry's leading executive, optimized. Similarly, the rise of Thomas Stallkamp, a principal architect of the new Chrysler approach, to the presidency of Chrysler and then to the jobs of president and vice-chairman of DaimlerChrysler, illustrates how highly valued his Extended Enterprise model was to corporate success.

As suggested by the enormous interest in online business-to-business marketplaces, networked communications will significantly affect the economic structure of supply networks as well as the costs of the underlying activities. This has a number of components.

Transaction costs of purchasing will undoubtedly fall. Clerical work will become automated and take place both faster and more reliably. Processes—needs identification, vendor selection, review and approval—will go on very much faster and more efficiently.

The new communications technologies also offer opportunities for aggregating orders that will likely drive costs down. The three main elements that will effect change derive from the fact that web-based procurement makes advertising requirements and terms inexpensive and enhances the likelihood of receiving comparable bids. The pool of potential bidders will expand. This is a matter of the first importance in an industry with a typical cost-share of materials of nearly 50 percent for many companies and products.

Orders can be consolidated and placed strategically at the nth tier of the supply chain. That is, the car firm can use the technology to gather and keep current information about supplier capabilities and performance and use this to direct orders to the most efficient suppliers. If information about the whole supply chain is available in a transparent fashion, the firm may be able to use the scale of its overall orders to obtain advantages for many of its higher-tier suppliers at all n tiers (that is, by pointing out to suppliers upstream how many of the apparently independent orders are in fact emanating from its final business), as well as to extend the use of advanced scheduling software and the like.

The process of consolidation need not stop there. As discussed above, OEMs have joined together to create Covisint to pool their purchasing power and to develop technology platforms to exploit networked technologies in many arenas, including procurement and engineering. The recent decision by the Federal Trade Commission suggests that this venture will actually go forward.

Consolidating orders could enable consolidating shipping. Effectively, larger orders with more lead time and certainty might allow the assets of transportation providers to be used more effectively. This could yield significant economies. In addition, network technologies should also lead to greater price competition in the supply chain. This would have beneficial effects for the OEMs through two distinct channels, both of which would show up in the productivity statistics as currently calculated. The first is that supplier margins would decline given the basic structure of costs: there would be more direct competition for orders. The second is that suppliers would be motivated—if not forced—to invest more in cost-reducing innovation: in the long run, costs would go down too.

There is a final element of supply cost that would be affected, and this because of the lower cost of obtaining and using up-to-date information about demand. With more current information, there would be greater forecast accuracy and a clearer understanding upstream about what demands were coming. This would lead to fewer rush orders. Rush orders are almost always filled and shipped in high-cost ways.

Opportunities in Manufacturing

The manufacturing system itself may well change in highly significant ways. Here, there are at least three important possibilities. First, networked communications may lead to improved manufacturability within the set of activities the OEMs continue to carry out. Such improvements may result as an added benefit of networked product development activities in enhancing design for manufacturability. In turn, improved manufacturability may reduce scrap and setup/changeover times as well as reduce assembly times and complexity, all resulting from the shortened amount of real-time process engineering required by factory personnel who often must find ways to compensate for difficult-to-manufacture designs.

Second, having electronic linkages permeate the factory floor should enhance real-time quality improvement, downtime reduction, and every other communication-intensive function in the factory.

In addition, due to reduced transaction and search costs, an environment of fast and flexible communication across the automotive supply chain may lead to a greater use of common modules across automotive manufacturers and first-tier suppliers. This modularity, in turn, can encourage firms to outsource greater portions of the manufacturing enterprise as supply firms begin to specialize in certain kinds of modules.[14]

Opportunities in the Order-to-Delivery Cycle

Dramatic changes seem likely to occur in the vehicle order-to-delivery cycle in two broad categories. The first concerns cycle times per se, the second channel costs.

As mentioned earlier, Internet penetration into households seems to have stimulated a demand for more goods that can be configured and purchased through a World Wide Web interface and delivered by a rapid ser-

---

14. See, for example, Fine (1998).

vice delivery provider. In response, on the supply side, we believe that net-worked communications have the potential to reduce order-to-delivery cycle times in the automobile industry, although probably not at the level achieved by Dell. Network technology will make it possible for suppliers to "see" customer orders as soon as they are placed, reducing the historically significant delays in transmitting this information along the supply chain. Conversely, order takers should have much better insight into the capacity and inventory available in the chain so that prices can be proactively adjusted to steer demand toward product configurations that can be delivered within shorter time windows. Better information about demand even without complete make-to-order fulfillment will lead to smaller, efficient levels of finished goods inventory. The amount of money tied up in such inventories now is very large, with forty to eighty days' worth of distribution-chain inventory a typical range for many models.

The effect of better information will also turn up in the revenue line. Desired stock (that is, stock made to order) should bring higher prices because it will be precisely what is desired by a given customer. The magnitude of severe discounting of difficult-to-sell configurations as well as the reduction of all promotional expenditure of overstock should be reduced.

The costs of operating the retail channel should also decline, perhaps dramatically. Sales commissions should fall since the information-conveying role of the sales force seems likely to melt away. (From a more sour perspective, customers will know so much that competition will force commissions down.) Indeed, with consumers seeking out information over the web, manufacturers may become very much better informed about consumer tastes. This would be valuable information throughout the value chain.

For the same reason that fewer salesmen are required, fewer dealerships may be in order (and thus total value-chain overhead may decline). With fewer dealers, there will be fewer stock points and lower industry shipping costs. Some scale economies may be lost getting cars to customers, but there will be very much less moving cars around from one storage area to another or to customers in another place.

Estimating the Size of These Opportunities

The most thorough study to date of these matters is the Goldman Sachs study.[15] The numbers given below are theirs unless otherwise stated. We

15. Lapidus (2000).

note that these do not represent all of the components of their calculations (we do not discuss about 20 percent of the savings they identify) and that we sometimes aggregate the primitive elements rather differently than they do. Neither of these considerations affects the substance of our argument. The overall estimates below are given as possible cost reductions relative to present average costs, which they put at $26,000. We explore later the extent to which these represent productivity improvements in the sense the phrase is usually used. But they are a start toward understanding the industry's present situation; and they are thought provoking because the magnitudes they suggest are not small.

Under the heading of product development, all analysts see some prospects for improvement. But there is so little consensus as to suggest a lack of detailed analysis. Goldman puts the potential cost reductions at this stage at $388, Deutsche Bank–Alex Brown at more than two-and-a-half times that sum.[16] Neither seems to have considered the process itself analytically: the numbers represent savings from superior designs as reflected, for example, in lower warranty and other expenses due to improved quality. On the basis of our description of the process and its expense above, we certainly think there are unconsidered elements here. For a $2 billion vehicle development project that yields one million production units over its lifetime, $388 represents a savings of 19 percent. In our opinion, this figure may be optimistic but it does not seem impossible.

Under procurement and supply, Goldman sees a slightly larger but basically similar-sized opportunity. It sees $160 in reduced transaction costs (others' estimates come to roughly comparable dollar sums). It also sees $70 in firm-based bulk buying and another $47 from inter-OEM coordination. Declines in supplier margins would contribute another $94, it says, for a total of $331. It does not consider web-enabled economies in shipping expenses, nor does it seem to think that web procurement will lead to significant cost-reducing innovation from suppliers. The whole issue of rush-order-related costs is not recognized. This too suggests underestimation.

Goldman sees manufacturing as the same size opportunity. Their analysis suggests a total of $302 of savings from improved manufacturability. They do not seem to see important advantages coming from a change in outsourcing behavior in itself, despite the different cost structures OEMs and supplier firms typically have.

16. Lapidus (2000); Blaschke and others (2000).

The order-to-delivery cycle is, in Goldman's view, where the big money is. It sees $575 in savings due to lower inventory in the channels (though others' estimates of this run as low as $150) and $832 in savings due to better matching of supply and demand. In retail, it predicts $381 for lower sales commissions, $387 for the reduced burden of fewer dealerships, and $50 for lower overall shipping costs, for a subtotal of $818. Altogether, the total for this stage (in our categories) is $2,225.

All in all, then, Goldman sees (on our terms) potential reductions of $3,446, that is, in excess of 13 percent. And there are reasons to believe that important potential savings must still be incorporated into this. So even if one imagined the figures to be biased high for the reasons described above, the true figure appears likely to be very substantial.

In a subsequent publication more focused on European manufacturers, Goldman offered a focused but more detailed financial analysis (based on one disguised actual manufacturer).[17] This study places some weight in the discussion on the possibility that revenue will actually rise but does not factor this consideration into the computations. The gist of those are as follows. Reductions Goldman thinks perfectly feasible in channel inventories would boost the return on capital by about 11 percent by the second year out. These reductions, plus what Goldman takes to be a feasible cut in sales incentives on 40 percent of the cars sold, would push the return up an incremental 18 percent. Cutting sales incentives on 100 percent of the cars (that is, moving to complete build to order) would add another 29 percent to the return. While we take these calculations to be merely illustrative, they clearly make the point that a great deal of money and time is tied up in the order-to-delivery cycle and much lost opportunity in selling cars with specifications not preferred by the customer.

Relationship between Anticipated Changes and Ongoing Improvements

Traditional measures of total factor productivity and productivity per head (that is, the average product of labor) measure output in value terms rather than in physical units. Any factors that affect sale prices will thus affect measured productivity. This is a desirable feature of an index if improved

17. Hayes and Warburton (2000).

quality—not measured by the statistician but recognized by the consumer—enhances, say, product operating life in ways recognized by the consumer who is willing to pay: the index goes up as economic reality says it ought to. But there are circumstances—increased competition, for example—under which such an index might go down with true productivity either not changing or actually rising. Such measures should therefore be interpreted cautiously.

The statistical productivity indexes available for this industry (the best are compiled on an ongoing basis by the Bureau of Labor Statistics) possess these vulnerabilities and more. Most important, they are available currently only through 1994. This may well not be enough history to show the size of the effect of important innovations. The general pattern the series does show is noisy trend growth in multifactor productivity through the early 1970s, a steep drop-off and recovery in levels over the next fifteen years or so, and a distinctly sharper upward trend emerging roughly as the real diffusion of lean production got under way. This is, of course, consistent with the continuous improvement emphasis of lean production. Suppose that is what it is. The question then naturally arises of what is likely to happen next.

It is not possible, unfortunately, to go from the cost reduction estimates of the previous section to productivity growth estimates over the same five-year interval without more information than is really available at present. Multifactor productivity growth is a weighted average, and the Goldman study does not give or suggest key information about the balance of cost savings across factors of production. Industry sources seem disinclined to speculate. The suggested cost declines are quite large by historical standards, and so one would naturally suspect a substantial uptick. But we lack the raw data to propose a number appropriate to compare to the carefully calculated time series of the BLS even were we confident we could make appropriate assumptions about the future course of extraneous conditions affecting measured productivity.

Yet the discussions above suggest that this is not, in fact, the most interesting question. The changes networked communications seem likely to bring to the automobile industry's value chain and to the structure of its costs might affect true productivity in the same sort of ongoing way as lean production. Alternatively, in contrast, they might be merely transitional, essentially one-shot changes (however long the new equilibrium may take to establish itself) where they affect productivity at all, predominantly representing a transfer of surplus from one stage of the value-chain-plus consumers to another (or at least putting them up for grabs in competition between firms). The discussion above concerning costs and supply suggests that there will ultimately be some quantum of each type of change but that the predominant effect of networked communications will be to rescue the industry from what was once a great advance—make-to-stock-oriented mass production—which has become outdated as living standards have risen and alternatives have grown more diverse. The predominant effect thus seems likely to be to wring inefficiency out of a value chain through what is basically a one-shot improvement in forecasting, communication, and coordination. The automobile sector of the manufacturing economy is large, and this could well have a discernible effect on productivity growth while it is happening; but the effect does not seem likely to be long term.

A transition of the vast and lumbering automotive manufacturing system and supply chain to a taut and focused one such as this might be difficult to bring about and impossible in any short time frame. This is so not least because the underlying innovations themselves are still evolving. It would be difficult to predict with any confidence what numbers to expect and over what time period even if we knew the possibilities with certainty. And we certainly do not know them. But this much is clear: even if the potential cost savings discussed above were twice or three times too high, the true numbers would still be large. They might not attract so much attention from stock analysts and journalists, but they would still command the attention of firm decisionmakers. That the automobile manufacturing sector will be affected on an important scale seems thus beyond doubting. To whom it will matter, and for how long, is still up for grabs.

References

Blaschke, Kenneth, and others. 2000. *E-Auto Supply—Release 1.0.* San Francisco: Deutsche Bank–Alex Brown.

Chandler, Alfred D., Jr., ed. 1964. *Giant Enterprise: Ford, General Motors, and the Automobile Industry.* Harcourt, Brace, and World.

Chandler, Alfred D., Jr., and Stephen Salsbury. 1971. *Pierre S. Du Pont and the Making of the Modern Corporation.* Harper and Row.

Clark, Kim, and Takahiro Fujimoto. 1991. *Product Development Performance.* Harvard Business School Press.

Fine, Charles. 1998. *Clockspeed.* New York: Perseus Books.

Fine, Charles H., and Evan L. Porteus. 1989. "Dynamic Process Improvement." *Operations Research* 37 (4): 580–91.

Girsky, Stephen J., and Susan Quilty. 2000. *Automotive Internet.* New York: Morgan Stanley Dean Witter.

Hayes, Keith, and Max Warburton. 2000. *Automobiles: Europe.* London: Goldman Sachs.

Helper, Susan 1991. "Strategy and Irreversibility in Supplier Relations: The Case of the U.S. Automobile Industry." *Business History Review* 65 (Winter): 781–824.

Hymowitz, Jordan, and Justin Highes. 2000. *The eAuto Report.* Boston: Robertson Stephens.

Lapidus, Gary. 2000. *Gentlemen, Start Your Search Engines.* New York: Goldman Sachs.

Nelson, Richard, Benn Steil, and David Victor. 2001. *Technological Innovation and Economic Performance.* Princeton University Press.

O'Brien, Anthony Patrick. 1997. "The Importance of Adjusting Production to Sales in the Early Automobile Industry." *Explorations in Economic History* 34 (April): 195–219.

Raff, Daniel M. G. 1996. "Productivity Growth at Ford in the Coming of Mass Production: A Preliminary Analysis." *Business and Economic History* 25 (1): 176–85.

Sloan, Alfred P., Jr. 1964. *My Years with General Motors.* Garden City, N.Y.: Doubleday.

Sorensen, Charles. 1956. *My Forty Years with Ford.* Norton.

Williams, Karel, and others. 1994. *Cars: Analysis, History, Cases.* Providence: Berghahn Books.

4

ERIC K. CLEMONS
LORIN M. HITT

Financial Services: Transparency, Differential Pricing, and Disintermediation

THE INTERNET HAS had a profound effect on the financial services sector, dramatically changing the cost of and capabilities for marketing, distributing, and servicing financial products and enabling new types of products and services to be developed. This is especially true for retail financial services, where widespread adoption of the Internet, the standardization provided by the World Wide Web, and the low cost of Internet communications and transactions have made it possible to reach customers electronically in ways that were prohibitively costly even five years ago. Indeed, pre-Internet attempts at the online distribution of retail financial services were outright failures in the mid-1980s.[1]

Starting from a base of essentially zero in 1995, the growth in Internet-enabled products and services has been rapid in some sectors and slower in others. Retail brokerage has seen a dramatic change, with more than $800 billion of brokerage assets now managed in online trading accounts, and substantially more if "traditional" brokerage accounts and mutual funds

We would like to thank Bob Litan and workshop participants at Brookings Institution and the Wharton School for valuable comments on earlier drafts of this paper.

1. In 1968, the Chemical Bank Proto System failed due to high operational cost and slow consumer adoption (Clemons, 1991). A similar fate befell early attempts to provide banking services through Prodigy and CompuServe.

with online access are included.[2] Similarly, approximately 10 million U.S. customers currently use online banking, and thirty-nine of the top 100 banks offer fully functional Internet banking.[3] Many banks and brokerages are on the second or third release of their online delivery platforms. Credit cards, while not radically transformed in operational aspects, have begun to see some volume of new origination online.[4] In addition, leading credit card companies, such as Capital One Financial, have been some of the largest users of Internet advertising among "traditional" companies.[5]

More regulated and complex financial products, such as mortgages and insurance, have had some origination volume on the Internet: it has been estimated $17 billion of mortgages would be originated and about $400 million in insurance premiums would be sold online in 2000.[6] For these sectors, the adoption of online origination has been much slower and concentrated in entrants, rather than in incumbent firms. However despite the small level of originations, the Internet has become a significant and growing source of product information. This may ultimately affect purchase and pricing structures for financial products, irrespective of the delivery channel. Internet companies have also played a role in many other segments of the industry, such as financial information and news, rating and comparison services, and even, perhaps surprisingly, financial planning and investment banking. While future growth rates are uncertain and penetration of the more complex products does not yet appear to be widespread, it is safe to conclude that the Internet will play a significant role in consumer financial services for a large subset of customers, and that this role will be significantly different across different subsectors of the financial industry.

2. Online trading data are from Salomon Smith Barney (2000).

3. For online banking, see Jeanne O'Brien, "Study: E-Banking User Base Slipping," *Bank Systems and Technology,* May 2000 (New York). For Internet banking, see ePaynews, "Online Banking Statistics" (www.epaynews.com/statistics/bankstats.html#10 [September 2000]).

4. NextCard, the first purely online credit card, has accumulated 400,000 customer accounts in the two years following its launch in February, 1998. The company claims that it captures approximately 25 percent of all online credit card applications. See NextCard, "About Us" (www.nextcard.com [November 2000]).

5. See (http://adres.internet.com/statistics/advertising/article/0,9231_442781,00.html [March 2001]).

6. The Tower Group estimated that by the end of 2000 about 1 percent of mortgages would have been originated over the Internet, representing about $17 billion in loan production (Beidl, 2000). Forrester Research projected that in 2000 the Internet would account for about $440 million in new insurance premiums, 70 percent of which would be auto insurance.

In discussions of the Internet's impact on the financial services sector, the emphasis has often been placed on the direct cost saving effects of using the Internet to provide transaction services. These potential savings are indeed considerable and in the long term may lead to significant creation of value. However, there are also substantial barriers to realizing much of this value. In some sectors, such as the credit card industry, many of the potential gains from automation have already been realized, and in others, the gains may be concentrated in only a few areas of the value chain. For products that are sold through branches or agents (banking, mortgages, and insurance), realization of cost savings will require a difficult and time-consuming redesign of the retail delivery system. Finally, many of these efficiencies are accompanied by improved customer convenience. To the extent that consumers respond by consuming more services, particularly those that generate costs but not revenue, overall costs may not be substantially reduced. This has been the experience of previous innovations in retail financial service delivery such as automated teller machines (ATMs).

Computers, and more recently the Internet, are best described as "general purpose technologies," like the electric motor or the telegraph.[7] With general purpose technologies, most of the economic value created is associated with their ability to enable complementary innovations in organization, market structure, and products and services. However, these complementary changes are often disruptive to the existing structure of an industry, leading to significant redistribution of value among industry participants and between producers and consumers.[8]

To understand the impact of the Internet on the financial services industry, it is therefore necessary to identify how the Internet affects the critical drivers of industry structure and how it enables or necessitates changes in products and services. Admittedly, it is not easy to isolate the contribution of the Internet from the effects of other complementary innovations, or to distinguish Internet effects from other long-term industry trends and exogenous factors. But while it is difficult to obtain precise numerical estimates of the productivity effects (although later in this chapter we show a partial attempt to do so), in many cases the direction and general magnitude of the Internet's impact on productivity, profitability, and consumer surplus (consumer value) will be clear.

7. Brynjolfsson and Hitt (2000); Bresnahan and Trajtenberg (1995).
8. Tushman and Anderson (1986); Bower and Christensen (1995).

We identify three principal issues that will determine the transformation of retail financial services:

—*transparency,* or the ability of all market participants to determine the available range of prices and product characteristics for financial instruments and financial services;

—*differential pricing,* in which increasingly finer distinctions must be made among groups of customers, setting prices for them based on the revenue streams they generate, the costs to serve them, and the resulting profitability of their accounts; and

—*disintermediation,* or bypass, in which net-based direct interaction eliminates the need for financial advisers, retail stock brokers, and insurance agents.

Each of these factors will affect the roles to be played by financial service providers, the sources of profits available to them, and the strategies they may choose to pursue in order to earn those profits. However, the nature and significance of these drivers will vary substantially across industries. In addition, these factors are often interdependent—for example, differential pricing is often a necessary response to increasing price transparency to prevent erosion of margins, and the ability to deliver sophisticated (although typically not complex) pricing strategies to customers may be affected by the incentive programs and structure of the distribution system. For these reasons, in this chapter we discuss these effects as they apply within different sectors in financial services.

Our analysis focuses on the primary sectors in retail financial services: credit cards, deposit banking, mortgages, brokerage, and insurance. We choose the retail segment because it has been the most radically transformed by the Internet, primarily because it has had the most to benefit from the reduction in customer interaction costs, the ability to reach mass markets, and the reduction in the role of geography in determining the strategies of financial services providers. By contrast, much of the computing- and communications-enabled transformation in the relationships among financial institutions or between financial institutions and consumers of wholesale financial services (for example, brokerage houses and exchanges, or large firms and their commercial lenders) had already occurred or was well underway before the Internet was commercialized. For these markets, the economics of computing and networking were favorable under previous generations of technology. Many of the commercial financial services that are likely to be transformed by the Internet, at least in the medium term (three to five years), closely resemble retail services; for example, commercial mortgages, short-term lending, leasing, cash management, and so forth. That is not to deny that business-to-business (B2B) e-commerce opportunities exist in the financial sector—but many of the medium-term opportunities resulting directly from the Internet are closely analogous to changes in the retail sector; the others are probably more closely related to organizational and market innovation independent of the Internet, rather than resulting from ubiquitous and low-cost communications technology.

Credit Cards

The credit card industry had been radically transformed by the increasing availability of information both for credit card companies and for consumers before the Internet was a relevant factor. However, the Internet has accelerated general trends that were already present in the industry. Because the distribution structure—principally direct marketing and centralized operations—is much simpler than that of other financial services products, producers have had much more flexibility to respond to technological developments with changes in product design. While this sector has experienced significant secondary effects due to the Internet—on demand, marketing strategy, and the emergence of alternative payment systems— these primarily reflect drivers of demand and cost on the margin. The increase in transparency and the increased utilization of differential pricing strategies represent potentially large effects on profitability (on the order of several hundred basis points), as well as the availability and pricing of credit card services to a substantial segment of the population.[9]

General Trends and Productivity Effects on the Margin

Fundamental demand for credit card services is closely linked to final consumer demand, the structure of interest rates, and overall economic conditions, especially personal income and consumer debt levels. In the long term, these demand drivers are likely to be affected by the Internet due to increased productivity and economic growth, and even more directly through the increase in incremental retail sales generated by the Internet,

---

9. A basis point represents 1/100 of 1 percent, typically in relation to the face value of a transaction. Therefore, 100 basis points equal 1 percent of a loan or deposit balance.

where credit cards are the dominant transaction medium.[10] However, in aggregate these effects are not likely to have wide-ranging impact on the structure of the sector. There is a multitude of macroeconomic drivers of interest rates, and it is reasonable to assume that the Internet represents only a small fraction of these.[11] Retail consumer spending on the Internet still accounts for only a small fraction of overall charge volume. For instance, Visa reports that about 2 percent of its total charge volume was attributed to online sales in 2000. This proportion is expected to grow to around 10 percent by 2005.[12] In addition, online transactions are associated with significant levels of fraud and "chargebacks" (where a consumer successfully disputes a charge), which may offset any gains in efficiency due to increased volume of online purchases. The emergence of consumer-to-consumer payment systems (for example, Paypal) will shift to credit card some transactions that would otherwise be made by check, but again the volume is small and these services have ambiguous effects on overall productivity.[13]

While most of the operational costs of credit cards are centrally managed and are not greatly affected by the Internet, the Internet may offer an opportunity to reduce the cost of generating, mailing, and processing monthly statements and payments. Because many consumers may prefer online billing, and, once technical issues are resolved, it should ultimately lead to cost savings, it is likely that online bill presentment and payment will become a competitive necessity. All firms will offer the service, many

10. At present, it is estimated that 97 percent of consumer purchases on the Internet are made using a credit card. Leslie Beyer, "The Internet Revolution," *Credit Card Management*, November 1999.

11. Estimates of the contribution of all information technology to productivity growth have been on the order of 1 percent a year. Economic and productivity growth are significant contributors to interest rates and inflation. See Brynjolfsson and Hitt (2000) and Gordon (2000) for a discussion of the role of computers in productivity growth at the firm and macroeconomic levels. Existing consumer debt levels play a substantial role as well, and these were rising rapidly long before the Internet became significant.

12. Frederick H. Lowe, "Why Credit Will Still Rule the Web," *Credit Card Management*, February 2001, p. 24.

13. While credit card transactions are operationally less costly to process than checks, the "float" that a purchaser enjoys until the next billing cycle and the costs and losses due to fraud and chargebacks make the total cost of using credit cards substantially higher than that of using checks, at least from the perspective of the intermediary. Thus in the short run the effect on productivity is ambiguous. If one factors in consumer convenience, it is possible that productivity is actually increasing. However, it is difficult to assess the value of consumer convenience as these benefits are highly subjective and "revealed preference" arguments (that is, people use it because it is productive) cannot be applied because the service is currently subsidized.

consumers will adopt it, and the cost savings will accrue primarily to consumers and to a lesser extent to the vendors who provide these services.

Marketing costs play a significant role in the economics of credit cards.[14] The Internet may have a favorable effect on these costs in two ways. First, Internet advertising may become an efficient way to target credit card offers to individual consumers, although there has been limited use of this technology to date. Second, Internet companies also provide marketing partnership opportunities to credit card firms, such as "preferred" card status at some online merchants. On balance, there is no clear evidence that the Internet provides a lower cost distribution channel than direct mail, which is currently the preferred means of customer acquisition. To the extent that online advertising and promotion enable differential pricing strategies or greater levels of product customization, the Internet is likely to play a significant role in the overall marketing mix. In the longer term, differential pricing strategies may ultimately reduce card switching and the acquisition of customers who do not use their cards, and origination expenses may be substantially reduced due to decreased volume, leading to some additional efficiencies. However, this scenario would not necessarily be favorable to the industry—the improved efficiency is likely to be accompanied by very low margins, as customers are increasingly priced closer to the cost of serving them and see no reason to switch providers.

Industry Transformation

As most of the operations of credit card issuers are centralized, including marketing and distribution, disintermediation is unlikely to play a role in the industry, now or in the future. However, the two other critical factors, differential pricing and price transparency, have had major effects on the industry both before and after the Internet became commercialized.

Research on the credit card industry has documented the wide dispersion of profitability across different customers, even within the same issuer and demographic segment.[15] The best two deciles ("love 'ems") account for roughly 125 percent of profits earned by credit card issuers, while the worst two deciles ("kill you's") are loss making. The remaining population,

14. Marketing costs for "pureplay" Internet credit card companies, like many business-to-consumer companies, can be extremely large. For example, according to its 10-Q reports, in the first half of 2000 NextCard's marketing expenses alone were approximately equal to its revenue (net of interest charges).

15. Clemons and Thatcher (1997).

representing the vast majority of accounts, are generally break-even. Unlike other industries, where profitability dynamics are extremely complex, the factors that affect customer profitability in credit cards are well understood: love 'ems pay finance charges, other customers do not. Kill you's further distinguish themselves from break-even accounts by not paying back principal and creating expensive charge-offs and significant operational costs in collections.

Until the mid- to late 1980s, these fundamental differences in profitability were exacerbated by the marketing and operational practices common in the industry. Typically, borrowers were offered a single price point (~19.8 percent annual percentage rate [APR]), and growth primarily came through mass marketing, where any customer who could pass the credit screen was considered attractive. Success in this era meant efficient direct marketing operations and transaction processing systems, in general achieved through economies of scale.[16] Uniform pricing and mass marketing in the face of enormous intrinsic differences in customer profitability created massive cross-subsidies: the best accounts were being overcharged to subsidize losses incurred in servicing the worst accounts.

This difference in customer profitability, however, created an opportunity for a company that could devise strategies to attract only profitable customers. Capital One Financial (at that time the credit card division of Signet Bank) pioneered the following strategy to exploit these differences, which ultimately proved to be enormously profitable:

—Identify profitable customers, through a combination of data mining and product design, that is, a mixture of target marketing and price discrimination.[17]

—Offer them incentives to switch providers.

16. Credit assessment is also an important driver of overall profitability, but assessment techniques rapidly became similar across issuers as credit analysts used similar methods of evaluation, and later, nearly identical computer-based credit scoring models. Technological innovation has created periods of differentiation in the industry—for example, the early adoption of fraud prevention systems by American Express provided some advantages in charge-off rates—but such innovations are typically copied within a few years.

17. Examples included identifying correlations between the use of certain products (for example, specific magazine subscriptions) and borrowing habits through experimentation and data mining—essentially, third-degree price discrimination). Capital One's first major innovation was the balance transfer product, where a lower interest rate was offered to customers who transferred outstanding balances from other credit cards. Because this offer is only attractive to customers who both have credit balances and intend to pay them back slowly, it makes use of customer self-selection to attract only profitable accounts—that is, second-degree price discrimination.

—Endure slightly higher than average processing costs, primarily to ensure flexibility in account management, data analysis, and customer retention.

It is interesting to note that the productivity and consumer surplus effects of this innovation are atypical for a "technology" investment. All three steps, especially product R&D and flexible but inefficient data processing operations, would lead to an apparent decrease in measured productivity. In terms of consumer surplus, there is a substantial reduction in interest costs to those customers who pay finance charges and potentially an increase in charges (explicit or implicit) to customers who do not. Some customers, especially those most likely to default, may find their access to credit has been curtailed. In the short term, the change in consumer surplus will be positive: some customers will receive lower rates; others will continue to be subsidized by firms that are unable to distinguish profitable from unprofitable accounts.

A by-product of this strategy is that all issuers will ultimately be forced either to offer differential pricing or to exit the business—persistence with uniform pricing, especially as consumers become better informed about prevailing prices and offers, will ensure that a firm's credit portfolio is composed solely of unprofitable accounts.[18] As all surviving firms will become increasingly adept at differential pricing, these losses will be reduced, cross-subsidies will shrink, and some consumers may opt out of the market. However, the market has shown an unusual ability to create profitable products even for the highest risk segments (including those with bankruptcies or convictions for credit card fraud), limited primarily by regulatory restrictions. Thus over the long term this transformation will typically not lead to a denial of credit, although some consumers will find that credit may be available on much less favorable terms than they enjoyed in the past.

Although the major strategic innovation, differential pricing and elimination of cross-subsidies, occurred before the Internet was a significant factor in the credit card industry, the Internet has direct implications on how these strategies will look in the years to come and how they will affect the productivity and profitability of the sector. A primary source of advantage for firms like Capital One Financial (and those that followed them) was that competitors were slower to respond to their innovations than customers

18. Clemons, Croson, and Weber (1996).

were to adopt their products. Given the Internet's ability to reach customers rapidly, agile competitors can target consumers electronically with new offers and observe responses almost immediately, further increasing the gap between the fast and slow competitors. In addition, Capital One has more than 10,000 price points for credit cards (combining fees, APR, other ancillary benefits and services)—a degree of price complexity that can only be implemented through direct contact with consumers.

However, the profitability of these strategies will be eroded over time as consumers are increasingly priced at their risk-adjusted cost to serve. As customers become more informed about prices, competition will eventually squeeze out the margins in each segment, making profitability more difficult to sustain in the future. This margin compression will occur first through product pricing, which is easier to alter, and later through increased expenditure on convenience and service improvements. Increasing consumer informedness also has a strong negative consequence. Poorly designed products that offer a disproportionate share of the surplus to consumers will be rapidly identified and adopted, making pricing mistakes much more costly. While the current generation of "shopbots" in financial services are relatively rudimentary, some of the price search agents in retail have already begun to target firms that offer "loss leader" products, either intentionally or inadvertently, and others, such as Gomez Advisors and Bizrate, are increasingly making service quality information available to consumers.[19]

The trade-offs among pricing complexity, competition, and price transparency will ultimately determine the ability to earn above-normal profits within the sector. As differential pricing increasingly provides prices tailored to individual customers, and competition drives down margins within each customer segment, one would generally expect significant gains (albeit declining on the margin) in consumer surplus over time and long-term reductions in the profitability of the sector, although possibly offset somewhat by increased utilization resulting from more efficient pricing. The firms that are more successful at this game will probably delay the profit impact while still providing the market the benefits of allocative efficiency (consumers making correct decisions resulting from correct pricing), but the general long-run trend is toward compressed margins. Exact estimates of this change are difficult to make, but current evidence suggests

19. For loss leader information, see, for example, www.pricegrabber.com.

that the numbers are large.[20] Measured productivity for the sector, calculated using traditional measures such as cost per customer, may indeed decline as the support infrastructure for differential pricing and customer retention continue to add incremental costs that did not previously exist, although general progress in software and computing may help offset these costs.

Retail Banking

As with the credit card industry, the Internet has enabled cost reductions in many of the service aspects of retail banking that are likely to create both productivity and service improvements. However, the fundamental transformational effects of the Internet in this industry are driven by two critical factors, neither of which are present in the credit card industry. First, a significant component of the cost structure is embedded in the retail delivery system—principally branches, and to a lesser extent automated teller machines (ATMs). Second, unlike credit cards and most other financial services products, there is a much more limited customer profitability gradient. On the one hand, while there are customers who are enormously profitable (for example, those who leave large balances in non-interest-bearing accounts), they are much less common; and on the other hand, it is difficult for a customer to become a "kill you," especially if modest steps are taken in product design to charge for transaction services. As a result, much of the innovation in the use of the Internet in retail banking has been in increasing the convenience and availability of banking services and in reducing costs by off-loading transactional activity from high-cost bank branches to other channels.[21]

Alternative Service Delivery

There has been a long history of innovation in service delivery in U.S. banks, beginning in the 1970s with ATMs and including touch-tone telephone

20. In the first half of 2000, Capital One Financial earned about 850 basis points (after credit loss provision) of interest margin on its loans. In contrast, the comparable figure for Internet start-up NextCard, which competes almost entirely on the Internet and is probably less experienced at differential pricing, is 200 basis points.

21. For example, Booz-Allen reports that the marginal cost of an online banking transaction is $0.04 and of a call center transaction is $0.70, whereas a traditional teller-based transaction costs $1.44 (McQuivey and others, 1998).

banking, voice response units, centralized telephone call centers, co-located branches (for example, in supermarkets), and most recently, online banking. All of these investments resulted in lower costs per transaction and substantial increases in customer convenience, although these benefits were typically tempered by increases in customer transaction volume and limited ability to use these efficiencies to reduce costs in other channels. For example, in the early 1990s, twenty years after ATMs were introduced, the number of bank branches in the United States was still increasing and ATMs were viewed largely as a competitive necessity rather than a source of incremental profit or competitive advantage.[22] R. Steiner and D. Teixiera suggest that this is a general trend for many types of technology innovations in banking, which are "creating value, destroying profits."[23]

These observations are largely consistent with the experience of home banking. The first large-scale attempt at home banking was the Chemical Bank Pronto system introduced in 1986, which failed because of high infrastructure costs and low consumer adoption due to the need to impose fees.[24] The next significant innovation was the introduction of "PC banking" in the mid-1990s. This service allowed customers to perform simple transactions, make inquiries, and in some cases, pay bills and generate checks using a software application on their personal computer and a dial-up connection to a proprietary network.[25] Over time, these systems increasingly utilized off-the-shelf personal financial management software (PFM) that was customized slightly for the bank, and the proprietary dial-up networks were replaced by the Internet.[26] The economics of such products were mixed. Although PC banking operations appeared to be highly profitable, this was primarily due to already profitable customers adopting the product, with minimal change in their overall profitability.[27] In addition, there were significant operational costs for software licensing, network operations, and customer support, totaling $5 to $15 per month and only partially offset by fees. Outsourcing fees played a substantial role in these costs, especially for electronic payments, which were typically pro-

22. On bank branches, see Osterberg and Sterk (1997); on the perception of ATMs, see Clemons (1990).

23. Steiner and Teixiera (1992).

24. Clemons (1990).

25. Kalakota and Frei (1997).

26. The three most common PFM products were Quicken, Microsoft Money, and MECA, a package created by a consortium of banks expressly for online banking applications. In some cases, the only customization is a bank logo on the "splash screen" when the product loads.

27. Hitt and Frei (1999).

vided by an outside service such as CheckFree.[28] Customer fees even for the third-party vendors do not necessarily represent excess profits, since service and fulfillment costs can be significant in online banking, especially as the technology and operational practices evolve.

By 1998 most banks were shifting these proprietary systems toward Internet banking, which had substantially different economics on the cost side. The use of a web browser (or Internet-enabled PFM) has eliminated most of the network and software costs, although the costs of centralized servers, electronic payment fulfillment, and customer service remain. Nonetheless, this cost reduction has enabled banks to provide basic inquiry-only service at no cost, while charging nominal fees for online bill payment ($5–$10). As a result, adoption of online banking increased rapidly, from around 3 percent of customers for PC banking to more than 10 percent for Internet banking.[29] For example, by year end 2000, Wells Fargo bank had more than 1.4 million customers utilizing online access, 1.3 million of whom (more than 20 percent of all customers) did so through the web. There are also several online-only banks, but by the end of 2000 their services had been adopted by only 7 percent of online banking users—less than 1 percent of banking households and even less in terms of assets, since few customers use online banks exclusively.[30]

In the near term, the overall impact of cost efficiencies from online banking is probably neutral to slightly cost saving, although it has clearly increased consumer convenience. Evidence in the banking trade press is mixed. While banks such as Wells Fargo and Citicorp appear to be comfortable with the progress of their online banking operations, other reports suggest that Internet banking disproportionately attracts unprofitable customers.[31] These equivocal reports are probably due to the relatively small penetration of online banking, the difficulty of measuring the impact of a single channel in the presence of multiple alternatives, and the

28. Only 10 to 15 percent of electronic bill payment and presentment transactions are processed by banks. The majority—about 55 to 70 percent—are fulfilled by third-party service providers, and the remainder by billers. See ePaynews, "Online Banking Statistics" (www.epaynews.com/statistics/bankstats.html#10 [September 2000]).

29. ePaynews, "Online Banking Statistics" (www.epaynews.com/statistics/bankstats.html#10 [September 2000]).

30. Online Banking Report (www.onlinebankingreport.com/resources/toc.html#67 [March 2001]).

31. For positive assessments, see Thomas Hoffman, "Are On-Line Banks Profitable?" *Computerworld,* January 3, 2000, p. 33; for negative assessments, see Jessica Toonkel, "Bank Web Sites Draw Bargain Hunters, Study Says," *American Banker,* March 24, 2000, p. 14.

concentration in inquiry-only services that are likely to be incremental rather than substitutes for other channel usage. While growth in the use of online banking will increase the potential cost reduction benefits, significant gains in productivity from direct cost savings will require greater adoption of higher-value transaction services such as bill payment and presentment, which have not yet seen widespread acceptance, and the restructuring of other delivery channels to capture the savings created by online efficiencies.[32] A much more negative scenario is that a reduction in cost to consumers in performing inquiries and transactions causes them to consume more transactions (raising costs elsewhere), while making them better able to maximize their interest earnings by shifting money among accounts or to different financial services providers (for example, mutual funds) which offer more attractive yields. Thus it is not clear that overall costs are improved, and in an increasingly competitive market revenues are likely to be reduced for these products.

Industry Transformation: Disintermediation and Commoditization

The combination of a limited customer profitability gradient and relatively simple and standardized product design has made banks tremendously susceptible to problems of price transparency. This has historically been offset by geographic differentiation (most customers bank within two miles of where they live or work), differences in quality of service, and modest switching costs, although resulting in a proliferation of bank branches and other investments in improving service and convenience.[33] Another strategy was the development of "relationship banking," where banks tried to maximize the number of products used by a customer through promotional efforts and cross-subsidies among products.

The emergence of online banking has eroded many of the underpinnings of such strategies. Online banking has reduced the role of geography in consumers' choice of banking services. Online availability of rates and large expenditures on advertising that emphasizes pricing by banks with direct distribution, like Telebank, have informed consumers of the best prices for these products and created downward pressure on margins. The

32. In addition, for online only players, customer acquisition costs are also an issue. For now, acquisition costs outweigh any possible cost savings in the short term. A key issue is whether customer retention is such that these investments are ultimately productivity and profit increasing.

33. Switching costs represent the explicit or implicit costs of changing providers (see Chen and Hitt, 2000) for a discussion in a financial services context.

advantages of bundling products have also declined: the ease of online money management and the interoperability across institutions of many personal financial management software packages (for example, Quicken) make it possible to replicate many of the advantages of consolidating accounts in one institution. Consumers can now find the best price products and services from a variety of providers (including brokerage houses and mutual funds) and coordinate these activities online. The sustainability of cross-subsidies in this type of environment is highly dubious—customers will increasingly identify and disproportionately adopt the "loss leaders," and customers in products that are overpriced will be targeted by specialist firms offering better pricing or service. In contrast to the credit card industry, and to a lesser extent commercial banking, which have embraced differential pricing, retail banks are typically reluctant to offer customized pricing which may make these difficulties even more acute. Part of this reluctance is due to the inflexibility of banking software platforms, some of which cannot effectively handle customized pricing; the remainder is probably due to the service costs and price erosion that would occur if customers discovered that rates and fees for their bank accounts were negotiable.

It is unlikely that all customers will ultimately choose to bank exclusively online, and many customers may never use online channels. As a result, bank branches will still play a significant role in the delivery of banking services. This will have a mixed impact on profitability. On the one hand, geography will still have a role in service differentiation. On the other hand, as customers move online, banks will be continually adjusting and reconfiguring their branch networks, a task that has often proven managerially and socially difficult. One counterstrategy has been to increase the sale of alternative financial services products through bank branches; for example, brokerage accounts, mutual funds, and annuities. However, such products often fail to match up to the best available offerings in the market, and may face even more severe pressures from the Internet, as we discuss below.

In summary, it is likely that in terms of operational efficiencies there will be opportunities for cost savings, but that much of this gain will be passed on to consumers in the form of reduced margins and increased convenience and dissipated through increased transaction volume and revenue reductions due to more efficient money management by consumers. Due to the complexity of altering the branch system and the slow consumer adoption of online variants of high-cost and high-value transactions, these effects will play out more slowly than in some other industries, such as brokerage and credit cards. However, as in the credit card industry, the impact of price transparency is likely to be more rapid and declines in overall margins will begin to put pressure on banks to eliminate cross-subsidies and reduce costs.

Mortgage Lending

While the overall level of mortgages originated over the Internet is still small—1.5 percent—the mortgage sector has seen a substantial amount of Internet activity.[34] The attraction has been the cost structure and perceived lack of entry barriers. The mortgage origination process is a collection of activities that involve consumer counseling and sales at one end, and application acceptance, credit evaluation, and document processing at the other. This part of the overall mortgage value chain consumes about 200 basis points of the value of a typical mortgage, of which about a third is marketing, and the remainder is "fulfillment," the document processing required to issue a mortgage.[35] Most of the other areas of mortgage operations involve interfirm transactions among mortgage banks, mortgage servicers, securitization agencies, investment banks, and institutional investors. Automation and developments in communications technology have facilitated the optimization of activity in the value chain, although this has principally been due to transaction standardization and private networks rather than to the Internet.[36]

Both the informational and sales aspects and the operational aspects of mortgage origination have moved online. Many sites provide information services, especially services that allow customers to calculate payments, evaluate their purchasing power, and search for lenders and rates. These sites typically earn income from advertising and referral fees. A few sites also have the ability to take online mortgage applications, typically for a single online or traditional mortgage broker or lender. Finally, multilender sites aggregate information from several lenders and enable consumers to submit a single application to more than one lender, promoting competi-

34. Beidl (2000).
35. Posner and Courtian (2000).
36. Jacobides (2000).

tion for customer business. The most notable example of this type of site is LendingTree.com.

The structure of the mortgage product is such that there are not significant advantages to automating service operations; typically the only post-origination service is payment processing and refinancing. The overall demand for mortgages is determined by housing sales, interest rates, and changes in interest rates, and is not greatly affected by the efficiency of the origination process. This suggests that most of the demand for "online mortgages" is a replacement for mortgages that would have been originated in traditional channels. Therefore we expect that most of the economic impact of the Internet on the mortgage sector will be determined by how the Internet affects two long-standing trends in the industry: the continued disintermediation of the mortgage origination function and the impact of price transparency on pricing, margins, and allocative efficiency.

Transparency

The presence of informational sites and competition among online mortgage originators, who often bundle information services as part of their offerings, has created an ease of price search that will ultimately lead to greater price transparency. Given that the number of shoppers for online mortgages outweighs the number of customers who actually purchase mortgages online by an order of magnitude, price transparency will put pressure on margins long before online origination is prevalent. The limited range of product dimensions (interest rate, fixed versus variable, term, down payment requirements, documentation requirements) make this product ideal for an Internet search because the process is easily standardized but multidimensional, potentially resulting in a large number of combinations that can be handled efficiently by online search technology. Moreover, mortgages are a product bought only periodically, making it less likely that customers favor a particular mortgage provider with whom they have a special relationship. Multilender sites, which enable consumers to receive the benefits of price search without actually conducting a search themselves, will further expand the population of consumers who can benefit from transparency and competition.

One would expect mortgage lenders to respond with differential pricing strategies, particularly when the profitability of individual loans (like other credit products) can vary substantially across consumers. However, the characteristics of the product, and to a lesser extent prices, are constrained by government regulation, as well as by conditions imposed by the agencies and enterprises that securitize loans, such as Fannie Mae. Since more than half of residential mortgages originated in the United States in the past several years have been securitized and sold in secondary markets, lenders have less incentive to create unique products that cannot securitized.[37] Similarly, lenders are more concerned about average profitability over all their loans than about the profitability of individual loans, since these differences will be eliminated when the loans are pooled—and this further decreases incentives for differential pricing or product innovation. The situation could change if some firms begin to aggressively identify and target low-risk loan opportunities, potentially enabled by the Internet. This industry may be particularly attractive to other financial services providers such as retail brokers and insurance companies, who may have substantial information about the risk or other characteristics of a potential borrower from his or her use of other products. In this scenario, the ultimate effects would be similar to the credit card industry, with an increasing profit disparity between firms that engage in differential pricing and those that do not. However, aggressive use of differential pricing currently is not prevalent in the mortgage lending industry and may not be in the future without significant change in the strategies of multiple participants in the mortgage value chain.

Disintermediation of Mortgage Origination

As mentioned earlier, in the longer term the attractiveness of high potential margins will create a significant interest in the disintermediation of mortgage origination. Unlike almost all other banking services, where most activity occurs in a "captive" branch system or is centralized, the mortgage origination process has a mixed distribution channel. Currently, about half of all mortgage loans in the United States are originated through mortgage brokers (independent representatives of the mortgage companies), and the others are originated directly by the captive distribution arm of mortgage banks or branches of traditional banks, which typically operate through mortgage banking subsidiaries. Fees for sales and origination (or the operational costs of the captives) consume about 200

37. See Mortgage Bankers Association of America, "Mortgage and Market Data, " table I-4 (www.mbaa.org/marketdata/data2000/mbs_83%20-%2099.html [March 2001]).

basis points of the typical mortgage loan, and therefore offer much potential for disintermediation.[38]

Most of the Internet-based mortgage businesses focus on the sales process—identifying customers, counseling them about loan options, and encouraging the submission of a loan application—while operations activities are often off-loaded to traditional mortgage lenders (although some Internet lenders also provide software designed to streamline the origination process). However, to the extent that this sales component of the origination processes justifies relatively high fees for the other origination activities which are complex but standardized, Internet-enabled origination represents a real threat, particularly to independent brokers who rely on these fees for their profitability and in cases where the Internet may offer significant economies in reaching customers more efficiently.[39] This threat is even more significant when combined with price transparency, because mortgage lenders will increasingly look for cost savings in distribution efficiency to offset declining margins, and customers may ultimately be able to perform many of the preapplication processes themselves, cutting out agents and brokers entirely.

Even though it is predicted that the cost structure of origination will fall substantially over time, much of this gain is due to the use of standardized loan processing software that has been available for some time. Most of the functionality of this software existed before the Internet was widely used, and the cost savings, while facilitated by the Internet, are largely driven by the ability of brokers to assimilate existing technology.

Overall, the long-term trends on productivity and profitability in the mortgage lending sector are moderately clear. With industry-imposed constraints on pricing structure, increased price transparency, and the entry of online competitors with a potentially lower cost structure for distribution, margins will be squeezed, at least on mortgage origination. Measured productivity will increase, partly because consumers will increasingly take

---

38. Posner and Courtian (2000).

39. The experience of Internet-based lenders to date provides little information about the ultimate efficiency of this sector. Their economics are currently dominated by advertising and customer acquisition costs, which have created substantial losses for all of the publicly traded companies (for example, E-loan, LendingTree, and Mortgage.com). In contrast with other businesses, which initially incur losses for customer acquisition to ultimately support a more efficient operational cost structure, acquisition costs are a critical cost driver of mortgage origination efficiency, suggesting that these Internet-based lenders have not created any gains in aggregate productivity thus far.

responsibility for the front end of the process in return for cost savings (coproduction), and also because price pressures will force firms to reduce costs or exit this segment of the business. The net effect is that productivity will increase in this segment of the value chain. It is not obvious that there are substantial cost savings to be achieved through Internet origination alone in the current industry structure, making margin pressures even more acute.

Brokerage

Among the retail financial service industries, the retail brokerage sector has been the most radically transformed by the Internet, principally by the emergence of low-price online securities trading and free financial information services.[40] Over 200 retail brokers now operate online, typically providing a limited array of standardized information services along with low-cost trading.[41] Prices for a "market order" (an order to buy or sell a security at the prevailing price) range from $5 to around $30 with online brokers compared to on the order of $100 to $300 for a typical retail-size order at a full service broker. In aggregate, analysts at Morgan Stanley Dean Witter calculate that the price of an average retail stock trade—including all channels—has dropped from an average of $80 in 1998 to an average of $50 in 2000, and they predict continued drops for at least the next five years.[42]

Overall, the industry has experienced dramatic growth. From a base of essentially zero in 1995, online brokers managed more than $800 billion in customer assets, accounted for more than 30 percent of retail stock trades, and had in excess of 10 million accounts in 2000.[43] Two of the most prominent full-service brokers, Morgan Stanley Dean Witter and Merrill Lynch, initiated online access and trading services to their full-service

40. Many of these services were not originally free, but aggressive competition among content providers of all types of information, especially financial information, has forced many sites to abandon a fee-based model in favor of advertising and partnerships to facilitate customer acquisition.

41. For the Gomez Advisors profile of the major online brokers, see (www.gomez.com). Allstocks.com listed the telephone numbers of 211 brokers as of March 2001.

42. Henry McVey, "On-Line Financial Services," presentation, Morgan Stanley Dean Witter, July 2000 (www.msdw.com [September 2000]).

43. Salomon Smith Barney (2000), pp. 2, 4.

clients in 1999 at discounted commissions comparable to the high end of pricing at online firms. Despite the large number of online brokers, the market share of this industry is heavily concentrated, with the top nine firms accounting for approximately 95 percent of online brokerage assets. Among the three largest, Fidelity and Schwab were leading firms in the mutual fund and discount brokerage industries, respectively; the third, E*trade, is the largest of the new online entrants.

In many respects the Internet has a natural fit with the retail brokerage industry. Customers require a great deal of timely, text-based, and numeric information that can be easily delivered through a website. From a retail investor's perspective, the trading process is relatively standardized, with the actual transaction typically requiring no intervention by a market professional. The previous generation technology—direct phone calls to order taking brokers—was fraught with inefficiencies, such as errors in the communication of orders, limited ability to authenticate the customer, access problems (especially at peak trading times), and overall high costs, both to the customer and to the firm. Particularly for active traders who do not want or need advice from a market professional, Internet-based trading offers significant advantages. The ability to unbundle high cost advisory and service aspects from trading services enabled firms to profitably charge significantly lower prices, and the volume created by this price reduction has allowed them to offset the relatively high fixed costs of the technology infrastructure.

These changes have created substantial productivity improvements in front office operations of firms, which are primarily devoted to online trading, while increasing the volume to scale-intensive back office operations, which have remained largely unchanged, possibly providing a small productivity boost. Full-service brokers have also realized some of these efficiencies through improved communications with customers over the Internet, although the magnitude of these savings is less significant.

Offsetting the operational cost savings are extremely high investments in customer acquisition. The average of over 50 percent annual growth in the number of online brokerage accounts has been fueled by an advertising blitz that frequently consumes more than 100 percent of the revenue of start-up online brokers. The most aggressive advertiser of the online-only firms, E*trade, spent more than $120 million in 1999 alone promoting its online brokerage services, and its spending continues to rise. While productivity has increased in aggregate, to date much of this value is being transferred to consumers in the form of adoption subsidies, some of which have been quite large, and to advertisers in promoting these sites.[44] The fundamental economics of these investments can be favorable if customers are retained—with a one- to two-year payback for an *active* customer. Over 1998–2000, the market capitalization of a typical online broker is on the order of $1,000 to $3,000 per customer, suggesting that external investors had been willing to finance customer acquisition.

Different Intermediation, Transparency, and Alternative Revenue Sources

Disintermediation, price transparency, and differential pricing all play significant roles in the implications of the Internet for the long-term structure of the brokerage sector.

In this industry, pure disintermediation of the entire value chain is not a relevant threat—for the most part, customers are not able to access the financial markets directly. However, there is a significant threat of "different intermediation," as online brokers have the potential to capture significant market share through lower prices due to cost efficiencies that result from unbundling trading, advising, and, to a lesser extent, operational costs. Perhaps the most serious threat to the current structure of the industry is that more full-service customers will choose the combination of low-cost online brokers and free or low-cost online information services instead of the traditional bundle of trading and information services. Ultimately, this will depend on the pricing differentials between online and other brokers and the ability of full-service brokers to respond with differential pricing and service offerings.

In addition, the business practices of online brokers have further enhanced the position of firms that operate off-exchange trading systems and electronic crossing networks (ECNs), encouraging the further disintermediation of the primary stock exchanges. As we will discuss below, many online brokers make use of alternative trading systems in an attempt to earn incremental profits on retail trades through "payments for order flow" from the operators of these systems.

44. In the first quarter of 2000, E*trade was offering those who signed up for an account $400 in free computer equipment purchased from a computer retailer. Various other brokers have offered free personal digital assistants (retail value about $200) for new accounts, in many cases with minimal initial investment requirements.

The emergence of online brokers (and their advertising expenditures) has educated customers on the prices that they need to pay for transaction services. This has created substantial downward pressure on prices, particularly for full-service brokers. In some respects, however, this price transparency is illusory. Customers in fact pay significant costs, many of which are difficult to understand or are hidden and almost impossible to identify. Since explicit transaction fees have been driven toward marginal cost, brokers have sought other ways to improve profitability.[45] There are at least three significant sources of additional revenue that are received directly from the customer in ways that are moderately or completely opaque. First, at most brokerages uninvested balances are invested in a house "money fund." Typically, the interest rates on such finds are well below prevailing short-term interest rates (sometimes by as much as 200 basis points), and some e-brokers pay no interest on uninvested balances.

Second, when customers borrow money "on margin" to make investments, they pay finance charges to the broker. The size of these finance charges varies substantially across brokers; a casual scan of several brokers revealed differences of 200 or more basis points across brokers and even larger differences within brokers. Customers with small balances are charged extremely aggressive interest rates, which is consistent with a form of price discrimination if smaller investors are less informed about the appropriate price for margin lending or have fewer alternative funding sources. Given that these loans are essentially zero risk, due to the security requirements, this interest can represent a significant source of income. Moreover, they are not subject to disintermediation—the margin lending function is only zero risk if it is tied to the brokerage account that holds the assets purchased on margin. This prevents third parties from disintermediating the broker to capture the rents that exist in margin lending.

Finally, a common practice in the industry is "payment for order flow," in which retail brokers receive fees from market-making firms in return for the right to handle their orders. These market makers are often able to match orders internally or trade on off-exchange ECNs and so capture a significant portion of the bid-ask spread (the difference between the highest price offered to buy a security in the market and the lowest offer to sell). Payments for order flow and market making revenues can represent

45. Informal estimates put the marginal cost of processing a stock trade at $3 to $5. See Thompson and Gamble (1988).

a significant component of revenue for many brokers.[46] The practice is legitimate because customers receive prices no worse than the prevailing price on the exchange, although as a result they may lose any ability to obtain better prices than the prevailing quote, as is often the case for actively traded stocks on major exchanges.[47] Thus while price transparency appears to be a critical issue and has put substantial pressure on margins, at least in the short term, brokers have responded by identifying other revenue opportunities that are more opaque to the customer.

Brokerage customers differ significantly in their profitability. Customers who trade actively, who do not create activities with high operational costs (for example, forced liquidations of margin positions), and who consume relatively little broker time can be extremely profitable, particularly at full-service brokerage rates. They are even more profitable if they also utilize fee-generating products with low operational costs, such as mutual funds. Customers who consume all the service options of full-service brokers but generate few trades, or worse, consume these services and then trade elsewhere at discount rates, can be extraordinarily unprofitable. In particular, full-service brokers are vulnerable to opportunistic "pick-off" of their high-profitability accounts. This has already placed pressure on margins, partly to close this price gap between online and traditional brokers. It has also forced full-service firms to offer Internet trading, which will further decrease profitability and total revenue to the industry, although this decline may be offset by increases in asset management fees from other products, such as mutual funds.[48]

However, full-service brokers have at least two advantages that may enable them to sustain their market share in the face of competition from online brokers. First, they offer a vertically differentiated service—a higher

46. Morgan Stanley Dean Witter (1999) estimates that these sources account for about 10 percent of total revenues. E*trade, for example, earned about 6 percent of revenues from this source (as reported in its 10-K filing for 2000).

47. On the New York Stock Exchange, about 13 percent of customer orders are intermediated by a specialist who captures the bid-ask spread. See "Market Quality Report" (www.nyse.com/pdfs/activity99.pdf [March 2001]). On the Nasdaq, an interdealer market, market makers would expect to be on the "correct" side of the trade half the time and to capture 50 percent of the spread on average—with the remainder going to the customer. On some of the off-exchange trading systems, the customer loses the spread almost 100 percent of the time.

48. A back-of-the-envelope calculation suggests that total revenue from trading fees in the industry is indeed shrinking. Prices have dropped from full-service rates by a factor of roughly 10. Trading in online accounts is typically 4 times as much as trading in regular accounts. This suggests a net revenue reduction to the industry of about 60 percent per customer defection to online brokers, or about 6 percent overall, primarily borne by full-service firms.

quality product at a higher price—that has withstood twenty years of onslaught from discount brokers, albeit with a somewhat smaller price gap and less aggressive marketing tactics. Many customers truly value the service they receive from full-service brokers, particularly high net worth individuals with complex financial planning needs. In addition, these brokers can often offer access to initial public offerings and other coveted investment opportunities that may not be made available to the broader retail market. Second, full-service brokers are already well informed about who is and who is not a profitable account and they have more pricing flexibility with which to respond to the loss of a potential customer. This makes it significantly more difficult for entrant online firms to target the most attractive full-service customers. In fact, over the long term the situations may be reversed, as full-service firms create Internet-based offerings that can profitably be sold to moderate wealth investors who could not have been serviced economically in the traditional full-service model.

Overall, the Internet has already created significant productivity gains and has expanded the consumption of trading services by customers who would traditionally have made use of discount brokers. This has created a substantial expansion of consumer surplus, due to reduced cost and increased consumption of trading services.[49] However, much of the gain to date has been dissipated by increases in advertising and promotional expenditures. The ultimate productivity effects are dependent on the extent to which customer retention strategies can be implemented at low cost. Preliminary research suggests that the customer attrition and switching rates among online brokers are significant (10 to 25 percent), especially for those firms with the highest advertising expenditures.[50] It has also placed price pressure on full-service brokers without dramatic changes in the cost structure and led to a loss of some customer accounts. As full-service brokers have begun to introduce online trading options, the rate of loss has apparently been slowing. However, the key question for the long-term productivity and viability of the full-service sector is the extent to which these firms will continue to attract new high-wealth clients—especially those who may have had their initial exposure to the financial markets through online brokerage firms.

---

49. Some, however, would argue that this is not true economic output because trading itself is, to a first approximation, a zero-sum game (except for the effects on corporate governance). See Bresnahan, Milgrom, and Paul (1992) for an analysis of the sources of consumer and producer surplus that arise from financial trading activity.

50. See Chen and Hitt (2000).

Insurance

While insurance shares many of the structural characteristics of other retail financial services sectors, particularly the large customer profitability gradient and a complex and high-cost distribution system, to date it has probably been the least affected by the Internet. Penetration of even simple commodity products, such as term life, has seen rapid growth but remains insignificant in relation to overall volume in the industry. For example, life insurance originations over the Internet represented less than 1 percent of total originations in 1999 and are not expected to exceed 15 percent by 2003.[51] Moreover the majority of these originations are in term life, the simplest insurance product and one of the least profitable. Similar trends are observed in the simplest property and casualty insurance products, auto and homeowner's, while the traditional whole life, annuity, and variable life products have not seen significant adoption by consumers through online channels.

The Internet transaction activity in insurance is dominated by price comparison services. Insuremarket and Quotesmith, for nonhealth products, and eHealthInsurance.com are examples of firms that offer "instant quotes" from a wide variety of providers. However, they are not insurance agents: they primarily provide leads to insurance company representatives or to a local general agent who will process the application and facilitate issuance of the policy. Several of these companies went public in 1999, presumably to support their extensive marketing budgets, but thus far their revenue and stock performance has been dismal. The emergence of these services probably accounts for the not insignificant number of customers (about 15 percent) who report using the Internet to search for insurance information, although this is a relatively small proportion compared to many other consumer search categories.

As with mortgages, the agency system consumes a significant portion of overall value in the insurance industry. Commissions are on the order of the entire first year's premium for most renewable contracts, with renewal premiums on the order of 5 to 10 percent of all future payments. Thus agencies are potentially attractive targets for disintermediation.

There have been some dramatic moves by incumbent firms, in particular, the decision by Allstate in early 2000 to renegotiate its agency agree-

51. Jeff Dunsavage, "Complexity Limits Life Sales on the Web," *Best's Review,* February 2000, p. 155.

ments to provide more flexibility in offering alternative, Internet-based products. Some of the direct writers (such as Geico), unencumbered by channel conflict issues, have placed applications for auto insurance online, although fulfillment still goes through their normal process and is primarily offline. Many firms have taken smaller steps, creating Internet-only products for delivery through existing insurance marketplaces, advertising on the Internet, or enhancing informational sites to provide agent locators, product information, and account self-service options. Some larger brokers have also provided online capabilities to their marketing partners, for example, offering online applications for auto loans at the point of sale at car dealerships. These types of initiatives appear to be successful in decreasing operational costs and increasing the cross-sell rates of car dealers for insurance products. However, this is an extension of capabilities that may have already existed and have been made less costly and more prevalent by the Internet.

The relatively slow penetration of pure Internet origination is due to a combination of factors that are unique to the insurance industry. First, by its nature the product does not lead to rapid consumer adoption of alternatives. Insurance is an event-driven product—prompted by buying a car or a house, changing jobs, getting married, and so forth—and the vast majority of customers renew their policies without reconsidering the product, the company, or the agency. Even for short-term products such as term life, at most one-twelfth of all policies are up for renewal in any given month, and only a small fraction of these are actually "in play." Second, while the application process and provision of an initial quote can be partially automated by the Internet, there is still a substantial offline underwriting process, preventing "instant quote" from shifting to "instant issuance." Finally, making insurance readily available to the mass market may encourage the acquisition of unprofitable customers. This "adverse selection" problem is probably more acute in insurance than any other industry, due to the large number of unobservable factors that drive profitability and strong regulatory restrictions on the use of certain types of information by underwriters, carriers, and agents.

The central role of agents in the distribution of insurance may also be a significant constraint on the disintermediation of agents. The industry adage, "Insurance is a product that is sold, not bought," suggests that agents are very important in generating demand for insurance products. In addition, most insurance customers identify their agent, rather than the company, as the provider of insurance. Any significant attempt to use the

Internet for direct distribution or to otherwise alter agents' interaction with their customers—such as the earlier attempts to improve customer service through call centers—is likely to meet with substantial resistance. Agents recognize that their commissions represent a substantial component of any cost savings from Internet distribution; in effect, they would largely fund the firms' savings. Resistance to online distribution will be particularly strong from general agents (independent commissioned sales representatives), who are in a position to move significant share away from any company that attempts to reduce commissions through a direct distribution strategy. Slow consumer adoption and the relative invisibility of the carrier will increase the threat of this shift. Even in firms with captive agency systems, where the agents are employees of the company, the agency force typically wields substantial political clout, both internally and externally. Significantly more agents vote than chief executive officers, and agents have a significant voice in decisions at most insurance companies.

Price transparency has also played a more limited role than in other financial industries. While online product and price comparison engines can provide a greater degree of price transparency, there is a greater degree of complexity to insurance products, which may make it difficult to compare products directly. Even the simplest insurance product, term life, requires the specification of age, smoking habits, duration, and coverage amount before an "instant quote" can be generated. Thus the rates shown on insurance comparison sites are conditional on a number of individual factors and quotes may not be valid for a significant fraction of consumers. In addition, in contrast to bank deposits, which have government guarantees and can be easily moved, most insurance purchases are long term (since even short-term contracts such as term life are typically renewed) and the stability of the provider can be a significant issue.

Differential pricing plays a major role in insurance due to the "rating" process, where prices are based on actuarial risk. However, additional use of differential pricing, particularly pricing based on characteristics of individuals, which could be facilitated by the Internet, is strongly limited by regulation. Insurance is one of the few industries subject to explicit prohibitions on many types of differential pricing as a matter of social policy. Practices that are generally permitted elsewhere, including those that can improve market efficiency or are commonplace in other financial industries, are frequently banned for insurance. This limits the ability to offer tailored pricing, which could lead to significant transformation of the industry.

Overall, the insurance sector has been only mildly affected by the Internet, due to many structural factors of the industry and the nature of its products. There are certainly opportunities for promotion on the Internet, as well as some small incremental cost savings through the simple automation of some types of service tasks. However, until there is a substantial change in regulatory practices or in the role of agents in the delivery and service processes, it is hard to envision significant effects on industry productivity or profitability. This will happen, but it will happen slowly. As a historical example, the erosion of the role of the travel agent in the distribution of air travel products, for example, and the subsequent reductions in commission, took more than twenty years to occur, and travel agents still wield considerable power, particularly those who have moved to a non-commissioned, fee-for-service model in the business travel segment of the market.[52]

Quantitative Analysis of Productivity Gains

It is very difficult, and perhaps impossible, to characterize objectively the gains from radical changes in the structure of the retail financial services industry. Much of this value will likely come through intangible improvements in products and the creation of new types of products, distributed in new ways.[53] It is similarly difficult to estimate the gains from structural changes when in many industries one observes only a limited diffusion of new practices, and the economics of the firms that are adapting are dominated by adjustment costs—advertising expenditures, technology development costs, and other start-up expenses—that may not reflect long-run performance. However, there are two types of changes for which one can obtain quantitative estimates (with a potentially wide margin of error) of the possible long-run impact: disintermediation and restructuring of the product origination process, and incremental savings on periodic operational activities, principally billing and statement presentment.

We do not believe that these fully exhaust the possible range of productivity gains, but they are very likely to occur and can be estimated with some degree of confidence. Some additional, small changes are likely but are very difficult to quantify; for example, firms may be able to persuade

52. See Clemons and Hann (1999).
53. Brynjolfsson and Hitt (2000).

Table 4-1. *Annual Productivity Impact of the Internet*
on Retail Financial Services Industries
Millions of dollars

Industry	Origination	Servicing	Total
Credit cards	1,260	3,899	5,159
Banking (deposit products)	255		255
Mortgage	2,891		2,891
Brokerage	5,156	223	5,379
Insurance	1,414		1,414
Other online billing	4,229		4,229
Total	10,722	8,606	19,328

Source: Authors' calculations.

customers to use Internet self-service procedures for some types of simple operational activities, rather than using the call center or branch. Other changes, such as the welfare gains from increased pricing efficiency, can be quantified, but that is beyond the scope of this paper. And still other, more speculative changes—such as long-term change in the distribution of mortgages and insurance products, or a dramatic increase in the use of differential pricing—are too uncertain in both timing and form to make any reasonable quantitative predictions.

Our approach to the quantification of operational savings and origination gains is straightforward. For each industry, we estimate the volume of activity, the present cost, and the future change in cost attributable to the Internet in each of the two categories. We focus primarily on productivity gains to avoid issues of distribution of value. However, our discussion above suggests that much, if not all, of these productivity gains will accrue to consumers. The quantitative estimates are presented in table 4-1 and the computation process is briefly described in the appendix. When assumptions or guesses were necessary we erred on the high side, to capture the maximum possible benefit.

Several observations are immediately apparent from table 4-1. Most of the large gains are related to the reduction in cost of origination in industries with complex distribution systems. The only exception is the credit card industry, where origination volume drops as a result of increasingly efficient pricing, without greatly changing the remaining industry structure. Pure operational efficiencies are indeed significant, but not large compared to industry size. Overall, all the savings we have been able to identify and quantify will contribute a one-time gain of about 0.25 percent in the aggregate productivity of the U.S. economy in the long term, or at most about $19 billion in annual cost savings.

Summary

This analysis of the various retail financial services industries suggests that three factors—price transparency, differential pricing, and disintermediation—will play a significant role in determining how the Internet affects the industry structure. These three factors will have different effects in the various segments of financial services; in particular, they will have different implications for productivity, profitability, and consumer surplus. Our principal findings are summarized in table 4-2.

For all industries, the increased price transparency enabled by the Internet will be a significant factor. It will be especially important for industries with relatively simple products that can be easily compared by consumers, such as credit cards and deposit products in banking. Direct comparisons of such products will increase simple price-based competition and will ultimately drive each market segment toward nearly perfect competition. Transparency will also be important where the market structure allows differential pricing, as this is one of the primary ways in which firms can respond to increased transparency. That is, when all consumers can find their best deals there is very limited margin for error in pricing. Targeting strategies, such as those pioneered by Capital One Financial, will become the norm, as companies make use of increased transparency concerning consumer attributes, which will also be enabled by the Internet. No consumer can reliably be expected to cross-subsidize another in a transparent and efficient market, and consequently each customer will need to be priced closer to his or her risk-adjusted rate of profitability (for credit cards), his cost to serve (for insurance and brokerage), or other related factors. Similarly, strategies based on cross-subsidies across products for the same customer are equally vulnerable without some form of lock-in, product complementarity, or other means of preventing customer opportunism.

Improved price transparency will typically favor consumers—leading to increased consumer surplus—at the expense of producers, who will have to make additional investments in service, differentiation, or retention, or redesign products more frequently to offset increased consumer informedness. This will be a cost of doing business, a requirement for dealing with

Table 4-2. *Transparency, Pricing, and Disintermediation and the Effect of the Internet on the Retail Financial Services Sector*

Industry	Transparency	Pricing	Disintermediation	Productivity or profitability and consumer surplus
Credit cards	High, due to product simplicity	—Acute competition, due to product simplicity and transparency —Accurate price discrimination, due to simplicity of activity-based cost accounting and accuracy of information —Adverse selection	—Disintermediation of local banks occurred before Internet, due to simplicity of product and ease of direct mail marketing —Possibility of re-disintermediation, as Internet enables new players	—Allocative efficiency is improved —Big users will use more as their price declines —Labor and other inputs will not increase —Least creditworthy will be denied access as adverse selection forces greater care
Banking	High, due to simplicity of individual products	—Acute competition in some products, due to product simplicity and transparency —Not yet accurate pricing in PC banking —Not yet rational pricing of individual product lines —More extreme adverse selection	—Disintermediation not a threat; with very few exceptions, C2C retail lending, borrowing, payment systems for settlement and clearing are not options —Re-intermediation or the end of local relationships, opportunistic pick-off of best rates available anywhere, will heighten competition	Two competing trends: —End of relationship banking, accurate individual product pricing, will make each product more like credit cards. Allocative efficiency, and so forth —Relationship pricing will reduce acute competition in pricing of individual products if sufficient value to consumer can come from bundling and interconnection of products via PC banking. Consumers will benefit from product design, banks will benefit from increased profitability

Mortgages	Already high, due to product transparency	—Currently limited competition, limited price discrimination, due to Fannie Mae and Freddie Mac —Large-scale securitization has created moral hazard, reduced or eliminated wish to rate on risk	—Re-intermediation of local banks has largely occured —Internet-based transparency may increase re-intermediation of local banks —Internet-based transparency may result in re-intermediation, as current players are also replaced —The current system is not stable; new players will replace current players (see next column)	—Current system is not stable. Even with the subsidies that Fannie Mae and Freddie Mac receive (as a result of governmental guarantees, which reduce the incentive to risk rate), cross-subsidies of highest risk from lowest risk borrowers charged the same rate creates opportunities for mortgages —This will increase allocative efficiency. However, consumption of mortgages will be affected only slightly. Some individuals will now be more able to buy a house or to buy a larger house. Others will be unable to purchase a home and will need to rent, resulting in commercial mortgages replacing some consumer mortgages
Brokerage	—Traansparency of trading service pricing is now high —Transparency of pricing for secondary services (margin loans, etc.) is less, perhaps due to reduced interest and understanding among investors	—Full competition and full efficiency in pricing for discount services, subject to fact that support service pricing is less transparent —Not yet full price discrimination. Two-tiered service: full-service and discount brokerage	—Some replacement of full-service intermediaries by discount brokers occurred even before the Internet —Process of replacement has been accelerated by the Internet —One mitigating factor is the need for coaching and explanation, financial planning, and confidence in investment management products among some segments of the market —Unlike in insurance (see below) customer adoption has been rapid, especially among those investors who are easiest to serve, and quite slow among more complex customers. Balancing act, trying to provide online services without alienating brokers and losing remaining customers	—Clear example of allocative efficiency. A large population of day traders now exists. More trading occurs, with far less labor —Productivity is improved as well —Profitability may or may not change —The distress of the industry demonstrates that new pricing strategies and new relationship value propositions will be required

(continued)

Table 4-2. *Transparency, Pricing, and Disintermediation and the Effect of the Internet on the Retail Financial Services Sector* (Continued)

Industry	Transparency	Pricing	Disintermediation	Productivity or profitability and consumer surplus
Insurance	—Transparency of simplest products becoming quite high —More complex products (universal life, etc.) remain largely unaffected by Internet —Nonprice attributes (company reputation, etc.) limit transparency of products	—Pricing has not achieved the full efficiency of credit cards or other financial services products —For different reasons than for mortgages, underlying cause is governmental interference with market efficiency, in this case by placing severe restrictions on the use of information in pricing	—Disintermediation has occurred to some extent in the simplest products, like term life, which are already often sold through professional associations via direct mail —Disintermediation can occur to a greater extent in the future, due to the Internet —One mitigating factor is the need for coaching and explanation, financial planning, and confidence in risk management products, which have a higher emotional content than pure investments —Another is the imbalance between speed of customer adoption of proposed e-channels (low and slightly favorable) and agent response to proposed e-channels (high and quite damaging) —Greatest threat comes from Internet-based offshore products that have looser regulatory regimes; best risks can get best prices, causing extreme adverse selection among more tightly regulated onshore issuers. May result in fundamental instability, as with mortgage industry	—Disintermediation of distribution of simple products (distribution channel simplification) will reduce labor costs and improve efficiency —Disintermediation of more complex products may occur only slowly, over time. Just as some products (socks) can readily be purchased online, and others (dress suits, tuxedos) require custom fitting, so too will some insurance products require custom fitting, at least in the near term. —The very plausible threat of agents to punish firms that introduce agentless channels will delay alternative distribution —However, as with mortgages, the current pricing system is unstable. In mortgages, some players may opt out of the current pricing system by giving up the right to resell with federal guarantees. In insurance, other players may attempt to escape state regulation by moving offshore —Allocative efficiency can be greatly increased by allowing more accurate pricing —Productivity will probably increase as well, due to efficiencies in distribution (where agents are not used) and in service (to keep cost of agent-based distribution manageable)

better-informed customers, who shop for their best price and locate the best service, and with better-informed competitors, who set their own prices accurately. As a result, overall costs will increase in these industries, leading to the possibility that measured productivity will actually decrease, although this trend will be partially offset by cost saving opportunities provided by the Internet. In sectors of the financial industry where these counterstrategies are not possible, firms must bundle (in ways that cannot lead to opportunistic pick-off or unbundling) other high-margin products that have less transparency or endure a sustained period of lower profits.

Differential pricing will be a factor wherever it is consistent with regulatory constraints or industry practices. Differential pricing strategies will tend to eliminate cross-subsidies among consumers, which should generally lead to increased consumer surplus in the long run, because the prices customers receive may better represent their actual cost to serve, creating allocative efficiency. This process also favors agile and informed competitors at the expense of uninformed and inflexible firms. Opportunistic pick-off by informed firms will leave uninformed firms with a portfolio increasingly composed of kill you's. Attempts to recapture profitability by raising average prices for all consumers will result in a self-defeating "death spiral," as even more customers become vulnerable to opportunistic repricing.[54] Thus these industries will also be characterized by substantial shifts in profitability across firms, although the general trend will be toward decreased margins and profitability, as competition enters finer and finer segments of customers.

Bypass or disintermediation, or at least the threat of bypass, will be significant in any industry that relies on a high-cost, agency-based distribution channel, whether the agents are employees or independent contractors. In particular, disintermediation will be important in cases where customer adoption of online alternatives is rapid, where agents lack any special information advantages over firms that would like to engage in direct distribution, where agents have limited influence over the purchasing behavior of their clients, or where new entrants present a great threat to the overall viability of a firm.[55] When agents wield substantial power and adoption is slow relative to the ability of agents to punish firms engaged in disintermediation, this practice will be present but very slow. It may also be concentrated in entrants rather than incumbent firms. Typically, much of

54. Clemons, Croson, and Weber (1996); Clemons (1997).
55. Clemons and Row (1998).

the benefits of Internet distribution in these industries will accrue to the agents and other participants in the distribution system.

Of the three products that have a significant agent-based distribution system, brokerage is the most likely to be disintermediated. That has always been a potential problem, and computer-enabled discount brokerage existed long before the Internet became commercialized. While full-service brokerage firms have not wanted to move toward alternative strategies too quickly, so as to avoid cannibalizing profitable business and offending their powerful brokers, they have been able to adapt. In the mortgage industry, brokers may encounter some disintermediation, but the current industry structure, the complexity of the application process and consumers' desire for assistance, and the resulting low customer adoption imply that any significant change will be slow. However, it is hardest to envision a significant transformation in the insurance industry over the medium term, except in the simplest products. The power of the broker, due in large measure to the complexity of high-end products, consumers' desire for assistance and need for a trusted intermediary, and the resulting slow rate of consumer adoption will deter aggressive efforts in disintermediation. This situation could change dramatically if new online entrants demonstrated true efficiencies in customer acquisition, enabling pricing and product distribution that were truly attractive to consumers. But to date this has not been the case.

The stronger the threat of disintermediation, the more likely the industry will realize cost savings in origination and sales activities. Consumer surplus typically will increase because competition will allocate these gains to the consumers, in the short term through subsidies for adoption and in the long term through production efficiencies. Profits for the sector will depend on the relative effectiveness of firms and their agents at capturing the value not allocated to consumers. Productivity should be strictly improved by successful disintermediation.

Transparency, differential pricing, and disintermediation are transforming all service sectors. They interact in complex ways—as we have shown, the possibility of differential pricing has made disintermediation much more rapid in brokerage than in mortgage. They will change market structures over time—the absence of differential pricing in mortgages or insurance will not be stable, and the pricing of mortgages and rating of insurance will need to become much more information intensive. Over time, the consumers who are the lowest risk, or easiest and most profitable to serve for other reasons, will enjoy better pricing, and as is evident from both theory and experience with industries such as telecommunications, the allocative efficiency that results will be good for consumers and will increase demand. The productivity of service providers, measured in terms of income per employee, or revenue per employee, or even product produced per employee, may appear to decline, and producer surplus may decline as well. Some consumers will be relatively disadvantaged; that is, those whose interest rates, premiums, or financial advisory fees are increased. Measured in aggregate, however, consumer welfare will increase.

Appendix
Quantitative Estimation of Productivity Gains

These estimates are intended as an outer bound for the possible long-term impacts of the Internet on selected segments of the retail financial services industries discussed in the paper to allow the reader to gauge potential magnitudes. Where exact or reasonable estimates were available from external sources, we made use of these. In other cases, we assumed *conservatively* (for our purposes) a maximal effect. Nevertheless, in most cases these numbers, while nontrivial, are not large.

Credit card origination. According to a 1999 estimate, the credit card industry currently generates 3.5 billion direct mail offers annually.[56] Success rates have ranged from 0.4 percent in the second quarter of 2000 to 1.2 percent for 1999 as a whole. We use the average success rate to estimate that there are approximately 28 million new card accounts originated each year. At a cost of $50 per origination, an estimate provided by a large, efficient issuer, this represents a cost to the industry of $1.4 billion. If 90 percent of all originations were eliminated due to decreased card switching and incremental adoption (the remaining 10 percent would be new adopters), the resulting cost savings would be $1.26 billion, which is clearly an outer bound.

Credit card servicing. There are approximately 550 million credit card accounts in the United States.[57] A survey by the Federal Reserve found that

56. Leslie Beyer, "Return to Sender," *Credit Card Management,* April 1999, pp. 33–37.

57. This number is based on a figure of 430 million for Visa and Mastercard reported at year end 1999 by the Federal Reserve. See "The Profitability of Credit Card Operations of Depository Institutions," Annual Report by the Board of Governors of the Federal Reserve System submitted to Congress pursuant to section 8 of the Fair Credit and Charge Card Disclosure Act of 1988 (June 1999). American Express is reported to have approximately an 18 percent share, according to litigation

66 percent of credit card consumers would someday be willing to use online bill payment and presentment. We use this as the actual figure to construct an outer bound of possible cost. The cost of a paper statement presentment and payment is estimated to be between $0.60 and $1.75; for this industry we choose the mean cost, or $1.18. The fees charged by outsourcing firms for online presentment are approximately $0.35, which, assuming a 20 percent margin to the outsourcing vendor, yields a cost of $0.28 for an online statement. Thus each of twelve monthly statements has a cost savings of $0.90, leading to an annual savings of $10.80. For the 363 million accounts (66 percent of 550 million) that may ultimately have online bill payment and presentment, this yields a total of $3.89 billion in annual savings.

Banking origination. We assume that there are no net gains in origination cost. Although the online channel is likely to lower cost, it is not clear that the data entry component is significant and that banks will be able to make significant adjustments to capture any cost savings in origination.

Banking servicing. There are already extensive servicing options in multiple channels, and there is little evidence of significant replacement of transaction activity by online channels. However, as with credit cards, there may be significant use of online statements, which may create some cost reduction. Since no payment is involved, we assume that a bank statement is at the low end of statement costs, which yields a cost of $0.60, and similarly, assume an online statement processing cost of $0.28. We assume that overall adoption of online statements is lower in banking than in the credit card industry, due to customers' preference for paper documents for archival record purposes, so we use a 33 percent rate of long-term adoption. There are approximately 120 million households in the United States, 84 percent of which have a transaction account at a bank, according to the Federal Reserve. If each banking household has a single statement per month (possibly representing multiple accounts), our calculation yields 1.2 billion statements per year at a savings of $0.32 per statement, or $256 million annually.

Mortgage origination. The principal gain is a reduction in the operational costs of mortgage origination through the use of the Internet in both

---

documents in proceedings between Visa and American Express, which implies an additional 90 million accounts (http://home3.americanexpress.com/corp/latestnews/mshare.asp [March 2001]). And we assume another 30 million for the remainder of the market.

traditional and online mortgage origination channels. There are incremental savings for the fraction of mortgages that are originated principally
over the Internet. The Mortgage Bankers Association estimates that
$1,285 billion worth of mortgages were originated in 1999. Kenneth
Posner and Michael Courtian estimate that the origination cost is currently
200 basis points and will drop to 120 basis points by 2005.[58] We guess,
conservatively, that about 25 percent of this drop is due to the Internet. In
addition, 10 percent of mortgages will have only Internet fulfillment,
which we assume will cut the cost of fulfillment (50 basis points) by an
additional 25 basis points. This yields a total Internet savings of 22.5 basis
points of origination volume in the long term. At today's volume, this represents annual savings of $2.89 billion, and it will grow with the mortgage
origination market over time.

Mortgage servicing. We assume that there are no incremental gains due
to the Internet for mortgage servicing. Most mortgages require minimal
servicing, and automated alternatives (for example, voice response units)
provide most of the necessary automated functionality. Automated payment already exists in the form of electronic funds transfer or direct debit.

Brokerage origination. We estimate that there is no significant savings in
origination cost, as the rate of new adoption will slow and the process is
still highly labor intensive, due to securities regulation.

Brokerage operations. There are expected to be approximately 88 million
brokerage accounts by 2005, 50 percent of which will be online. These
online accounts will trade, on average, 25 times a year, of which we assume
75 percent will be through the online channel (since some online accounts
are attached to full-service accounts). This implies there will be approximately 825 million online trades in 2005. Current brokers charge an additional $10 to $15 for phone-assisted trading, which is equivalent to a non-
Internet trade. Taking the midpoint of this range and assuming that the
cost of this service is approximately half the fee, this yields a savings of
$6.25 per trade, or a total savings of $5.16 billion. There are also additional savings from online statements; using the same set of assumptions as
for banking, we arrive at total savings of $224 million for statement gen-
eration and mailing.[59]

58. Posner and Courtian (2000).
59. The number of brokerage accounts in 2005 is from Morgan Stanley Dean Witter (1999), p. 17.
Current fees for phone-assisted trading are based on pricing by Charles Schwab, Morgan Stanley Dean
Witter, and E*trade.

Insurance origination. The size of the current market in insurance is estimated to be $2.4 billion in new term life premiums, $15.6 billion in renewal premiums, and annual auto premiums of $125 billion.[60] Commission rates are approximately 13.5 percent for new issues of auto, 50 percent for new issues of term life, and 5 percent for term life renewal, which yields a total commission of $18.8 billion in annual premium. Long-term estimates place the total online insurance segment at about 15 percent of originations. If we assume, optimistically, that there is a 50 percent savings in commissions due to cost savings, this yields $1.41 billion in savings, of which 90 percent is in auto insurance.

Insurance operations. Currently we do not believe that significant operational savings will be achieved through the Internet. There is limited statement generation, and in many cases the broker is the preferred provider of information or transactions services.

Online billing. The approximately 120 million households in the United States receive between six and twelve bills a month. We assume the upper limit. In 1999, approximately 55 percent of large-scale billers announced online billing initiatives.[61] Moreover, surveys suggest that between 40 and 55 percent of consumers would reportedly be willing to receive online bills for various types of payments. (We presume that this is lower than the Federal Reserve's estimate of 66 percent for credit card customers because alternatives such as direct debit are typically available for simple billing transactions.) We assume that bills are of intermediate complexity, with costs between a simple statement ($0.60 as above) and a credit card statement ($1.18 as above), yielding an estimated original cost of $0.89 per bill, with a 50 percent savings due to online payment. This yields a total outer bound of savings of $4.3 billion. This is likely an overstatement, since it does not fully account for existing substitutes (direct debit and credit cards) that have for some time been available for the payment of simple bills.

References

Beidl, Richard A. 2000. "Housing Finance on the Internet: The Battle for Global Dominance." *Housing Finance International* (March).

60. Morgan Stanley Dean Witter (1999), pp. 32–36.
61. Jackie Cohen, "Are Consumers Going for On-Line Billing?" *Industry Standard,* January 27, 1999.

Bower, Joseph L., and Clayton M. Christensen. 1995. "Disruptive Technologies: Catching the Wave." *Harvard Business Review* 73 (1): 43–53.

Bresnahan, T. F., P. Milgrom, and J. Paul. 1992. "The Real Output of the Stock Exchange." In *Output Measurement in the Service Sectors,* edited by Zvi Griliches, Ernst Berndt, and Marilyn Manser. University of Chicago Press.

Bresnahan, T. F., and M. Trajtenberg. 1995. "General Purpose Technologies: 'Engines of Growth'?" *Journal of Econometrics* 65 (1): 83–108.

Brynjolfsson, E., and Lorin M. Hitt. 2000. "Beyond Computation: Information Technology, Organizational Transformation and Business Performance." *Journal of Economic Perspectives* 14 (4): 23–48.

Chen, Pei-Yu, and Lorin M. Hitt. 2000. "Switching Cost and Brand Loyalty in Electronic Markets: Evidence from On-Line Retail Brokers." Paper prepared for the 21st Annual International Conference on Information Systems. Brisbane, Australia, December 10–13.

Clemons, Eric K. 1990. "MAC–Philadelphia National Bank's Strategic Venture in Shared ATM Networks." *Journal of Management Information Systems* 7 (Summer): 5–25.

———. 1991. "Evaluation of Strategic Investments in Information Technology." *Communications of the ACM* 34 (1): 22–36.

———. 1997. "Technology-Driven Environmental Shifts and the Sustainable Competitive Advantage of Previously Dominant Service Companies." In *Wharton on Dynamic Competitive Strategy,* edited by G. Day, R. E. Gunther, and D. Reibstein, 99–121. John Wiley.

Clemons, Eric K., David C. Croson, and Bruce Weber. 1996. "Market Dominance as a Precursor of a Firm's Failure: Emerging Technologies and the Competitive Advantage of New Entrants." *Journal of Management Information Systems* 13 (2): 59–75.

Clemons, Eric K., and Il-Horn Hann. 1999. "Rosenbluth International: Strategic Management of Technology-Driven Discontinuous Change at a Successful Global Enterprise." *Journal of Management Information Systems* (Fall).

Clemons, Eric K., and M. C. Row. 1998. "Electronic Consumer Interaction, Technology-Enabled Encroachment, and Channel Power." Working Paper 97-09-09. Wharton School, University of Pennsylvania.

Clemons, Eric K., and Matt E. Thatcher. 1997. "Capital One." *Proceedings of the Hawaii International Conference on Systems Sciences.* University of Hawaii.

Gordon, Robert J. 2000. "Does the 'New Economy' Measure up to the Great Inventions of the Past?" *Journal of Economic Perspectives* 14 (4): 49–74.

Hitt, Lorin M., and Frances X. Frei. 1999. "Do Better Customers Utilize Electronic Distribution? The Case of PC Banking." Working paper. Wharton School, University of Pennsylvania, and Harvard Business School.

Jacobides, Michael J. 2000. "Small Numbers Outsourcing: Efficient Procurement Mechanisms." Ph.D. diss., Wharton School, University of Pennsylvania.

Kalakota, R., and Frances X. Frei. 1997. "Frontiers of Online Financial Services." In *Banking and Finance on the Internet,* edited by Mary J. Cronin. New York: Van Nostrand Reinhold.

Mayo, Michael A., James Marks, and Haakon Boenes. 2000. "Financial Services Companies and the Internet." Research report. Credit Suisse First Boston (May 31).

McQuivey, J., and others. 1998. *Retail's Growth Spiral.* Forrester Report. Cambridge, Mass.: Forrester Research.

Morgan Stanley Dean Witter. 1999. "The Internet and Financial Services." Research report (August).

Osterberg, William P., and Sandy A. Sterk. 1997. "Do More Banking Offices Mean More Banking Services?" Economic Commentary Series. Federal Reserve Bank of Cleveland (December).

Posner, Kenneth A., and Michael D. Courtian. 2000. "The Internet Mortgage Report II: Focus on Fulfillment." Research report. Morgan Stanley Dean Witter (February).

Salomon Smith Barney. 2000. *Research Report: Online Brokers.* (February.)

Steiner, R., and D. Teixiera. 1992. *Technology in Banking: Creating Value and Destroying Profits.* MIT Press.

Thompson, Arthur A., and John Gamble. 1988. "Competition in the Electronic Brokerage Industry." Unpublished paper. University of South Alabama.

Tushman, Michael L., and Philip Anderson. 1986. "Technological Discontinuities and Organizational Environments." *Administrative Science Quarterly* 31 (3): 439–65.

5

ANURADHA NAGARAJAN
ENRIQUE CANESSA
WILL MITCHELL
C. C. WHITE III

Trucking Industry: Challenges to Keep Pace

THE INFORMATION HIGHWAY is changing the business practices of the trucking industry and, in the process, is reshaping the way the trucking industry affects the rest of the economy. As e-commerce transforms the economic landscape, Internet-enabled new business practices in the trucking industry are changing the revenue and cost structure of the industry. In addition, because other sectors of the economy, such as manufacturing and wholesale and retail trade, depend on the value added by trucking services, the trucking industry contributes to the growth in the general economy. We define e-commerce to include business processes that permit transactions and trade to take place on the World Wide Web, as well as processes that use the Internet as a repository, an enabler, and a conduit of information.[1] Trucking firms are using the Internet's strategic building blocks of distributed access to valuable information, quick communication, and boundary-defying connectivity to exploit current resources and capabilities and to explore new Internet-enabled business opportunities.

We greatly appreciate assistance from Mike Belzer, Steve Burks, Maciek Nowak, Pete Swan, Cliff Winston, and staff members of the U.S. Bureau of Transportation Statistics. The responsibility for interpretation is ours.
    1. Sampler (1998); Rayport and Sviokla (1995).

The highly competitive and volatile trucking industry makes a significant contribution to the national economy. Data and examples from multiple sources confirm that information availability stemming from the Internet is stimulating demands to exploit existing skills in order to serve existing customers better as well as creating opportunities to explore new transportation markets and services. Emerging changes in industry structure are also arising as the result of acquisition activity. Many of these changes in industry structure stem from firms' attempts to gain access to new resources and to coordinate the use of heterogeneous capabilities. Our quantitative assessment of the financial impact of the Internet on the operations of trucking firms leads us to conclude that the Internet is currently having greater impact on growth than on cost reduction. The net impact of the revenue and cost trends may lead to larger trucking businesses with profitability that is similar to current levels. We estimate that revenue growth in the trucking industry resulting from these changes will have modest but notable impact on economic activity. The value added contributions of trucking to other industries mean that the trucking industry is also likely to have a substantial impact on other sectors of the economy, quite possibly to a degree greater than the within-industry impact. The full impact of these changes will depend on how Internet-related policy issues concerning merger policy, labor policy, and technology policy are resolved.

Trucking Industry Background

Freight transportation, particularly by truck, is central to the health of the U.S. economy. The transportation sector moved more than 12 billion tons of freight in the United States during 1998, with 7.7 billion tons being transported by the trucking industry in primary and secondary shipments.[2] These shipments generated more than $486 billion in revenue for the domestic trucking industry. In 1997, the most recent year for which aggregate modal data are available, trucks provided nearly 60 percent of shipment volume and nearly 82 percent of shipment revenue in the trans-

---

2. Primary shipments usually cover freight on long hauls to manufacturers and processors and product shipments from there to warehouses and distributors. They account for the greatest portion of the mileage a shipment travels. Secondary shipments mainly cover local and short haul movements. They connect product shipments from a warehousing or other transshipment points to their final destination.

portation sector, making the trucking industry the dominant mode for freight movement.[3] Trucking is a major employer in the United States, with 9.7 million people working in trucking or trucking-related jobs in 1998.[4]

The trucking industry has gone through a long cycle of regulation and deregulation, leading to high industry volatility. Following the Motor Carrier Act of 1935, for-hire companies that wanted to haul freight across state lines had to obtain authority from the Interstate Commerce Commission (ICC). Most carriers set prices for their services through a collective rate-making process made legal by federal antitrust exemption. Passage of the Motor Carrier Act of 1980 did not eliminate state-based regulation of trucking companies, but the federal law initiated substantial changes at the interstate level by allowing easier entry, providing greater pricing flexibility, eliminating restrictions on how many customers a contract carrier could serve, and reducing restrictions on private fleets. The rapid expansion by entrants and incumbents after 1980 quickly increased industry capacity, and by the late 1990s, more than 3,000 carriers a year were gaining new or additional operating authority.[5]

Competition has held down the rates that trucking firms charge shippers, and typical operating ratios now fall in the mid-90 percent range (the operating ratio, which is the ratio of operating expenses to operating revenue, is a key efficiency measure in the industry). In the three years before 1980, the trucking industry operating ratio averaged approximately 94.9 percent for ICC-regulated carriers. In 1991 the average ratio was 96.8 percent, and in 1997 the average ratio was just over 95 percent—less than five cents operating margin per revenue dollar. About 48,000 carriers went out of business between 1980 and 1999, including 74 of the top 100 revenue-generating firms in 1984.[6]

The trucking industry is both highly segmented and extremely fragmented. Within the industry, freight movement is distinguished by shipment size: truckload (TL), less than truckload (LTL), and private fleets. A reasonable approximation of the number of U.S. trucking firms, combining information from several sources, is that there were more than 500,000 interstate motor carriers in the United States in 2000; about 30,000 of these were for-hire carriers; the remainder were private fleets. Of the

3. Standard & Poor's (1999); American Trucking Association (2000).
4. American Trucking Association (2000).
5. Newport Communications (1999).
6. Newport Communications (1999).

30,000 for-hire carriers, about 21,000 (69 percent) were TL specialists, about 8,000 (28 percent) handled both LTL and TL shipments, and 1,000 (3 percent) were LTL specialists. Most trucking firms are quite small. More than 70 percent of the interstate carriers operated six or fewer trucks, while 80 percent had twenty or fewer trucks. Nearly two-thirds of the 30,000 for-hire carriers had annual revenues of less than $1 million.[7]

Truckload carriers specialize in hauling large shipments long distances. Most TL shipments are 10,000 pounds or more, with the average TL ship-ment weighing about 27,000 pounds. The national truckload market is further segmented into national dry van, regional dry van, refrigerated/temperature controlled, flatbed, tank truck, and specialized operators. In the TL segment, an owner-operator or a driver employed by a TL firm picks up a load from a shipper and carries the load directly to the con-signee, without transferring the freight from one trailer to another.[8] Thus, TL carriers do not need a network of terminals. The TL segment of the industry consists of highly competitive operations, which typically are nonunion facilities that use owner-operators to minimize fixed costs and focus on achieving high vehicle productivity. The TL segment moves 45 percent of primary shipment volume, while accounting for only 37 per-cent of shipment revenue.[9] TL firms concentrate on high-density corridors and balanced freight flows to ensure high vehicle use and low costs.

Less-than-truckload carriers haul shipments that tend to weigh between 150 and 10,000 pounds. The average LTL shipment weighs slightly more than 1,000 pounds. Key economies of scale and density for an LTL carrier come from consolidating many shipments that are going to the same area. Such consolidation requires a network of freight terminals. Therefore, LTL carriers are characterized by networks of consolidation centers and satellite terminals. The average length of haul for national LTL firms is about 650 miles, and the average for regional LTL firms is about 250 miles. Thus, a pickup-and-delivery truck typically transports an LTL shipment from the shipper's dock to the trucking firm's local terminal, where workers

7. American Trucking Association (1999, 2000); Newport Communications (1999); Standard & Poor's (1999). Estimates of numbers of U.S. trucking firms vary substantially, because of the size and fragmentation of the industry. There were 501,744 interstate motor carriers on file with the Office of the Motor Carriers as of March 2000.

8. An owner-operator is a sole proprietorship or other small company whose primary purpose is to operate one or more trucks for-hire.

9. Standard & Poor's (1999, p. 12).

unload and recombine the shipment with other shipments that are going to similar destinations, most often a destination terminal in another city. The process of moving groups of shipments from one terminal to a terminal at another destination is known as line-haul operations, which may be accomplished by large trucks or by another transportation mode (such as rail or ship), depending on price and service considerations. Once the shipment arrives at its destination terminal, the load is processed, moved to a pickup-and-delivery truck, and then hauled to the consignee. LTL shipments accounted for 3 percent of U.S. shipment volume and 16 percent of revenue in 1997.[10]

Table 5-1 provides a view of the financial structure of TL and LTL trucking firms, using the most recent Form M data available from the Bureau of Transportation Statistics. The number of firms included in the table is moderate (113 firms), but we believe that the information provides insight into the current state of the industry.[11] In 1999 the operating ratio for the LTL firms was 93.9 percent. TL firms had a mean operating ratio of 94.7 percent. Firms that reported operating in both TL and LTL had the highest operating ratios among the segments (95.5 percent). The higher operating ratio could indicate, as we discuss later, that trucking firms are responding to customer demands for integrated trucking services, but that additional coordination costs needed to create the integration are lowering the firms' profitability. When the firms from all the segments are combined, the operating ratio is 94.5 percent, indicating that on average a trucking firm makes an operating profit of just over five cents for every operating revenue dollar. As of the second quarter of 2000, many of the public TL firms indicated significant increases in revenue but declines in

10. Standard & Poor's (1999, p. 12). In the past few years, largely as a result of the emergence of the Internet economy discussed in this paper, package express (PX) companies such as UPS have become a highly visible part of the LTL segment (indeed, many of the larger package express firms have merged with "traditional" LTL companies). There are several key differences between PX and the rest of LTL, including the equipment needed to move goods and the volume of material picked up and delivered. PX has more items to deliver, but the goods are lighter; PX pick-up-and-delivery vehicle drivers do not need to operate fork lifts. PX drivers usually make ten to fifteen pick-ups or deliveries an hour, whereas LTL drivers make two to five an hour. PX and traditional LTL share key similarities, though, in aggregating shipments from multiple sources and then disaggregating them to multiple consignees.

11. According to the American Trucking Association the operating ratio for trucking firms, based on reports to the U.S. Department of Transportation of 1,500 firms with $3 million or more in annual revenue, was 96.4 percent in 1990, 95.8 percent in 1992, 95.0 percent in 1994, 96.9 percent in 1996, and 94.5 percent in 1998.

Table 5-1. *Financial Statistics for LTL, TL, and Combined Firms, 1999*

Firm	Mean	Percent	Maxi-mum	Mini-mum	Standard deviation
LTL (21 firms)					
Operating revenue	468.8	100.0	2,219.4	6.7	642.4
Operating expenses (operating ratio)	440.3	93.9	2,217.6	8.3	610.9
Operating income	28.5	6.1	215.9	−3.3	52.2
Total assets (N = 20)	285.5	. . .	1,215.7	2.0	363.6
Total employment, in thousands (N = 20)	5,392	. . .	23,009	32	6,645
TL (80 firms)					
Operating revenue	152.4	100	1,559.6	0.15	252.1
Operating expenses (operating ratio)	144.3	94.7	1,541.6	0.15	241.4
Operating income	8.1	5.3	102.2	−3.87	15.8
Total assets (N = 57)	78.9	. . .	699.5	0.03	120.6
Total employment, in thousands (N = 54)	1,199	. . .	12,032	11	2,395
Combined firms (12 firms)					
Operating revenue	373.0	100	2,590.7	12.8	719.5
Operating expenses (operating ratio)	356.4	95.5	2,506.9	12.5	695.2
Operating income	16.6	4.5	83.7	−10.0	28.3
Total assets (N = 8)	142.8	. . .	749.4	5.1	256.1
Total employment, in thousands (N = 7)	4,226	. . .	23,279	54	8,588
Pooled sample (113 firms)					
Operating revenue	234.6	100	2,590.7	0.15	431.9
Operating expenses (operating ratio)	221.8	94.5	2,506.9	0.15	412.8
Operating income	12.8	5.5	215.9	−10.0	28.4
Total assets (N = 85)	133.5	. . .	1,215.7	0.03	229.3
Total employment, in thousands (N = 81)	2,496	. . .	23,279	11	4,828

Source: Authors' calculations based on Form M data for 1999 from the Bureau of Transportation Statistics.

net income, while LTL firms showed increases in revenue and small increases in net income.[12] The key conclusion is that operating ratios are tight throughout the industry, particularly among firms that are offering integrated services.

Despite competition and over-capacity in the for-hire segments, private fleets operated by manufacturers or distributors still account for about half of U.S. volume (52 percent in 1997) and revenue (47 percent in 1997) of general freight shipments. Private fleets typically focus on medium to short hauls, while outsourcing the lengthier hauls to the for-hire market. The private trucking market share grew following deregulation but has been declining recently. Reasons for the decline include the availability of low-price alternatives, inefficiencies that arise when private carriers have difficulties obtaining backhauls (that is, a shipment that originates near a delivery point so that the trucking company does not incur the costs of operating an empty truck on the return trip), and the complexity of the logistics process required for increased imports and exports.

The Impact of Trucking on the U.S. Economy

The trucking industry is an integral part of the U.S. economy. Our earlier figures noted that trucking services make up well more than half of the volume and revenue of transportation volume in the United States. For goods produced in the United States, trucking services begin with the transport of raw materials to manufacturers and continue through shipments to distributors, retailers, and, in increasing numbers of cases, to end consumers. For imported goods, trucks transport freight from the docks to break-bulk terminals and from there to manufacturers, distributors, and retailers. Moreover, trucks serve as key conduits within intermodal transportation systems of train, air, ship, and pipeline, making the trucking presence ubiquitous in all parts of the transportation sector.

Although identifying the importance of the trucking industry is straightforward, measuring the impact of trucking on the U.S. economy is more difficult, because trucking services are so intertwined with all sectors of the economy. Following are summary estimates of the measurable share of the economy that trucking services represent. These estimates provide

12. Jonathan S. Reiskin, "Truckload Profits Fall, LTLs Rise in Second Quarter," *Transport Topics,* August 7, 2000, p. 3.

Table 5-2. *Share of Trucking in the U.S. Economy, 1996*

Category	Dollars (billions)	Share of GDP (percent)
Gross domestic product (GDP)	7,825	4.8
Total transportation	378	4.8
Other transportation (rail, pipe, air, water, transit)	135	1.7
For-hire motor freight, warehousing	101	1.3
Own-account (in-house) trucking	142	1.8
Contribution of trucking industry	243	3.1
Total intermediate inputs (all industries)	6,176	
For-hire motor freight, warehousing	111	1.8
Own-account (in-house) trucking	58	0.9
Contribution of trucking industry	169	2.7
Total industry output	14,001	
For-hire motor freight, warehousing	212	1.5
Own-account (in-house) trucking	200	1.4
Contribution of trucking industry	412	2.9
Total commodity output	13,989	
For-hire motor freight, warehousing	200	1.4
In-house trucking	200	1.4
Contribution of trucking industry	400	2.9

Sources: Bureau of Transportation Statistics (1998); Fang and others (2000, table 2).

Note: Across all industries, total commodity output equals GDP plus intermediate inputs.

the basis of our later estimates of the impact of Internet-based trucking services on the economy. In that later section, we also attempt to approximate how the trucking industry's use of the Internet may affect the economy through the less-measurable, but critically important, intertwining of trucking services with disparate economic activities.

Several sets of figures help measure the contribution of trucking services to the economy. We start by considering the share of trucking in the gross domestic product (GDP) (table 5-2). According to figures that the U.S. Department of Transportation released on July 10, 2000, all modes of commercial transportation services contributed 4.8 percent of GDP ($378 billion) to the national economy in 1996, which is the most recent year for which reliable figures are available. Comparable figures for 1992 were 5.0 percent of GDP ($313 billion). These figures, which are based on the Transportation Satellite Accounts, include both the end-user expenditure on transportation services and the intermediate expenditure on transportation services that arise during production stages in other sectors. In a change from previous practice, the Department of Transportation figures include in-house provision of private commercial transportation services as well as for-hire segments of the transportation sector.[13] As our earlier figures show, private fleet trucking services are important elements of the transportation sector, so including in-house commercial transport is critical to measuring the full contribution of the industry to the economy.[14]

As the table shows, trucking represents a substantial majority of the transportation sector value added, accounting for about 3.1 percent of the U.S. GDP in 1996 ($243 billion, or about 65 percent of transportation services).[15] For-hire trucking and warehousing accounted for 1.3 percent of GDP ($101 billion), while in-house trucking added 1.8 percent of GDP ($142 billion) in 1996.

Another way to measure the impact of trucking is to consider its share of intermediate inputs in the economy and, in turn, its share of total industry output. Intermediate inputs are the goods and services that contribute to value added processes within industries. Total industry output is the sum of each industry's intermediate inputs to other industries, in addition to an industry's contribution to GDP. In 1996 trucking services accounted for 2.7 percent of total industry inputs, 2.9 percent of total industry output, and 2.9 percent of total commodity output across all industries.[16] Thus, on multiple measures, including both end-product output and

13. The magnitude of transportation services has long been underrepresented in U.S. economic data. Until recently, national measures of transportation services counted only the value of for-hire transportation, ignoring the contribution of in-house private transportation. The Transportation Satellite Accounts (TSA), developed jointly by the Bureau of Transportation Statistics of the Department of Transportation and the Bureau of Economic Analysis of the Department of Commerce, provide more comprehensive estimates. Including in-house transportation adds $142 billion to the 1996 estimates derived from traditional accounts that emphasized for-hire services. The TSA is statistically and conceptually consistent with the national accounts used to calculate gross domestic product (GDP). These accounts are based on the five-year Economic Census; 1992 and 1996 are the most recent years for which complete data are available.

14. For the purposes of this paper, we use the terms "in-house," "own-account," and "private" transportation interchangeably. We attribute all the value added by own-account transportation to in-house trucking (this attribution means that we include in-house bus, which contributes less than 1 percent of the value added of own-account transportation, within in-house trucking).

15. Bureau of Transportation Statistics (1998).

16. Across the full economy, industry inputs and commodity output are the same. At the industry level, however, industry inputs and commodity output may vary.

Table 5-3. *TSA Direct Requirements for Transportation Services per Dollar of Additional Output, by Industry, 1996*

| | Industry (output sector) | | | | | | |
| | | | | | Transportation | | |
Commodity (service sector)	Agriculture, forestry, fisheries	Mining	Construction	Manufacturing	Railroad and passenger ground	Motor freight and warehousing	Water
Railroad and passenger ground	0.006	0.006	0.002	0.005	0.043	0.002	0.000
Motor freight and warehousing	0.014	0.007	0.015	0.016	0.007	0.185	0.003
Water transportation	0.001	0.001	0.000	0.000	0.000	0.005	0.193
Air transportation	0.002	0.002	0.001	0.004	0.004	0.009	0.002
Pipelines and freight forwarders	0.000	0.000	0.000	0.001	0.008	0.031	0.047
Own-account transportation	0.052	0.021	0.056	0.006	0.000	0.000	0.000
Total value added	0.357	0.443	0.416	0.365	0.605	0.477	0.322
Total output (percent)	1.000	1.000	1.000	1.000	1.000	1.000	1.000
Total industry output (in billions)	290	173	868	3,666	69	212	35
Summaries							
Truck share (motor freight and own-account) (percent)	6.6	2.8	7.1	2.2	0.7		0.3
Truck share × total industry output (in billions)	19.2	4.8	61.5	79.3	0.5		0.1

inputs to intermediate production, trucking services account for a notable proportion of economic activity in the country.

It is also useful to consider how trucking services contribute to different sectors of the economy, in addition to their aggregate contributions to economic activity. Table 5-3 reports the demand for trucking services by different industries. On average (weighted by industry output), trucking ser-

				Industry (output sector)				
	Transportation							
Air	*Pipelines, freight forwarders*	*Public transit*	*Own-account trans-portation*	*Com-muni-cations, utilities*	*Whole-sale, retail trade*	*Finance, insurance, real estate*	*Services*	*Other*
0.001	0.001	0.021	0.001	0.009	0.001	0.001	0.001	0.001
0.002	0.006	0.011	0.006	0.002	0.003	0.003	0.004	0.002
0.000	0.001	0.002	0.001	0.001	0.000	0.000	0.000	0.002
0.061	0.006	0.001	0.000	0.003	0.004	0.002	0.004	0.002
0.085	0.023	0.004	0.001	0.002	0.000	0.000	0.001	0.000
0.000	0.000	0.000	0.000	0.002	0.038	0.001	0.018	0.001
0.501	0.557	−0.066	71.1	0.521	0.654	0.694	0.594	0.930
1.000	1.000	1.000	100.0	1.000	1.000	1.000	1.000	1.000
118	42	7	200	661	1,454	2,148	2,962	1,085
0.2	0.6	1.1		0.4	4.1	0.4	2.1	0.3
0.3	0.2	0.1		2.6	59.7	7.6	63.5	3.2

Source: Fang and others (2000, tables 1, 2, 3).

This table reports the contribution (direct requirement) of each commodity in producing a dollar of ouput from an industry, in provider prices. For example, "manufacturing" requires 1.6 cents of "motor freight" and 0.6 cents "own-account" transport to generate one dollar of output. Total industry output in 1996 was $13,989 billion; trucking's share was $302.6 billion. The weighted mean of trucking's share (omitting intratrucking) of total industry output was 2.2 percent.

vices contribute about 2.2 percent of the intermediate inputs to other industries. The agriculture, forestry and fisheries (1.4 cents per dollar of cost), construction (1.5 cents), and manufacturing (1.6 cents) industries are among the largest users of for-hire trucking. The agriculture, forestry and fisheries (5.2 cents), construction (5.6 cents), and wholesale and retail trade (3.8 cents) industries have the largest requirement for private trucking services. The central conclusion, illustrated in table 5-3, is that trucking services are important parts of the inputs that other industries require in order to produce their own goods.

Changes in end-product demand for other commodities also affect the demand for trucking services. This approach helps show how trucking services change as the economy changes. Table 5-4 shows how much additional services from intermediate industries will be required for each dollar increase in final demand for a commodity. Averaging across all industries (weighted by industry commodity output), a dollar increase in demand for commodities other than trucking leads to an increase of 4.6 cents for trucking services (about 2.0 cents for for-hire motor freight; 2.6 cents for own-service trucking). Overall, the table shows that trucking services are key parts of other commodities.

Several specific elements of table 5-4 stand out. Commodities for which for-hire trucking plays an integral role include communications and utilities (3.9 cents per dollar), manufacturing (3.7 cents), and agriculture, forestry, and fisheries (3.5 cents). Considering the commodities for which private fleet services are needed, agriculture, forestry, and fisheries (8.0 cents), construction (7.1 cents), and wholesale and retail trade (4.5 cents) commodities have the largest draw in terms of the service output that every dollar of final demand requires. Notably, changes in demand for other transportation modes (rail, water, pipeline, air) also create the need for additional trucking services, including both for-hire motor freight and own-account transport (incremental demand ranges from 1.0 cents for pipeline demand for own-account trucking to 2.1 cents for railroad demand for motor freight). In turn, changes in motor freight demand lead to needs for additional services from other transportation modes, especially pipelines (5.2 cents) and air transport (1.3 cents). Again, trucking services are important inputs throughout the economy. In addition, the role of trucking in cross-border transport has become critical as international trade has grown. In 1996 trucking had a dominant share of transportation for exports (74 percent to Canada, 85 percent to Mexico) and imports (63 percent from Canada, 77 percent from Mexico).

Thus, the trucking industry clearly plays a vital role throughout the U.S. economy. Not only do substantial contributions come from both for-hire and in-house trucking services, but the trucking industry also plays a critical support role for other transportation modes and for other sectors of the economy, particularly the resource, manufacturing, construction, and wholesale and retail trade industries.

Internet Usage in Trucking

An article in the July 31, 2000, issue of *Transport Topics* called 1999 the "Year of the Internet" for trucking, a claim confirmed by three independent sources that surveyed Internet usage in the trucking industry. First, a survey conducted in 1998 by the ATA Foundation and the National Private Truck Council found that 51 percent of TL carriers were using Internet technology in 1998, compared with 11 percent in 1996. Among the LTL carriers, 61 percent were using Internet technology in 1998, compared with 14 percent in 1996.[17] Second, a more recent mail survey, which we conducted for the University of Michigan Trucking Industry Program (UMTIP), and which covered late 1999 and early 2000, found that three-quarters of the 177 respondents were using the Internet (79 percent of the TL respondents, 72 percent of LTL respondents, 75 percent of the firms that participate in more than one segment, and 75 percent of the private fleets).[18] Third, in August 2000, we searched the web for public Internet sites at 132 for-hire trucking firms for which we had 1999 Form M data. Of these firms, 80 percent had public websites in August 2000 (75 percent of 97 TL firms; 95 percent of 24 LTL firms; and 82 percent of 11 firms that operated in multiple segments).

The key reason that the Internet is affecting the industry stems from the availability of more detailed information to customers and competitors about goods and services, prices, and timing. Firms are changing the way they gather, process, and disseminate information. The changes in information result in both potential for greater efficiency in traditional transportation activities and in the creation of demand for new types of transportation activities. The immediate consequences of increased dissemination of information include greater price pressure and greater incentives for efficiency. Moreover, increased information is also leading to more fine-grained market segmentation, as well as to demands for new goods and services by trucking companies. Following are vignettes showing how firms in the trucking industry are using the Internet to exploit existing opportunities and to explore new opportunities.

17. Daniel P. Bearth, "Industry Use of Internet Blossoms," *Transport Topics,* July 31, 2000, p. 18.

18. We conducted the survey during early 2000, with the sponsorship of the University of Michigan Trucking Industry Program (UMTIP). UMTIP receives generous support from the Sloan Foundation and from trucking industry corporations.

Table 5-4. *TSA Total Direct and Indirect Requirements for Transportation Services per Dollar of Additional Commodity Demand, by Industry, 1996*

| | Industry (output sector) | | | | | |
| | | | | | Transportation | |
Industry (service sector)	Agri- culture, forestry, fisheries	Mining	Con- struction	Manu- facturing	Railroad and passenger ground	Motor freight and ware- housing
Railroad and passenger ground	0.011	0.010	0.005	0.009	0.939	0.006
Motor freight and warehousing	0.035	0.019	0.033	0.037	0.021	1.222
Water transportation	0.003	0.001	0.001	0.001	0.001	0.008
Air transportation	0.007	0.006	0.006	0.009	0.007	0.013
Pipelines and freight forwarders	0.004	0.002	0.003	0.005	0.020	0.052
State and local pass- enger transit	0.001	0.001	0.001	0.001	0.096	0.000
Own-account transportation	0.080	0.034	0.071	0.025	0.014	0.009
Total industry output multiplier	2.340	2.050	2.189	2.353	1.928	1.996
Total commodity output (in billions)	288	162	868	3,593	75	200
Summaries						
Truck share (motor freight and own- account) (percent)	11.4	5.4	10.4	6.2	3.5	
Truck share × total commodity output (in billions)	32.9	8.7	90.2	222.3	2.6	

| | Industry (output sector) | | | | | | | | |
| | Transportation | | | | | | | | |
Water	Air	Pipelines, freight forwarders	Own-account transportation	Communications, utilities	Wholesale, retail trade	Finance, insurance, real estate	Services	Other
0.003	0.003	0.003	0.003	0.011	0.002	0.002	0.003	0.002
0.013	0.012	0.015	0.014	0.039	0.010	0.008	0.014	0.005
1.158	0.001	0.002	0.001	0.002	0.000	0.000	0.000	0.003
0.006	1.013	0.009	0.002	0.006	0.006	0.003	0.007	0.002
0.066	0.119	1.025	0.002	0.004	0.002	0.001	0.002	0.001
0.000	0.000	0.000	0.000	0.001	0.000	0.000	0.000	0.000
0.010	0.008	0.010	1.008	0.014	0.045	0.007	0.026	0.003
2.204	1.892	1.800	1.563	1.852	1.610	1.515	1.770	1.139
37	124	36	200	691	1,457	2,115	3,134	1,009
2.3	2.0	2.5		5.3	5.5	1.5	4.0	0.8
0.8	2.5	0.9		36.6	79.8	31.1	124.1	7.7

Source: Fang and others (2000, tables 1, 4).

Note: this table shows how much demand for each industry's output will increase for an increase of a dollar in demand for each of the commodities, in producer prices. For example, a dollar increase in demand for "manufacturing" commodities would generate 3.7 cents new demand for "motor freight" and 2.5 cents new demand for "own-account" transportation. Total commodity output in 1996 was $13,988 billion; trucking's share of total commodity was $640 billion. The weighted mean of trucking's share (omitting intratrucking) of total industry output was 4.6 percent.

Vignettes of Internet Use in the Trucking Industry

Because it increases customer demands for greater speed, reliability, efficiency, and innovative services, the Internet is causing substantial pressure on the capabilities of trucking companies. Firms are able to respond to some demands through incremental expansion of their existing expertise.[19] The example of ABFreight (ABF) illustrates such changes. Many changes, however, require major changes in business routines and resources.[20] Arnold Industries is an example of a firm that is exploring new opportunities by both building on its existing repertoire of skills and acquiring new skills. In some cases, the new skills are destroying firms' existing competencies.[21] Transplace.com and freightquote.com are examples of ways the new competitive environment threatens the existence of traditional freight brokers. We then discuss the tendency for customers of trucking services to demand one-stop trucking, leading firms in the industry to respond by restructuring, consolidation, mergers, and acquisitions. These examples show that the trucking industry structure is changing as firms respond to the new economy.

ABF FREIGHT SYSTEM. ABF is an example of a trucking firm that gradually exploited the web to improve its existing capabilities. Starting about 1994 ABF initially offered downloadable personal computer rating software, along with routing and zip code directories, and general marketing information to its customers. Since then ABF has added a rating guide, and the ability to track shipments, create bills of lading, and request pickups, all online. ABF also offers customer-specific pricing quotations over the Internet. In 1998 the company introduced an ABF Toolkit to help customers navigate through the site. Customers could also retrieve shipping documents, as well as review loss and damage claims online. In 1999 ABF introduced "Transparent Direct Links," which enables shippers to incorporate data from ABF's Internet site directly into their own site. In January 2000 ABF introduced the "Shipment Planner," which is a patented program that displays shipment reports on a calendar, and the "Dynamic Rerouting" module, which is a program that allows customers to reroute in-transit shipments. ABF has made the Internet a focal point of its growth strategy, expanding and exploiting existing capabilities to

19. Richardson (1972); Langlois and Robertson (1995).
20. Karim and Mitchell (2000).
21. Tushman and Anderson (1986).

improve both its interactions with customers and its internal processes.[22] The impact of the actions taken by ABF will be felt primarily by their business customers, particularly in the areas of "just-in-time" and "lean" manufacturing.

ARNOLD INDUSTRIES. Arnold Industries illustrates a trucking company that is exploring the new competitive environment and redefining the boundaries of the services it offers in the Internet-enabled economy. Long a profitable LTL company, Arnold Industries during the 1990s expanded into the regional TL segment by acquiring TL firms. The company is now combining its trucking and warehouse operations to offer one-stop order fulfillment services for e-tailers and mail order catalog companies. These services include order processing, inventory management, and small package shipping. In this process, the company has transformed its business to improve its ability to fill orders quickly and precisely. The firm has turned its warehouses into logistics hubs where more than six hundred people are involved in the order fulfillment process. The process involves receiving goods from manufacturers or suppliers, processing, packaging, and delivering to customers. Arnold Logistics, a subsidiary, also provides value added services by comparing freight rates and handling customer returns. Further, the company takes online orders on behalf of its shippers and also provides live-chat and e-mail support for customers.

The traditional LTL and TL segments of Arnold Industries have benefited from the new business activities, because shipments to the firm's logistics warehouses use TL and LTL services. In addition, and at least as important, the company has expanded substantially into new transportation services that emphasize information management rather than physical handling of goods. Thus, Arnold Industries has transformed the company's definition of the transportation business to extend far beyond movement of freight. The firm has leveraged its knowledge and expertise to become "an information transfer point" in the new economy.[23] During the winter 1999 shopping holiday season, when consumers spent $7.3 billion online, Internet retailers failed to fulfill 16 percent of orders and filled an additional 24 percent late.[24] Online retailing is projected to grow in the retail

22. Daniel P. Bearth, "ABF Website Wins Kudos," *Transport Topics,* July 31, 2000, p. 16.

23. Daniel P. Bearth, "Arnold Industries Hits Vein in Logistics," *Transport Topics,* January 24, 2000, pp. 10–12.

24. Gerry Gottlieb, "Fulfillment, It's What's Needed to Deliver the Goods" (www. netcommercemag.com/oct00/oct_if1.html [February 2001]).

landscape, but its long-term success will depend on the extent to which firms such as Arnold Industries enable timely fulfillment and provide customers value added services as representatives of online retailers.[25]

TRANSPLACE.COM. In the trucking industry, productivity gains, given legal restrictions on size and weight, come mainly from two sources: fewer empty miles and higher cubic space utilization; and less idle time—less waiting time at the dock, for example.[26] Because the trucking industry is so fragmented and geographically dispersed, load-matching and other logistics services that coordinate disparate fleets and drivers are critically important. Load-matching services provide information that matches available shipments with trucks that have available cargo space, thus increasing trailer utilization and decreasing waiting times. Load-matching information is valuable to small firms and owner-operators, as well as to large firms that are interested in increasing productivity by reducing empty backhauls.

Load matching traditionally has been the business of freight brokers (freight forwarders), which act as transportation intermediaries to manage the coordination of information and freight. New types of electronic brokers such as Transplace.com and freightquote.com are threatening the future of traditional information brokers, both from within the industry and through entry to the industry. Transplace.com is an example of how industry incumbents are combining asset rationalization and the management of information to gain efficiencies.

Transplace.com was created when six of the largest publicly held TL carriers formed an alliance in March 2000 to explore new web-based business opportunities. Representing unprecedented cooperation in the trucking industry, the venture will combine the firms' logistics services and negotiate discounts for fuel, equipment, maintenance and parts, insurance, credit, and other services for its equity partners and other carriers that choose to join the purchasing cooperative. The founding firms hope to leverage their bricks-and-mortar experience, physical assets, industry-specific information technology expertise, brand equity, and customer relations in the electronic marketplace.

FREIGHTQUOTE.COM. While Transplace.com leverages its traditional transportation asset base in the e-business environment, a new genre of

25. Giga Information group predicts that online retailing will capture $39 billion in 2002 and $49 billion in 2004 (www.gigaweb.com/Content/Adhoc/RAH-072000-00018.html [February 2001]).

26. Space utilization is particularly important for LTL shipments—especially for those LTL companies providing national service—but it also applies to TL carriers. The benefits from reducing empty miles arise in both segments.

Table 5-5. *Internet-Based Load Matching Exchanges*

Exchange name, web address	Representative fees[a]
EFlatbed (specialty) www.eflatbed.com	$24.95 a month
Efr8 (TL) www.efr8.com	$50 a month
Freightquote (LTL) www.freightquote.com	Commission-based; no enrollment fee
Getloaded (TL & LTL) www.getloaded.com	$35 a month
Internet Freight Terminal (TL) www.freight-terminal.com	$125 a year
Loaddock (TL) www.loaddock.com	$20 a month
Massmotion (LTL) www.massmotion.com	Basic fee $40 a month
National Transportation Exchange (TL & LTL) www.nte.net	No membership fee
Nettrans (TL) www.nettrans.com	$35 a month
Truckstop (TL & LTL) www.truckstop.com	$35 a month for regular service
Tranzlink (TL) www.tranzlink.com	$14.95 a month + 0.15% revenue when shipment is awarded

Source: Internet search by authors.
a. Prices as of January 23, 2001.

information brokers is emerging solely on the Internet. Freightquote.com is an example of an industry entrant that is using the Internet to integrate information and offer load-matching services. Table 5-5 lists some of the other load-matching exchanges spawned by the Internet. The geographic dispersion of the industry and the small size of most carriers contribute to the rise of these new Internet exchanges, which are challenging traditional freight brokers in managing the coordination of information and freight. At the annual convention of the Transportation Intermediaries Association in March 2000, the dominant topic of discussion was the two-pronged threat posed to incumbent brokers by the Internet and new load-matching software. First, in shipper-driven brokerage substitution, the Internet enables many shippers to post loads and solicit competitive bids directly from carriers, which use the Internet to identify backhauls. This process combines load-matching with competitive pricing. In the process, the shipper receives the advantage of a low bid and the carrier increases productivity by reducing empty miles. In this scenario, however, the traditional freight broker has no role. Instead, shippers function as their own brokers, dealing directly with freight companies.

Second, the Internet allows new intermediaries to aggregate loads and obtain volume discounts. Freightquote.com is an Internet-based "infomediary" that specializes in the trucking industry. Freightquote.com targets smaller shippers that do not have enough volume to negotiate discounts on their shipments. On its Internet site, shippers can identify prices and order deliveries. Membership is free for shippers, although membership information provides freightquote.com with valuable shipper and carrier data. Shippers pay a fee each time they use the service to ship a load of goods. Freightquote.com handles arrangements for pickup, paperwork, and online billing. This scenario provides a critical role for freight brokers in the changing industry, unlike the emergence of shipper-driven brokerage substitution, but it requires brokers to develop new information technology skills and management abilities.

According to some estimates, business-to business (B2B) transactions on the Internet should boost long-run gross domestic product (GDP) by almost 5 percent in the major industrialized countries.[27] As B2B exchanges increase their presence on the Internet landscape, however, their sustainability has been questioned. The primary concern about these exchanges is whether they can acquire and maintain liquidity. Because Transplace.com is owned by the six largest firms in the industry, the participation of these firms is ensured, and liquidity concerns are neutralized. In contrast, freightquote.com serves as a common interface for shippers while pooling the resources of member owner-operators and organizations. Although particular Internet exchanges may enter and exit, it seems clear that this new way of doing business will remain. Truckload firms operate in an environment of tight margins. Efficiencies offered by exchanges such as Transplace.com and freightquote.com in terms of load matching, reduction of empty backhauls, volume efficiencies in purchasing and negotiating, and other value added services should help improve profitability in the truckload sector.

27. Brookes and Wahhaj (2000).

INTEGRATED SERVICES: MERGERS AND ACQUISITIONS. In the e-commerce environment, customers tend to demand transportation as an integrated service, with no regard to segments or length of haul. Faced with stringent demands for shipment time and quality, shippers would like to deal with one company for most or all of their inbound and outbound shipping needs. The new customer mandate requires routines that the firms cannot create from their existing repertoires of routines.[28] As a result, acquisition activity is becoming increasingly common in the industry, as a complement to internal development, with acquisitions arising from the need to gain access to new resources and coordinate the use of heterogeneous resources.[29] Thus, through combinations of internal development and acquisitions, firms are attempting to exploit their existing skills while also exploring new business opportunities.[30]

Many incumbents in the trucking industry are restructuring to offer integrated transportation solutions by including logistics and other transportation options in their corporate portfolio of asset-based transportation management services.[31] These firms are now offering suites of "one call, one carrier" services including TL, LTL, logistics, package express, and intermodal services. Several trucking firms have developed portfolios of asset-based transportation management services through mergers and acquisitions. Examples include CNF Transportation, Caliber Systems, USFreightways, and CRST International. The operating units of CNF Transportation include a package express firm (Emery Worldwide), an LTL firm (Con-Way Transportation Services), and a logistics provider (Menlo Logistics). Similarly, the operating portfolio of Caliber Systems includes a package express firm (RPS), an LTL firm (Viking Freight), and a logistics provider (Caliber Logistics). Caliber, in turn, was acquired in late 1997 by Federal Express, as FedEx sought to become a more broadly integrated carrier. USFreightways has expanded its primary business of providing regional LTL by acquiring a domestic and international freight forwarder, a logistics firm, and a regional truckload carrier. Its recent acquisition of Transport Corp. of America made it one of the nation's largest truckload carriers. Similarly, CRST International has recently restructured itself into a single transportation services company by combining its six units into

28. Nelson and Winter (1982).
29. Capron, Mitchell, and Oxley (2000).
30. March (1991).
31. Nagarajan and others (2000).

one operating unit. In the past, each unit served customers separately in their niche markets. Through the restructuring, CRST International combines CRST for TL, Malone Freight lines and the Three 1 truck line for flatbed services, CRST Logistics for logistics services, and an express LTL service. According to company president John Smith, "It didn't take a genius to figure out it was better approaching this as one team of professionals totally focused on the customer and making transportation as easy as possible for our customers."[32]

Competitively, these companies have to contend with the challenges posed in each of the segments in which the firms participate. Many of the firms began restructuring and consolidating when logistics software became widely available and increasing cross-border shipments with Canada and Mexico caused shippers to demand multiple services from their trucking vendors.[33] As more firms present themselves as providing integrated transportation management services, the formidable task that lies ahead of them is to achieve the close coordination that is required to capture the benefits of being a single entity. Firms can sometimes use alliances for these purposes, such as the Transplace.com example above. In many cases, however, it is likely that the needs for coordination will involve sufficiently complicated interactions among the firms that alliances will provide only partial solutions.[34] Instead, we believe that there will be increased reliance on business acquisitions in order to undertake the substantial changes that Internet-based business will require.

Survey Data on Internet Usage in the Trucking Industry

To ascertain the extent to which Internet technology is being used in the trucking industry, we conducted a survey, mentioned earlier, gathering information on Internet usage in late 1999 and early 2000 from 177 respondents. We sought not only to identify how the firms were using Internet technology, but also to gain an understanding of how early Internet usage is affecting firm performance and profitability. The respondents represent a cross-section of the trucking industry—TL (40 percent of the respondents), LTL (71 percent), logistics services (20 percent), package express (9 percent), and private fleet (30 percent) operators. About 55 per-

32. Schulz (1997).
33. Nagarajan, Bander, and White (1999).
34. Nagarajan and Mitchell (1998); Capron, Mitchell, and Oxley (2000).

cent of the firms participate in two or more of these segments of the industry. The size distribution of respondents was also useful, with about 65 percent of the firms operating 100 or fewer trucks and 35 percent operating more than 100 trucks.

As noted earlier, 75 percent of the respondents report at least minimal Internet activity by early 2000. At the same time, however, the impact is at very early stages of both investment and customer activity. The firms on average devoted only about 12 percent of their investment in new technology to Internet-related projects. Internet sales activity is even lower; on average the firms with Internet activity procured only about 5 percent of their shipments by the Internet in 1999. Thus, although Internet applications are diffusing widely among trucking firms, they still account for only small portions of the firms' business activities.

Table 5-6 lists the most frequently used applications of the Internet. As we noted earlier, most firms use the Internet to exploit many aspects of their existing capabilities and improve customer relationships and internal processes. In addition, many firms go beyond skill exploitation and look for new ways to identify new markets and customers using the Internet as a springboard. Accordingly, we classify the features in one of three categories—"Exploration," "Exploitation of existing skills: Customer-related," and "Exploitation of existing skills: Process-related"—to understand how firms are using the Internet. The most common exploration features are attracting new customers (72 percent), followed by service customization (27 percent). The most commonly used *skill exploitation* features that firms use to improve the *customer experience* are marketing services (75 percent), followed by online shipment orders from existing customers (37 percent), online pricing and rating software (31 percent), and freight pickup request (29 percent). The most commonly used *skill exploitation* features for *internal process improvement* are office communications (61 percent), followed by recruiting drivers (39 percent) and recruiting personnel other than drivers (37 percent).

The Impact of the Internet on the Trucking Industry

This section presents data on the association between Internet use, change of business activities, and firm performance. The data suggest that the Internet is having a greater impact on business activities that enable growth than on cost reduction.

Table 5-6. *Internet Applications Available at U.S. Trucking Firms,*
1999–2000

Percent

Internet application	Firms with application (percent)
Exploration	
Attracting new customers	72
Service customization	27
Exploitation of existing skills: customer-related	
Marketing your company's services	75
Online shipment orders from existing customers	37
Online pricing and rating software	31
Freight pickup request	29
Dedicated customer service	26
Cargo claims status	16
Offering special discounts	10
Exploitation of existing skills: process-related	
Office communications	61
Recruiting drivers	39
Recruiting personnel other than drivers	37
Real time shipment tracking	30
Forms and permits	30
Online bill of lading and proof of delivery	28
Load viewing and availability	23
Recruiting owner-operators	18
Online bill payment	17
Real time routing	14
Real time trailer tracking	12
Posting real time driver schedules	10

Source: UMTIP survey of U.S. trucking firms. The table shows results from 130 respondents that reported at least one Internet application.

Impact on Business Functions

Trucking firms are using the Internet in a variety of ways. The Internet helps firms explore new opportunities by aggressive sales and marketing. By giving customers immediate access to routine information and documents, the Internet allows marketing personnel to offer exceptional service to existing customers and to explore venues for new markets and growth. As the physical conduits of e-commerce, trucking firms have access to customer-specific data. Trucking firms are combining new data management capabilities, network management capabilities, and existing warehouses and mobile assets to offer integrated transportation services within the supply chain. The Internet also allows firms to exploit existing skills by improving the quantity and quality of information available to customers in real time and in a customized manner.

As in other economic sectors, the Internet has also become instrumental in process improvement in the trucking industry. The incremental cost of transacting on the Internet is as much as fifteen times less expensive than paper transactions, and trucking firms are aggressively moving to the net, in some cases replacing existing systems and in many cases creating new electronic interfaces. For instance, traditional electronic data interchange (EDI) services such as load tendering, status reporting, and invoicing can cost tens of thousands of dollars to set up and run, while also requiring substantial ongoing effort to maintain interfirm system compatibility. These costs and difficulties prohibited small carriers from adopting EDI systems and thus hurt their capacity to work with large shippers that mandated EDI transactions. Now, some shippers are using systems that allow EDI transactions over an Extranet, which is a secured Internet location that reduces setup costs. Still in its nascent phase, web-based EDI systems require manual entry and have not yet been widely adopted, but the potential low cost and standardized accessibility of EDI over the Internet levels the playing field for carriers that had been excluded from many freight opportunities earlier. The freight-matching transparency of the Internet also enables smaller firms to obtain loads and conduct more business than they might have otherwise. Tables 5-7 and 5-8 present findings from the UMTIP survey, showing the use of the Internet for different business functions and describing how the Internet has helped firms change their business activities. Table 5-7 reports the use of the Internet for various business functions. We find that the Internet has been used the most to enhance company image (mean of 2.8, on a scale of 1 to 5, where 1 indicates no use). The wide reach of the Internet has facilitated the broadcast of information in an environment where all the constituents are geographically dispersed. The connectivity enabled by the Internet also has facilitated the exchange of information with shipper and consignees (2.7), and third parties (2.5). Thus, the Internet has contributed to multiple business functions needed for offering new services, dealing with existing customers, and operating internal processes.

Table 5-8 presents the findings on the ways that the Internet has changed the business activities of trucking firms since 1996. Firms were

Table 5-7. *Use of Internet for Business Functions, 1999–2000*

Business activity	Mean effect
Exploration	
Variety of services increase	2.3
Customization of services	2.3
Exploitation of existing skills: customer-related	
Company image enhancement	2.8
Exchange of information with shippers and consignees	2.7
Market share	2.0
Exploitation of existing skills: process-related	
Process improvement	2.6
Exchange of information with third parties	2.5
Exchange of information with other trucking firms	2.1
Service quality improvement	2.1
Security of transactions	1.7

Source: UMTIP survey of U.S. trucking firms. The table shows impact of Internet on business functions for 130 respondents. 1 = no use; 5 = significant use, thus a higher mean signifies more use.

asked about the extent to which changes in different business activities were attributable to their Internet activities. Possible responses were that none, some, or most of the change was attributable to the Internet or that the question was not applicable. We found that 72 percent of the respondents said that some or most of the change in acquisition of new customers was due to the Internet. Trucking firms also reported that the Internet has helped them improve relationships with their shippers (67 percent) and consignees (63 percent) as well as provide quicker service (57 percent). In improving processes, many firms said that the Internet helped facilitate internal process improvements (72 percent), improve relationships with third parties (64 percent), and enhance the management of change (64 percent). The key conclusion here is that the Internet has helped facilitate recent improvement on many dimensions, although the Internet is far from the sole source of improvements.

Impact on trucking firm performance

As table 5-7 shows, firms in the industry have adopted the Internet at different levels. The differential adoption by firms within the industry allows

Table 5-8. *Role of Internet in Changes of Business Activity at Firms since 1996*
Percent

Area where changed occurred	Firms reporting some change due to Internet
Exploration	
Acquisition of new customers	72
Addition of new services	51
Acquisition of new markets	45
Exploitation of existing skills: customer-related	
Improved shipper relationships	67
Improved consignee relationships	63
Enabled quicker service	57
Enabled customer analysis	51
Improved dedicated services	50
Increased dependability	48
Improved on-time delivery	46
Exploitation of existing skills: process-related	
Provided quality improvements in internal processes	72
Improved third-party relationships	64
Enhanced the management of change	64
Provided time improvements in internal processes	59

Source: UMTIP survey of U.S. trucking firms, 177 responses. The higher the percentage the more common the Internet role in the change.

us to investigate the association between firm-level Internet adoption and firm-level changes in performance, by determining whether firms that have undertaken greater Internet adoption tend to have greater or lesser performance than firms that have undertaken less Internet adoption.[35]

Table 5-9 presents data from the UMTIP survey, showing the correlation between indicators of firm performance and the number of Internet features the firms report using. We use the number of Internet features as a measure of the extent to which a firm uses the Internet. We find that

35. Internet adoption is currently in a disequilibrium state within the trucking industry. The disequilibrium, which involves many factors, makes identifying relationships between Internet adoption and performance highly preliminary. At the same time, the disequilibrium allows a comparison of adoption and performance across firms, in order to investigate the initial impact of the Internet on firms in the industry.

Table 5-9. *Correlation of Number of Internet Features in 1999/2000 with Change in Firm Performance since 1996*

Performance measure	Correlation
Total assets increase	0.21
Profit increase	0.15
Market share increase	0.13
Revenue increase	0.12
Miles operated increase	0.12
Number of shipments increase	0.12
Operating income increase	0.11
Tons of freight carried increase	0.10
Labor cost	0.04
Total costs including labor	0.02

Source: UMTIP survey of U.S. trucking firms, 177 responses. In this survey, 1 = a decrease in performance change, 2 = no change in performance, and 3 = an increase. The higher the correlation, the more Internet features.

greater Internet use correlates positively with growth on many dimensions, including assets, market share, revenue, miles operated, number of shipments, and tons of freight. Greater use of Internet features also correlates positively with reported increases in profits. The correlations suggest that Internet usage associates closely with growth and the level of profits of trucking firms. Notably, though, Internet usage does not correlate closely with costs, whether labor cost or total cost. The results suggest that Internet investments along with other related activities are helping firms grow but are not reducing service costs, at least not so far. At the same time, the growth appears to recover the expense of the Internet investment, so that relative costs do not increase, even if they do not decline.

Table 5-10 reports data from our complementary analysis of Form-M reports from the Bureau of Transportation Statistics and firms' public web sites. As we noted earlier, we undertook a web search for survey respondents for which we were able to obtain Form M financial data.[36] We identified whether each of these firms offered a public web site and what skill exploitation and exploration features were present on the site. The table presents the correlation between the number of features available on the sites and financial measures based on data available in the Form M reports

36. The Form M–web analysis is largely independent of the survey, as only 8 percent of the firms in the Form M analysis were respondents to the survey.

Table 5-10. *Descriptive Statistics for Financial Indicators
and Correlations with Number of Internet Features Used by Firms*

| | Correlation with number of Internet features[a] | | | |
Financial indicator	All features	Exploration	Customer-related	Process-related
Operating revenue, 1999[b]	0.59	0.51	0.30	0.59
Profitability: return on operating revenue (income/revenue), 1999[b]	0.27	0.31	0.18	0.22
Three-year growth, operating revenue (percent), 1996–1999[c]	0.10	0.11	0.07	0.07
Three-year growth, return on operating revenue (percent), 1996–1999[c]	0.02	0.03	−0.08	0.03

Sources: Financial figures from Form M data from the Bureau of Transportation Statistics; Internet features from Internet search by authors.

a. Exploration Internet features included specialty service descriptions and summaries of charges. Customer-related features included general marketing information, shipping information and general help, pickup requests, status reports, e-mail notice of shipment status and delivery, contract information, and freight bill review with e-mail reply. Process-related features included creation of bills of lading, ratings, downloading base rates, tracking, retrieving documents such as bills of lading and packing slips, filing and checking status of cargo claims, locating terminals and service centers, and viewing and printing carrier forms and documents.

b. 1999 figures: $N = 113$ firms (21 LTL, 80 TL, 12 combined).

c. 1996–1999 figures: $N = 97$ (18 LTL, 70 TL, 9 combined).

for 1999 and 1996, including operating revenue and operating income. The table presents the data pooled from the firms for which we were able to obtain data on multiple measures.[37]

Several correlations in table 5-10 are notable. First, there is a strong correlation between firm revenue in 1999 and web activity in all three categories of skill utilization, suggesting that larger firms are undertaking more extensive web-based services. Second, there is a substantial correlation between 1999 profitability and web utilization. The causality of the profitability relationship likely stems both from the contribution of web activities to profitability and from the ability of more profitable firms to invest in web activity. Third, there is a modest positive relationship between web utilization and revenue growth from 1996 to 1999, with the strongest

37. The reported analysis pools the TL and LTL firms, because there were no material differences in the segment-specific correlation.

growth relationship arising from use of the web for exploration opportunities. Fourth, there is little relationship between web utilization and growth in profitability between 1996 and 1999. Indeed, the strongest of the weak relationships lies with lower profitability (that is, higher expenses) and greater utilization of customer-related web features.

Implications

Several implications arise from this quantitative investigation, coupled with the descriptive information from earlier sections. At this point of Internet service development, web usage is supporting growth more than improving efficiency. Web usage is facilitating growth of individual trucking firms—and the industry as a whole—by allowing firms to offer more services to their existing customers and to offer services to new customers. For instance, several firms offer online package tracking applications to inform customers of package status, which has helped firms keep old customers and attract new ones. So far, though, the evidence suggests that trucking firm costs have not declined as a result of the Internet, as operating margins have not improved at firms that use the Internet extensively.[38]

The contrast between the initial effects on growth and efficiency raises the issue of future growth and expense trends. Clearly, Internet usage will continue to support ongoing growth of trucking services. A key question, though, is whether greater efficiency benefits should be expected to emerge in the future. Certainly, there are potential efficiency gains from minimizing waiting times, maximizing trailer utilization, avoiding traffic congestion and bad weather, substituting EDI for paper-based transactions, managing intermodal relationships, and improving other business processes. Although the data suggest that such benefits have not yet emerged on any large scale, it may simply be too early for the benefits to have reached critical mass. It is likely that some such efficiencies will emerge.

It seems quite possible, though, that many costs of providing trucking services will not decline substantially in the future. The industry has

---

38. An alternative argument would be that costs of traditional trucking services have in fact declined, but that customers have demanded consequent rate reductions, so that operating ratios remain constant even though the firms are more efficient. To date, however, there is little evidence of such rent-seeking behavior by shippers and consignees. The null relationship between cost and Internet adoption shown in table 5-9 reinforces the conclusion that trucking firms' customers have not simply stripped away efficiency benefits of the Internet.

reached a high level of efficiency in the twenty years of deregulated competition. Although the Internet certainly will yield some future efficiency benefits, there also will be ongoing investment costs in Internet technology and quite possibly somewhat higher unit costs for the fine-grained services that the Internet supports. In addition, employment costs may well rise, given the need of increased skills in the work force. Web-based EDI, meanwhile, may tend to supplement traditional systems rather than replace them. So far, the evidence from the UMTIP survey and the Form-M data suggests that the benefits and costs appear to be in balance, continuing traditional operating efficiencies. Although the trends could change in the future, much of the future growth in demand for trucking services appears likely to be in the realm of services that would be too costly or impossible to provide at present. As a result, the benefits of the Internet may arise primarily in creating more shipments and, especially, new types of services, rather than in making traditional services more efficient. In parallel, the Internet may allow smaller firms to use more sophisticated routing, dispatching, and other processes than they now undertake, again resulting in greater service but not in lower cost than present operations.

This conclusion is consistent with firms' experience with information technology investment during the past half-century, in which information technology (IT) often enabled change more than it made current activities more efficient.[39] In the banking industry, for instance, electronic services such as ATMs (automated teller machines) and online banking provide greater benefits to customers, but also represent higher costs for the banks. Thus, the benefits of IT often arise through allowing people and firms to do things that they could not do otherwise, rather than being more efficient in their traditional activities.

One possible venue for increased efficiency might occur with the rise of specialist trucking firms that provide "traditional" trucking services using Internet technology to gain operating efficiencies. For instance, web-based specialist TL firms that minimize waiting times and maximize trailer utilization might well be more efficient than current providers of similar services. Such specialization, however, conflicts with the trend for the major carriers to become asset-based transportation management service providers in response to their customers' demands for integrated services. These integrated services will often be more costly than existing services.

39. See, for instance, Wilson (1995) and Powell and Dent-Micallef (1997).

Thus, the efficiencies are unlikely to show up in aggregate firm data, because the integrated firms provide a mix of more efficient traditional services and more costly new services.

Rather than primarily realizing greater trucking firm efficiency, then, Internet usage may be more likely to fuel greater end-user productivity. Major benefits of end-user productivity will arise as business customers of trucking have better information on where their shipments are, are able to plan better, can manage their inventories better, and gain other operating advantages. That is, the trucking industry is producing a better product and the benefits will show up in the increased efficiency and effectiveness of their business customers, more than in lower costs of trucking services. Initial analyses suggest that business-to-business Internet usage might provide end-users with cost savings of 15 percent to 20 percent on their freight transport costs.[40] Such benefits will lead to improved productivity for some shippers and consignees, so the productivity improvements of web-enabled trucking services will spill over into the general economy.

Even in the case of end-user productivity, however, it is not clear that most business customers will enjoy lower costs for current practices as the result of improved trucking services. Instead, many of the gains to business customers may well show up in providing more-refined services to their own end-customers, say, for instance, in providing customized production and delivery of various products, rather than in cheaper provision of existing services. Thus, many of the economywide productivity benefits will show up not as lower costs for traditional services, but as the ability to provide new services, such as faster production, more agile "mass customized" production, quicker and more frequent deliveries, and effective delivery systems for new Internet-based business-to-business and business-to-consumer sales.[41] In turn, these new services will tend to fuel economic growth through the spillover demands that they create.

In addition, it is possible that some of the efficiency benefits of Internet-facilitated trucking services may arise from business and retail customers ordering existing goods directly from producers and bypassing intermediaries. Pure disintermediation is unlikely to be common, however, because many customers will lack the necessary skill and scale to manage such pur-

40. Brookes and Wahhaj (2000).

41. The same study that found that freight costs decline for users of business-to-business websites also concluded that "the long term impact of B2B will be higher volumes not lower prices" (Brookes and Wahhaj, 2000).

chases. Instead, new intermediaries to manage the order-production-delivery-service interface are likely to rise, either as operating units within producers or as distinct firms. Major e-tailers, for instance, are building warehouses to supplement (or replace) their "inventoryless" business models, using the availability of web-based just-in-time delivery services from trucking firms to facilitate their inventory activities. Another example is emerging with Internet-based auto orders and deliveries, where changes in existing dealer networks are beginning to occur as the use of the Internet to order vehicles increases. Rather than eliminate the concept of auto dealers, though, this evolution is much more likely to lead to the development of new or transformed dealers that can stock example vehicles, facilitate option choices, help arrange financing, organize delivery, and provide after-sales services. The availability of web-based trucking services clearly would play a vital role in such activities. The overall cost of dealer service, however, is unlikely to decline much, if at all. Instead, consumers will benefit by getting better service than they do currently. Thus, gains that stem from utilizing Internet-facilitated trucking services will tend to show up as service improvement for customers.

The Impact of the Internet-Driven Trucking Industry on the U.S. Economy

By necessity, any assessment of how these various uses of the Internet by trucking firms might affect economic growth in the United States is highly speculative. But several realistic scenarios suggest that there will be substantial impact. We first consider how changes within the industry may contribute to the economy through 2005. We then attempt to estimate how the changes within the industry might facilitate or inhibit growth throughout the larger economy through the benefits or difficulties that users derive from the trucking industry's Internet adoption.

Contribution of Changes within the Trucking Industry

First, we consider scenarios of GDP and trucking industry growth. The scenarios require assumptions for GDP growth, trucking share of GDP in 1999, and trucking services growth. At the time this chapter was written, the most recent estimate of GDP for 1999 was $9.3 trillion, while the most recent estimate of GDP growth (second quarter of 2000) was 5.2 percent.[42] An optimistic forecast might project a growth rate for GDP of 5 percent over the next three years. A modest forecast might project a 3 percent rate, while a pessimistic forecast might project a 1 percent rate.

The trucking industry's contribution to GDP, including both for-hire firms and private fleets, was about 3.3 percent in 1992 and 3.1 percent in 1996 (see table 5-2). We assume that the share in 1999 was 3.2 percent, which is a conservative assumption given the economic growth and growing demand for trucking services during the late 1990s. To project post-1999 growth in trucking services, we start by looking at trucking value added between 1992 and 1996, which was about 5 percent a year, about the same as GDP growth during the period. The 5 percent trucking growth figure provides a baseline forecast, arising as it does from a period of preliminary Internet usage in the industry.

Our studies suggest that growing Internet usage in the industry is likely to lead to increased trucking growth, at rates at least in keeping with GDP growth. Our analysis of Internet use by trucking firms suggests that, initially at least, web-based trucking services have led to revenue increases with relatively little change in relative costs, that is, to increased shipments with operating margins that are similar to traditional levels. Thus, the impact of the Internet on the trucking industry arises primarily through increased revenue, rather than through greater efficiency.

We note that the firm-level revenue effects include both exploration opportunities by attracting new customers and skill exploitation opportunities by providing more services to existing customers. While some of these additional revenues will simply shift shipments within the industry, from trucking companies that lag in providing Internet services to more innovative firms, additional revenues will come from increased overall usage of trucking services. Examples of such increased usage include existing end-users adopting more frequent shipments for just-in-time production and distribution, and new end-users using commercial shipping for retail deliveries of web-based distribution and retail sales. Therefore, our financial forecasts assume that growth in the trucking industry keeps pace with overall economic growth, but allow for the possibility that incremental cost savings may emerge during the next five years. We consider three scenarios, based on 5 percent, 3 percent, and 1 percent GDP growth. Table 5-11 summa-

---

42. BEA (2000).

Table 5-11. *Estimates of the Effect on the U.S. Economy of Internet Usage within the Trucking Industry*
Trillions of dollars unless otherwise noted

Year	Optimistic scenario			Modest scenario			Pessimistic scenario		
	GDP	Truck	Trucking as a percent of GDP	GDP	Truck	Trucking as a percent of GDP	GDP	Truck	Trucking as a percent of GDP
1992	5.3	0.20	3.2	6.3	0.20	3.2	6.3	0.20	3.2
1996	7.8	0.24	3.1	7.8	0.24	3.1	7.8	0.24	3.1
1999	9.3	0.30	3.2	9.3	0.30	3.2	9.3	0.30	3.2
2000	9.8	0.31	3.2	9.8	0.31	3.2	9.8	0.31	3.2
2001	10.3	0.33	3.2	10.3	0.33	3.2	10.3	0.33	3.2
2002	10.8	0.34	3.2	10.2	0.33	3.2	9.6	0.31	3.2
2003	11.3	0.36	3.2	10.5	0.33	3.2	9.7	0.31	3.2
2004	11.9	0.38	3.2	10.8	0.34	3.2	9.8	0.31	3.2
2005	12.5	0.40	3.2	11.1	0.36	3.2	9.9	0.32	3.2

Efficiency-based
contribution in 2005 (billions)

1 percent improvement in operating ratio[a]		4.0			3.6			3.2	
2 percent improvement in operating ratio[a]		8.0			7.1			6.3	

Source: GDP growth and trucking growth after 1999 are authors' simulations based on alternative growth scenarios. The optimistic scenario assumes annual GDP and trucking growth of 5 percent, the modest scenario assumes annual GDP and trucking growth of 3 percent, and the pessimistic scenario assumes annual GDP and trucking growth of 1 percent.

a. Assumes improvement of current operating ratios (costs/revenue) from 94.5 percent to 93.5 percent (1 percent gain) or 92.5 percent (2 percent gain).

rizes the output of these assumptions concerning GDP growth, trucking growth, and cost reductions.

We then estimate the impact of a five-year efficiency-based improvement in operating ratios (costs/revenues) from the current level of 94.5 percent to 93.5 percent or 92.5 percent by 2005.[43] Using the growth

43. This conservative estimate of a 1–2 percent improvement in operating ratios is appropriate given the current high level of efficiency in the industry and the incremental benefits that appear to arise from Internet adoption. The efficiency improvement could show up either as an increase in trucking firm profitability or as a reduction in prices to customers.

forecasts as a base, a 1 percent improvement in operating ratios by 2005 would save an additional $3.2 billion to $4.0 billion a year.[44] Similarly, a 2 percent improvement in operating ratios would save an additional $6.3 billion to $8.0 billion. These estimates of efficiency-based contributions from Internet-driven activities within the trucking industry are moderate but real contributions to economic productivity.

Estimates of Internet-Driven Contributions That Affect the Larger Economy

We now turn to considering how changes in trucking might affect the larger economy through the interconnected relationship of trucking with other industries. These contributions arise from the improvements that customers might derive from Internet-enabled trucking services or, conversely, the problems that might arise if Internet adoption by trucking firms is flawed and interferes with customers' business activities. Again, we note that these estimates are highly speculative but stem from reasonable estimates of the role of trucking services within the economy.

The starting point here is that trucking services intertwine with many sectors of the economy and that the availability of sophisticated web-based trucking services, offering fine-grained, faster, integrated services, is critical to continued growth of many sectors of the economy. That is, other industries require new types of trucking services to continue their own expansion. In the manufacturing and construction sectors, for instance, the availability of reliable just-in-time delivery services is essential to modern production systems. The ongoing redefinition of wholesale and retail trade that is occurring with the growth of business-to-business and business-to-consumer Internet commerce, moreover, depends critically on growing sophistication of transportation services, particularly on trucking services. These changes will require refinements in existing package express, LTL, and TL services. In addition, as we discussed earlier, Internet trade will require greater integration among the different types of trucking services, as well as the provision of complementary services such as logistics, warehousing, and customer service. Quite simply, effective adoption of Internet technology by trucking companies will be required for other sectors of the

44. This figure for improvement in operating ratios provides a benchmark to show the impact of each 1 percent efficiency gain, that is, a saving of about $4 billion annually for each 1 percent reduction in costs.

Table 5-12. *Estimates of Effects on the U.S. Economy from Trucking Industry Internet Usage That Affects Other Industries*
Trillions of dollars

	High-growth baseline economy			Modest-growth baseline economy		
Year	*Effective Internet use 5.1% GDP*	*Baseline 5% GDP*	*Flawed Internet use 4.9% GDP*	*Effective Internet use 3.05% GDP*	*Baseline 3% GDP*	*Flawed Internet use 2.95% GDP*
1999	9.3	9.3	9.3	9.3	9.3	9.3
2000	9.8	9.8	9.8	9.6	9.6	9.6
2001	10.3	10.3	10.2	9.9	9.9	9.9
2002	10.8	10.8	10.7	10.2	10.2	10.1
2003	11.3	11.3	11.3	10.5	10.5	10.4
2004	11.9	11.9	11.8	10.8	10.8	10.8
2005	12.53	12.46	12.39	11.14	11.10	11.07

Source: Author's simulations based on alternative assumptions. Under the high-growth baseline economy scenario, the contribution in 2005 to the U.S. economy from Internet usage in the trucking industry that affects other industries will be $71 billion more or less depending on whether the trucking industry's use of the Internet is effective or flawed, or 0.6 percent of GDP. Under the modest-growth baseline scenario, the difference is an estimated $32 trillion in 2005, or 0.3 percent of GDP.

economy to even approach the potential of their own Internet-based growth. Thus, adoption of web-based technology by trucking companies almost certainly will have an impact well beyond the contribution to GDP that arises from internal changes in the trucking industry. In addition to the internal contributions, trucking industry Internet usage will have multiplier effects on growth throughout the economy.

Attempting to quantify the multiplier effects is highly tentative. On the positive side, suppose that highly effective adoption of Internet technology by trucking firms might facilitate as much as 0.1 percent of additional GDP growth, that is, a multiplier of 1.02 times the optimistic baseline projection of 5 percent a year (the high-growth baseline scenario in table 5-12).[45] In that situation effective Internet usage by trucking firms would contribute as much as an additional $71 billion to the economy by 2005 (0.6 percent of GDP) through its multiplier effect on the industries that require trucking industry services.

45. The 1.02 multiplier is a conservative figure, based on the estimate that an additional dollar of end-product demand requires about 4.6 cents of trucking services (see table 5-4).

Conversely, suppose that flawed adoption of Internet technology by trucking firms inhibits potential growth in other sectors, by as much as 0.1 percent below the current high-growth baseline projection. Flawed adoption would arise from the failure for some reason of shippers and consignees to develop new business opportunities that require shipment innovation and, therefore, the economy would not be able to reach the Internet growth potential. One example might be the failure to develop effective web-based interfaces between trucking firms' IT systems and their customers' evolving web-based IT innovations. A second example would be problems in development of internal IT systems within the trucking firms that lead to delayed and inaccurate deliveries. In such a scenario, ineffective trucking industry Internet usage would depress the economy by as much as $71 billion by 2005. We pose this scenario not to forecast specific numbers, but rather to demonstrate that even a relatively small interference with innovation by shippers and consignees could translate into substantial negative impact, just as even a small facilitation translates into substantial benefits.

In the modest-growth scenario in table 5-12, we show the results for a 0.05 percent additional increase or decrease in GDP growth due to effective or flawed trucking industry adoption of Internet technology in a modest-growth economy. The modest-growth scenario results in contributions or losses of about $32 million.

Policy Implications

This discussion suggests several financial influences of Internet-based trucking services and consequent gains (or losses) of economic productivity. The financial influences include cost reductions in the trucking industry (about $3 billion to $8 billion in our conservative estimates) and possible contributions to other sectors of the economy that will show up as increased revenue and decreased costs in other industries (as much as $71 billion or, conversely, an equivalent negative impact if Internet adoption were highly flawed).[46] The main productivity gains for the economy

46. The potential impact of $71 billion in the growth scenario includes both efficiency savings and increased revenue. One calculation of the efficiency portion is to take the current share of trucking services in other sectors of the economy (4.6 percent, in table 5-4), multiply by the efficiency gain in the industry (mean = 1.5 percent, in table 5-11) on the assumption that the gains will be passed on as lower prices, and then multiply the 2005 GDP ($12.5 trillion in the optimistic growth scenario of table 5-11)

arise from the efficiency savings in the industry and the multiplier or decelerator on other sectors.

Two points are key here. First, the potential multiplier effect of the trucking industry, which affects cost and revenue in other sectors of the economy, outweighs the measured changes of reduced cost within the industry. Second, the impact of the industry on the rest of the economy can either raise or depress the overall economy as a result of how successfully trucking firms develop and adopt web-based services. Thus, adoption of Internet services has implications that range far beyond the profitability and survival of individual trucking companies.

Fortunately, our study provides evidence that trucking firms are already beginning to use the Internet very effectively. Nonetheless, continued improvements in Internet adoption are necessary if the U.S. economy is to reach its positive potential. In greatest part, these continued improvements depend on continuation of the managerial initiatives within individual trucking companies and private fleets. The effectiveness of trucking industry Internet usage could be increased with sensitive attention to public policies concerning mergers, labor, and Internet technical support.

U.S. antitrust policy and enforcement has long viewed mergers between firms in the same industry with suspicion. Traditionally, the primary concern was that mergers would lead to greater market power and consequent ability to raise prices. More recently, antitrust policy has added concerns about mergers inhibiting innovation. We believe that such suspicions would be misplaced in the trucking industry.

Many mergers have already taken place within the industry. Rather than leading to increased prices or reduced innovation, however, these mergers are necessary for firms to offer business innovations needed in the broader economy. Most critically, the mergers help firms create integrated transportation services that include TL, LTL, package express, logistics support, and other complements. The role of web-based services is critically important here, as integration of previously disparate trucking businesses facilitates firms' ability to develop and adopt sophisticated Internet features. Without the mergers, independent firms would need to attempt to coordinate both the provision of integrated trucking services and the development of Internet features for those integrated services. Quite simply, such

---

by this factor. This efficiency gain of $8.6 billion (0.046 × 0.015 × $12.5 trillion) would show up as productivity gains outside the trucking industry.

arm's-length coordination would be suboptimal or impossible in many cases, because of the complicated evolution that the development paths must follow. The key implication here is that antitrust merger policy must develop the sophistication to recognize most trucking industry mergers as opportunities to improve and innovate, rather than to inhibit competition and reduce technical advance.

A second policy concern is the availability of labor. Drivers and other personnel in the trucking industry must have the training and skills to operate the new electronic technologies. The booming economy has seen unemployment at among the lowest levels in decades. Trucking firms will need to address the pressing need for skilled labor in order to play their substantial role in the new economy. Increased emphasis on information technology skills in educational institutions clearly would benefit the industry.

Several regulatory initiatives that influence the availability of labor need thoughtful attention. A topic of great debate at the moment is the "hours of service" regulations that the trucking industry must follow. There is much opposition within the industry to the newly proposed rules since these rules could increase the difficulty of managing operations in an industry that already has very little room for error. The tension between the number of hours a driver can safely drive and the need for a firm to do more with less is exacerbated in the new competitive environment. As more physical goods are demanded in the electronically efficient environment, trucking firms are scrambling to move the freight in the most efficient way possible. Greater efficiency might somewhat ease the labor shortage—by reducing the time a driver spends waiting for the truck to be loaded at dockside, for example. Operational options to increase efficiencies that the industry and regulatory authorities are considering include increasing the number of axles and allowing longer trailers. The implications of these moves on the safety of drivers and the public, together with the impact on the highway infrastructure, need to be considered carefully.

The third public policy implication concerns technical support of Internet technology development. Our study found that most Internet usage by trucking companies derives from internal development.[47] We believe that the privately led internal development will continue to lead to growing sophistication and effectiveness of Internet systems. At the same

47. Nagarajan and others (2000).

time, there will continue to be opportunities for public support of technical development in this industry.

Conclusion

The Internet is posing the greatest challenge to the trucking industry since deregulation was enacted in 1980, and trucking firms are moving aggressively to respond. Many firms have adapted to the new demands of their customers by making major changes in business practices, involving both exploitation of existing skills and exploration of opportunities that require new capabilities. Trucking firms are using Internet-based technology to expand existing resources, adopt new technologies to enable Internet-based communication with their customers, and develop processes to improve service and efficiency. The freer flow of information, the connectivity, and the opportunity to aggregate dispersed information have spawned new web-enabled businesses and these new entrants are challenging many tra ditional assumptions and business practices. At the same time, trucking industry incumbents are using alliances and acquisitions to redefine themselves as asset-based transportation management companies. The actions of the trucking firms will affect far more than the performance of the trucking services industry alone. In addition, the response of trucking firms to Internet-based opportunities and challenges will have major influences on the economy as a whole.

The prediction that tomorrow will be much like today is based on forecasting in an environment of incremental change. Many of the predictions about the impact of the Internet are based on present trends. The Internet has created enormous turbulence, however, and is the harbinger of discontinuous change in the economy. We have attempted to estimate the impact of the Internet on the trucking industry and consequently on the economy using recent trend data. Given the dramatic and integral role of the Internet in the redefined economy, the past and the present may be pale imitations of what the future holds. No matter what the new rules of competition are, however, the future of e-commerce depends on how physical goods are transported within the constraints of time, cost, and quality. As a result, the response of trucking firms will play a significant role in determining the extent to which the full potential of e-commerce will be fulfilled in the economy.

References

American Trucking Association. 1999. *American Trucking Trends,* 1999 ed. Alexandria, Va.: Transport Topics Press.

———. 2000. *American Trucking Trends 2000.* Alexandria, Va.: Transport Topics Press.

Brookes, Martin, and Zaki Wahhaj. 2000. "The Shocking Economic Effect of B2B." Global Economics Paper 37. Goldman Sachs, New York (www.gs.com [February 3]).

Bureau of Economic Analysis. Department of Commerce. 2000. "BEA 00-22 National Income and Product Accounts." August 7.

Bureau of Transportation Statistics. U.S. Department of Transportation. 1998. "TransStats: The Economic Importance of Transportation Services: Highlight of the Transportation Satellite Accounts." BTS/98-TS/4R. April.

Capron, L., Will Mitchell, and J. Oxley. 2000. "Recreating the Company: Four Contexts for Change." In *Financial Times: Mastering Strategy: The Complete MBA Companion in Strategy,* pp. 384–90. London: Pearson Education Limited.

Fang, Bingsong, and others. 2000. "U.S. Transportation Satellite Accounts for 1996." *Survey of Current Business,* May, pp. 14–22.

Karim, Samina, and Will Mitchell. 2000. "Reconfiguring Business Resources following Acquisitions in the U.S. Medical Sector, 1978–1995." *Strategic Management Journal* (special issue on the "Evolution of Business Capabilities") 21 (10–11): 1061–81.

Langlois, R. N., and P. L. Robertson. 1995. *Firms, Markets, and Economic Change: A Dynamic Theory of Business Institutions.* London: Routledge.

March, J. G. 1991. "Exploration and Exploitation in Organizational Learning." *Organization Science* 2: 71–87.

Nagarajan, Anuradha, and others. 2001. "E-Commerce and the Changing Terms of Competition in the Trucking Industry: A Study of Firm Level Responses to Changing Industry Structure." In *Tracking a Transformation: E-Commerce and the Terms of Competition in Industries,* edited by BRIE-IGCC E-conomy Project Task Force on the Internet. Brookings.

Nagarajan, Anuradha, J. L. Bander, and C. C. White, III. 1999. "Trucking." In *U.S. Industry in 2000: Studies in Competitive Performance,* edited by David Mowery, pp. 123–53. Washington, D.C.: National Academy Press.

Nagarajan, Anuradha, and Will Mitchell. 1998. "Evolutionary Diffusion: Internal and External Methods Used to Acquire Encompassing, Complementary, and Incremental Technological Changes in the Lithotripsy Industry." *Strategic Management Journal* 19: 1063–79.

Nelson, R. R., and S. G. Winter. 1982. *An Evolutionary Theory of Economics Change.* Harvard University Press.

Newport Communications. 1999. *The Structure of the U.S. Trucking Industry* (www.heavytruck.com/newport/facts/structure).

Powell, T. C., and A. Dent-Micallef. 1997. "Information Technology as Competitive Advantage: The Role of Human, Business, and Technology Resources." *Strategic Management Journal* 18(5): 375–405.

Rayport, J. F., and J. J. Sviokla. 1995. "Exploiting the Virtual Value Chain." *Harvard Business Review* 73: 75–85.

Richardson, G. 1972. "The Organization of Industry." *Economic Journal* 82: 883–96.

Sampler, J. L. 1998. "Redefining Industry Structure for the Information Age." *Strategic Management Journal* 19: 343–55.

Schulz, John D. 1997. "A Transportation Solution." *Traffic World* 252 (7): 54.

Standard & Poor. 1999. *U.S. Freight Transportation Forecast . . . to 2007.* DRI Fourth Annual Report, American Trucking Associations, Alexandria, Va.

Tushman, M. L., and P. Anderson. 1986. "Technological Discontinuities and Organizational Environments." *Administrative Science Quarterly* 31: 439–65.

U.S. Bureau of the Census. 1997. "Commodity Flow Survey." Washington, D.C. (www.census.gov/econ/www/cfsmain.html [February 2001]).

Wilson, D. 1995. "IT Investment and Its Productivity Effects: An Organizational Sociologist's Perspective on Directions for Future Research." *Economics of Innovation and New Technology* 3: 235–51.

6

JOSEPH P. BAILEY

Retail Services: Continuing the Internet Success

THE INTERNET MAY change the future of retailing, but so far it has accounted for less than 1 percent of total retailing revenue. Even if Internet retailing undergoes tremendous growth in the future, Internet retailing revenues may never exceed more than 10 percent of total retailing revenue. The Internet may change the retail sector in significant ways, but those changes may not be measurable by examining revenues and profits of "pure-play" Internet retailers. Rather the Internet may force most retailers to have an Internet presence that, in essence, will blur the lines between pure-play Internet retailers and traditional retailers. As more Internet retailers adopt a physical presence and traditional firms adopt an Internet presence, they become hybrid retailers with two channels to their customers.

The Internet has successfully moved from a "fringe technology" to the mainstream popular culture. In such a period of excitement about a new technology, however, one must be careful not to forecast continued exponential growth indefinitely. At some point, the 100+ percent growth rates in revenue by electronic commerce (e-commerce) retailers *must* abate. A

I greatly appreciate my interactions with Erik Brynjolfsson, Samer Faraj, Elliot Rabinovich, Mike Smith, Oliver Yao, and participants of the E-Business Transformation conference in shaping this paper.

more difficult question is determining when the exponential growth has run its course.

The factors that determine how and why e-commerce slows down might be easy to discern if this exercise were taking place after the fact. This paper, however, tries to assess the best practices of Internet retailers in order to determine why they are currently experiencing exponential growth even while it is happening. The paper then tries to project the potential scale of such best practices to determine when growth will ultimately slow down and reach a relative steady state.

By the end of 2000, there was some indication that Internet retailers were not enjoying the outrageous revenue growth they once had. Market forces and the dwindling supply of capital have led some Internet retailers to shift from a "grow at any cost" mentality to a stance more driven by the quest for profits. This shifts the advantage from companies that are still relatively new to the retail sector to the more traditional retailers who have much better revenue (and profit) prospects.

This paper tries to maintain a perspective of the retail industry as a whole, although it explores some firm specific strategies or performance measures in order to extrapolate to an overall characterization of the retail sector of the U.S. economy. The effect of the Internet may be large in changing Amazon.com's strategy, but it may have little or no effect on the overall statistics for the entire retail sector.

This paper explores the state of the retail sector of the U.S. economy with respect to the use and adoption of the Internet. After describing the retail sector in the U.S. economy, the paper then discusses how the Internet may affect the retail market by identifying different sources of efficiency. Next, the paper examines fourteen firms that participate in varying forms of electronic commerce. It illustrates some of the best Internet practices of these firms by characterizing their business strategies through some financial and technical measures of performance. Although "pure" Internet retailers are continuing to experience significant growth, their competitors from the "bricks-and-mortar" world of physical retailing are making significant inroads to a complementary Internet and physical channel strategy. The paper concludes with the proposition that the future of retailing will be difficult to separate into Internet versus physical commerce as the Internet becomes ubiquitous. Although Internet-channel sales may never reach more than 10 percent of the total retail sector of the U.S. economy, the existence of the Internet will affect the physical channel as well.

Structure of the Retail Sector

The retail sector of the U.S. economy can also be thought of as the business-to-consumer (B2C) part of the value chain. It is the point at which a firm is supplying goods to consumers who value consuming the product (as opposed to reselling it). This portion of the economy makes up approximately 9 percent of the gross domestic product (GDP)—about $800 billion a year—and has been fairly constant over the past fifteen years, as figure 6-1 shows.

Although retailing has many subcategories, including grocery stores, home furnishings, auto parts, and gas stations, this paper focuses on the larger segments of the retail sector: clothing, shoe, and accessory retailing and wholesaling; department stores; and discount and variety retailing.[1] These segments make up the majority of the 9 percent of GDP. The aggregate retail statistics do not separate Internet-based transactions from physical transactions. That is partly because Internet retail sales are relatively small, accounting for approximately 0.7 percent of overall retail sales.[2] Even if Internet retailing were to grow to account for 1 percent of the retailing GDP, this would only be 0.09 percent of the overall U.S. GDP. As figure 6-1 shows, annual fluctuations much larger than 0.09 percent appeared in the late 1980s, which was before the advent of Internet-based e-commerce. Therefore, any effect e-commerce might have on the macroeconomic measurements would be difficult to discern given its relatively small magnitude.

Finally, it should be noted that measuring the size of the retail sector is a difficult and inexact science. As Haltiwanger and Jarmin point out, much of the retail data collected by the U.S. government is problematic because it is often outdated and measured at a very coarse level of granularity.[3] By not separating Internet sales from physical-channel sales, the aggregate statistics can show only overall growth in the retail sector. If Internet-based e-

---

1. According to Hoovers Online (www.hoovers.com [2000]), retailing includes the following eleven sectors: clothing, shoe, and accessory retailing and wholesaling; department stores; discount and variety retailing; drug, health, and beauty product retailing; grocery retailing; convenience stores and gas stations; consumer electronics and appliance retailing; building materials and gardening supplies retailing and wholesaling; home furnishings and housewares retailing; auto parts retailing and wholesaling; and nonstore retailing.

2. Michael Boldin, "Internet Sales," *The Dismal Scientist* (www.dismal.com [August 31, 2000]).

3. Haltiwanger and Jarmin (2000).

Figure 6-1. *U.S. Retail Sales as a Percentage of Gross Domestic Product, 1986–98*

Percent

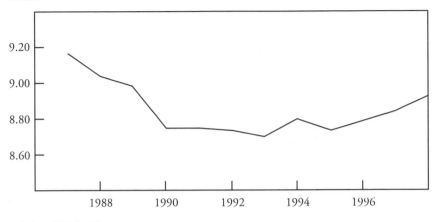

Source: BEA (2000).

commerce transactions are substituting for physical transactions, the aggregate statistics may miss the Internet's impact on the retail sector. Therefore, this paper assumes that the size of overall retail sales is fixed and that e-commerce retail sales can grow only at the expense of physical retail sales.

Sources of Internet Efficiency for Retailers

The Internet may enable greater efficiency in several different ways. This section explores efficiency in transactions with consumers, in transactions with suppliers, and in competition among retailers.

Efficiency in Transacting with Consumers

The Internet may reduce the costs of transacting with consumers, thereby lowering prices and reducing deadweight loss by eliminating some market friction. For example, high search costs to eliminate information asymmetries between the retailer and the consumer may cause market friction. When consumers have access to Internet search tools, such as search engines or shopbots, they can find products at the lowest price with little or no search costs.[4] The result is that consumers force price competition among retailers because retailers who set prices too high are unable to make any sales. This may lead to lower retail prices, as Brynjolfsson and Smith have shown empirically.[5] With lower prices and therefore a larger number of transactions, social welfare increases. One segment of the retail market where the Internet helps reduce transaction costs significantly may be the market for previously owned merchandise. Auction web sites, such as eBay, allow very small retailers (including individual households) to sell goods without having any appreciable transaction or inventory size.

Another possible source of Internet efficiency is a reduction in the internal operating costs of the firm, which then translates into lower prices in competitive markets. Internet firms may have an inherent advantage in being able to hire cheaper labor or have lower physical plant costs because their choice of physical location is not dependent on the location of their customers. In turn, the lower costs to the firm may then force the market supply to increase if the firm is in a competitive industry. The result of such a shift, holding the demand curve equal, is a reduction in prices for all consumers and an increase in social welfare with an increased number of transactions. Unfortunately, lower costs do not seem to be the case for many Internet firms. Many retail sectors have Internet firms that lose money on every sale because they may subsidize shipping costs and they have relatively high fulfillment costs.[6] The per-sale fulfillment costs, which include customer service and credit card processing costs, range from $5.00 for an Internet bookstore to $14.29 for an Internet drugstore. Finally, since all Internet retailers lack the size of a physical retailer like Wal-Mart, they are unable to negotiate lower product costs. The result of these relatively high costs is unprofitable Internet firms.

Even if Internet retailers do not offer lower prices, consumers may value the convenience of shopping on the Internet. Information asymmetries are not the only transaction costs between retailer and consumer; another is the cost of transportation for the consumer to travel to the retailer. The Internet many not eliminate transportation costs completely, but it can shift transportation costs from the consumer's side of the market to the retailer's side. The result may be a more efficient allocation of costs because

4. A shopbot is a price search intermediary that aggregates prices across many retailers and posts them on its web site.

5. Brynjolfsson and Smith (2000).

6. Mowrey (2000)

Internet retailers often outsource all their shipping to a carrier who has appreciable economies of scale, whereas some consumers have very high opportunity costs in traveling.

Finally, consumers may find that buying from an Internet retailer increases the "goodness of fit" they have with a product. Because Internet retailers are able to list large catalogs of products on their web sites without taking up valuable retail or warehouse space, they often have large product offerings. Consumers can then compare across a wider variety of products and find those from which they will derive the most utility. Purchasing from a physical store may result in a transaction as well, and perhaps at a lower price, but the consumer may have settled for a product she did not value as highly. The net result from having a better fit is increased consumer surplus.

One potential source of inefficiency for Internet retailers may be the return channel. Consumers not satisfied with their purchase may have very high transaction costs when returning merchandise to the retailer. Since consumers decide on a purchase without ever seeing the physical product, Internet retailers are faced with a higher percentage of returns. Like the transportation channel to the consumer, the return channel transportation is most likely outsourced to a shipping company. Most consumers, however, do not enjoy the relationship with a shipper that comes with a high volume of transactions. Therefore consumers are likely to find returning purchases to be both expensive and inconvenient.

Efficiency in Transacting with Suppliers

Retailers may find greater efficiency in their transactions with suppliers by automating ordering. Technologies that enable electronic business-to-business (B2B) transactions, such as electronic data interchange (EDI) and vendor-managed inventory, may increase the accuracy and timeliness of shipments. These technologies predate the web, but the Internet does enhance some B2B transactions. For example, a growing number of B2B exchanges on the Internet allow smaller firms to participate in B2B e-commerce. Larger retailers, including Wal-Mart and Amazon.com, still deal with their suppliers through EDI transactions rather than the Internet.

Internet retailers may be able to postpone ordering so that they can reduce their inventory size. Traditional retailers often stock shelves in anticipation of a sale so that consumers can examine the actual product when they shop and take it with them upon purchase. Internet retailers, in contrast, need only present consumers with a digital representation of the product. Internet retailers may not actually have the item in stock when the consumer orders it. Rather, they can postpone ordering from their suppliers until they are sure that the number of items they purchase will clear their inventory quickly. The benefit to retailers is that they can avoid some warehousing costs and increase the liquidity of product offerings.

Retailers with Internet capability may choose to disintermediate, or bypass, some of their more costly suppliers. As the suppliers to the retailer's suppliers develop an electronic presence, retailers can reach out directly to them and bypass their supplier altogether. For example, Amazon.com receives some books directly from publishers and not their distributor, Ingram. This is very difficult to do with traditional B2B e-commerce technologies, such as EDI, which were built specifically to handle transactions between neighboring echelons in the supply chain. Because the Internet spans the entire supply chain, retailers can interact directly with suppliers that are one or more echelons removed from their position in the supply chain. The result for the retailer is sometimes lower prices even if the supply chain is not disintermediated. For example, a distributor that knows that a retailer has an alternative sourcing channel may lower its prices to compete with the disintermediated supply chain. Another Internet benefit to retailers is increased product offerings. Now they can carry hard-to-find items that are unavailable from their distributors.

Efficiency in Competition among Retailers

There may be less differentiation among Internet retailers because their technology innovations are inherently transparent. An Internet retailer that comes up with an advanced website can diffuse it into the market quickly because the innovation is software. Unfortunately for the retailer, the innovation is apparent not only to its customers, but to its competitors as well. With such transparency of technological innovations, it is unlikely that a retailer will maintain a competitive advantage for a significant length of time.

With less differentiation, markets may become more efficient and approach the "law of one price." The Internet may eliminate market friction and force firms to compete on price if they have homogeneous offerings. Empirical evidence already shows that this is true in retail markets where the product is homogeneous, such as books and compact discs.[7] As markets tend to converge on a single price, price drops because of competitive pressures, and social welfare increases.

The Internet may also change entry and exit barriers so that markets adjust quickly to an efficient number of firms in a market. This is not to say that the number of retailers will always decrease. In fact, the economically efficient number of retailers might actually be larger with entry.[8] Entry may come from companies that are operating in different markets and are trying to find economies of scope by entering a new retailer market. Entry can also come from new companies with smaller fixed costs of entry because Internet retailing does not require physical retail stores. Exit may be easier because Internet retailers have increased the liquidity of their inventories by reducing their inventory size or by completely outsourcing their inventory operations.

Perhaps the most threatening change to traditional retailers posed by the introduction of the Internet is the potential for disintermediation of retailers themselves. Because retailers are inherently intermediaries between suppliers and consumers, they must be wary of any technology that might allow the retailer's customers to interact directly with the retailer's suppliers. Although very few retailers are likely be disintermediated because they do offer a valuable channel to consumers, the threat of disintermediation will keep retailers' profit margins in check.

Best Internet Practices among Retailers

As the Internet has become a business tool as important and ubiquitous as the telephone, there are no significant retailers that do not use the Internet. The differences among retailers are not whether they use the Internet, but rather how they use it. In this regard there are generally two types of retailers: those that built their business around the Internet—the so-called pure-play Internet retailers—and those who have a physical channel as their primary source of revenue but who increasingly use the Internet in their business practices—hybrid Internet retailers.

7. Smith, Bailey, and Brynjolfsson (2000).
8. Ba, Whinston, and Zhang (2000).

The Pure-Play Internet Retailer

To go beyond the macroeconomic measurements, the paper uses a set of fourteen retail firms to assess the impact that individual firms have had on displacing some traditional retail sales with Internet sales. Four of the firms are pure-play Internet retailers because they rely solely on the Internet as a distribution channel. As table 6-1 shows, the largest pure-play Internet retailer, Amazon.com, is still significantly smaller than the largest physical retailer, Wal-Mart. In fact Amazon.com's revenue is only 1 percent of Wal-Mart's.

The revenue figures may provide an adequate snapshot of firm size, but growth rates are much larger for the pure-play Internet retailers. As the table also shows, Buy.com and Amazon.com are far ahead of the other retailers in the percentage increase in revenue from 1998 to 1999.

Part of the reason why Amazon.com is incurring many more expenses than other pure players is that it is building warehouses and developing a greater physical presence.[9] Although building warehouses may not seem like the best business decision for a firm trying to leverage the benefits of the Internet, Amazon.com has realized the value of physical facilities. One benefit is that Amazon.com can now provide better customer service. For example, the company can now ship a product to its customer more quickly than it once did because Amazon.com is likely to have ownership of the product without relying on another firm upstream in the supply chain for fulfillment. Furthermore, Amazon.com is now able to take advantage of volume discounts it receives from the wholesalers by buying a larger quantity at one time and warehousing the inventory that will not be immediately sold. Although investment in physical assets may make retailers like Amazon less agile in changing their product offerings, these investments help companies lower their variable costs.

This is a very different strategy from the one employed by Buy.com, which relies on Ingram Micro for warehousing and distribution of all products that consumers buy on Buy.com. Although Buy.com is able to take advantage of some volume discounts through bulk buying, it is much more susceptible than Amazon.com to stock out and nonperformance problems. However, Buy.com tries to offset these problems with a very close and mutually beneficial relationship with Ingram Micro.

9. For an investigation into the business practices of Amazon.com, see Spector (2000).

Table 6-1. *Revenue, Net Income, and Revenue Growth
for Fourteen Selected Retailers, 1999*
Millions of dollars, unless otherwise indicated

Firm	Market	Revenue	Net income	Percent increase in revenues 1998–99
Wal-Mart	Discount	165,013	5,377	19.9
Sears	Department stores	41,071	1,453	–0.6
Kmart/BlueLight	Discount	35,925	1,300	6.7
Target	Discount	33,702	1,144	8.9
J.C. Penney	Department stores	32,510	336	6.0
Costco	Discount, wholesale club	27,456	397	13.1
Sam's Club	Discount, wholesale club	24,801	n.a.	8.4
May Dept. Stores	Department stores	13,866	927	3.4
Gap	Clothing	11,635	1,127	28.5
QVC	Discount, TV sales	2,847	n.a.	18.5
Amazon.com	Department stores, Internet	1,640	–720	168.8
Fingerhut	Discount, catalog	1,609[a]	76[a]	4.8
Buy.com	Department stores, Internet	597	–130	376.3
Netmarket	Department stores, Internet	n.a.	n.a.	n.a.

Source: (www.hoovers.com [2000])
n.a. Not available.
a. 1998 revenue data; 1997 to 1998 percent change.

The Hybrid Internet Retailer

As Amazon.com moves from its starting point as a pure-play Internet retailer toward a hybrid position, traditional retailers that have relied on a physical channel are finding ways to make their e-commerce efforts fit well into their existing assets. Although Amazon.com and other pure-play Internet retailers may have been in completely separate markets initially, the diffusion of e-commerce to the consuming public coupled with the recognition that it takes more than a good website to promote Internet sales has given physical retailers a strong incentive to find ways to use the Internet in their sales operations.

Physical retailers are finding that Internet and physical channels are in fact complementary. Customers can shop on the Internet to find the

Table 6-2. *Web Statistic Data*

Firm	Market	Web traffic	Web links	Web pages
Amazon.com	Department stores, Internet	2,404,080	10,183,456	12,587,950
Gap	Clothing	186,421	14,132	13,755
J.C. Penney	Department stores	181,115	9,494	14,895
QVC	Discount, TV sales	124,579	13,953	13,597
Wal-Mart	Discount	112,758	8,368	45
Buy.com	Department stores, Internet	104,204	36,399	n.a.
Sears	Department stores	95,383	8,950	5,555
Costco	Discount, wholesale club	66,561	2,185	227
Target	Discount	66,399	3,850	2,231
Kmart/ BlueLight	Department stores, Internet	62,713	6,452	36
Netmarket	Department stores, Internet	50,494	14,881	29,354
Fingerhut	Discount, catalog	21,119	1,775	260
Sam's Club	Discount, wholesale club	9,645	981	14
May Dept. Stores	Department stores	4,435	2,273	204

Source: (www.alexa.com [September 2, 2000]).

n.a. Not available.

a. Web traffic is the number of visits to a website, web links are a measure of how many other websites have links to the firm's website, and web pages are a count of the number of unique web pages that are listed in the search engine database and hosted on that particular firm's website.

product they want to buy, but they still might want to try on a garment or smell the food that they would like to purchase. The fact that physical retailers have both the convenience of a website for easy information navigation along with the possibility of immediate order fulfillment puts them in a very good position to compete with the pure-play retailers.

Physical retailers still have some catching up to do with regard to their website design and development. As table 6-2 shows, Amazon.com still leads the way in attracting users to its website.[10] But several traditional retailers have higher web traffic than does the fastest-growing pure-play Internet retailer, Buy.com. Kmart/BlueLight has only started exploring the

10. It should be noted that while traffic to a firm's website is an important performance metric for Internet retailers, it often overestimates sales. For example, only 10 percent of visitors to Amazon.com's website actually buy anything (Mowrey 2000). The traffic measures are presented here mostly for comparative analysis.

Table 6-3. *Web Performance Data*

Firm	Relationship services	On-site resources	Customer confidence	Ease of use	Overall
Amazon.com	6.67	7.74	6.90	7.64	7.26
QVC.com	2.95	6.61	7.87	6.58	6.19
Netmarket.com	2.84	6.36	6.23	6.83	5.73
Wal-Mart.com	2.68	5.70	7.51	7.51	6.07
J.C. Penney	3.12	5.37	8.10	4.92	5.53
Target	2.54	6.27	6.40	7.20	5.79
Fingerhut.com	3.31	4.34	5.29	6.27	4.92
Costco	2.09	3.24	6.24	4.39	4.15
Sam's Club	2.18	2.51	6.79	6.15	4.63
Kmart/BlueLight	2.93	4.67	7.13	6.70	5.55

Source: "Scorecards from General Merchandise Category" (www.gomez.com [September 2, 2000]).

complementarities between its physical (Kmart stores) and Internet (BlueLight.com) channels.

Over time, I would expect that the disparity in traffic between Amazon.com and the set of hybrid retailers to decline, indicating that physical retailers are catching up with the pure-play Internet retailers in their own game. Part of the reason why this is true is that the technology is more advanced today than it was when Amazon.com and Buy.com were first developing their websites. Now off-the-shelf software packages do a very good job of creating dynamically rendered web pages. And when an incumbent retailer makes a change to its website, competitors can easily copy that innovation.

At the same time, Internet retailers are finding it difficult to make the inroads in the physical channel. Clothing retail sales on the Internet seem to be concentrating much more on the traditional retailers as opposed to the Internet upstarts.[11] Furthermore, Internet retailers may have a harder time convincing new customers that they are trustworthy sites. As table 6-3 shows, the "customer confidence" value for Costco is higher than the value for Amazon.com.

Channel conflict is still an issue for hybrid retailers. Because they are trying to support an Internet and physical presence simultaneously, they

11. Lavanya Ramanathan, "Retail Sector Analysis," Hoover's Online (www.hoovers.com [2000]).

might find themselves giving inconsistent information or different prices that could alienate some customers. Furthermore, geographic price discrimination may not be possible for the Internet channel of a hybrid retailer.

The Case for the Ubiquitous Internet

Either directly or indirectly, retailers will be cognizant of the impact the Internet has on their business. If they choose not to develop their own Internet channel, they are likely to face some competition to lower prices or change services. Even firms that never fully implement a B2C sales channel are likely to be the direct or indirect beneficiaries of Internet use in their upstream supply chain. For example, through the use of the Internet, retailers may be able to increase their efficiency, as shown in table 6-4.

Buy.com and Amazon.com do very well in extracting relatively large revenue per employee. There may be some cost savings in replacing some of the large sales staffs with web content, call centers, or both. The area where there might not be an efficiency is the average revenue per inventory level. Amazon.com is eighth in this category, behind Target and even Sears. The one who still leads here is Buy.com because it carries no inventory. As Amazon and Buy.com illustrate, retailers may have a similar presence on the Web but vastly different inventory and order fulfillment policies.

The Future of Retailing

The success of the Internet in promoting retail transactions will likely continue. Many of the website features and functions of leaders such as Amazon.com have been copied by other retailers, and they are likely to continue to find complementary ways of using the Internet and a physical channel. Eventually hybrid retailers will become the dominant form of retailer. A growing proportion of the traditional physical firms will conduct more business using the Internet and the pure-play Internet firms will develop some form of physical presence in order to achieve the economies of scale necessary to enter into price competition with other hybrid Internet retailers.

Assuming a fixed gross product of retail sales of $800 billion and a starting point of $8 billion in Internet transactions, it is possible that, on aver-

Table 6-4. *Firm Efficiency Data*

Firm	Market	1999 revenue per employee	1999 revenue for every US$ of inventory
Buy.com	Department stores, Internet	2.59	∞
Costco	Discount, wholesale club	0.39	12.42
QVC	Discount, TV sales	0.30	n.a.
Amazon.com	Department stores, Internet	0.22	7.43
Fingerhut	Discount, catalog	0.17[a]	12.94[a]
Target	Discount	0.16	8.91
Wal-Mart	Discount	0.14	8.06
Kmart/BlueLight	Discount	0.13	5.15
Sears	Department stores	0.13	8.10
J.C. Penney	Department stores	0.11	5.09
May Dept. Stores	Department stores	0.10	5.05
Gap	Clothing	0.08	8.57
Netmarket	Department stores, Internet	n.a.	n.a.
Sam's Club	Discount, wholesale club	n.a.	n.a.

Source: (www.hoovers.com [February 2001, 2000]).
n.a. Not available.
a. 1998 data.

age, 10 percent of retail revenue would come through the Internet channel in five years. That would require an average of a 50 percent increase in Internet sales annually through 2005. This estimate is much larger than a recent projection of a 4 percent annual increase for retail clothing sales transacted using an Internet channel.[12] But it is at the lower bound of the projections made by four commercial research firms that estimated annual Internet retail sales of $75 billion–$144 billion by 2004.[13]

Some small retailers may never expand to the Internet. Retail stores with a handful of employees and a targeted geographic area may never take advantage of the Internet's scope because it runs counter to their strategy of remaining small and intimate. Furthermore, they might not have the

12. Lavanya Ramanathan, "Retail Sector Analysis," Hoover's Online (www.hoovers.com [2000]).
13. Thomson (1999).

personnel or the funds to launch an e-commerce initiative. As of June 2000 only 12 percent of small businesses participated in electronic commerce.[14]

The holiday season in 2000 supports the proposition that the hybrid retailers (also known as "bricks-and-clicks") have been growing much more than the pure-plays.[15] Between November 1999 and November 2000, some brick-and-click retailers' websites experienced a triple-digit growth in traffic; these included Kmart/BlueLight (438 percent), Target (215 percent), and Wal-Mart (152 percent). Meanwhile, many pure-play retailers had a much more modest increase over the same period, including Amazon.com (23 percent) and Buy.com (6 percent).

The fluidness of Internet retail competition is becoming more apparent as pure-play Internet retailers start exiting the market. Pets.com and Send.com once had a very optimistic view of the growth of Internet commerce. However, the abundance of retail price competition on the Internet, the financial stability of their hybrid retail competitors, and the evaporation of start-up funding was too much for these companies to survive.

Sophistication of technology will likely get better for the websites that have physical channel roots. Recent data indicate that these firms still have some room for improvement. Amazon.com and Buy.com are rated fifth and sixth, while Wal-Mart and Target are twentieth and twenty-first.[16]

Public Policy Issues and Conclusions

One public policy question that ought to be addressed with respect to the diffusion of the ubiquitous Internet among retailers is taxation. Some retailers that have physical and Internet channels, such as Barnes & Noble, try to keep their online and physical presences separated on purpose so that they may avoid charging an Internet customer a state sales tax. If the sales tax rules become well harmonized between the Internet and physical channels, retailers may become less averse to integrating their Internet and physical operations. Determining a tax jurisdiction is a significant issue for retailers because there are more than a thousand different tax jurisdictions

---

14. IDC, "Small Businesses Making Large Footprints on the Web." *IT Forecaster* (www.idc.com/itforecaster/itf20000613.stm [June 13, 2000]).

15. Helft (2001a).

16. Helft (2001b).

in the United States. Some authors have suggested, however, the possibility of tax schemes that do not require uniformity.[17]

Other public policy issues, such as Federal Trade Commission direct marketing rules and considerations about anticompetitive behavior, do not appear to be as much of a hindrance to convergence of a retailer's Internet and physical channels. This is not to say that these issues are trivial or unimportant. Rather, it is likely that efforts to promote competition and ensure trustworthy transactions on the Internet would strongly encourage physical retailers to develop an Internet presence. In fact, until recently many physical retailers have been reluctant to do more with the Internet because they did not want security uncertainty or technical problems to ruin their brand name in both the Internet and physical channels. Now that some pioneers such as Amazon.com have paved the way, the physical retailers can feel more comfortable with the Internet channel.

Perhaps the more difficult challenges lie ahead for Amazon.com and Buy.com. For them to move from a pure-play Internet retailer to a hybrid retailer requires significant investments in warehouses, distribution facilities, and maybe even physical retail locations. This would take a significant amount of capital if they tried to develop a physical geographic scope comparable to their Internet scope. Given the fact that both Amazon.com and Buy.com are still operating in the red, it might be difficult for them to make such a move.

References

Ba, Sulin, Andrew B. Whinston, and Han Zhang. 2000. "Small Companies in the Digital Economy." In *Understanding the Digital Economy*, edited by Erik Brynjolfsson and B. Kahin, pp. 185–200. MIT Press.

BEA (Bureau of Economic Analysis), U.S. Department of Commerce. 2000. "Industry Accounts Data: Gross Product by Industry" (www.bea.doc.gov/bea/dn2/gpoc.htm).

Brynjolfsson, Erik, and Michael D. Smith. 2000. "Frictionless Commerce? A Comparison of Internet and Conventional Retailers." *Management Science* 46: 563–85.

Choi, Soon-Yong, Dale O. Stahl, and Andrew B. Whinston. 1997. *The Economics of Electronic Commerce*. Indianapolis: Macmillan Technical Publishing.

Haltiwanger, John, and Ron S. Jarmin. 2000. "Measuring the Digital Economy." In *Understanding the Digital Economy*, edited by Erik Brynjolfsson and B. Kahin, pp. 13–33. MIT Press.

17. Choi, Stahl, and Whinston (1997, p. 495).

Helft, Miguel. 2001a. "Blue Christmas." *The Industry Standard* (January 1–8): 36–38 (www.thestandard.com/article/display/0,1151,21058,00.html).

———. 2001b. "A Rare Spot of Christmas Cheer." *The Industry Standard* (January 15): 61 (www.thestandard.com/article/display/0,1151,21303,00.html).

Mowrey, Mark A. 2000. "Pure-Play: Losing Model?" *The Industry Standard* (June 9) (www.thestandard.com/research/metrics/display/1,2799,16063,00.html).

Smith, M. D., Joseph Bailey, and Erik Brynjolfsson. 2000. "Understanding Digital Markets: Review and Assessment." In *Understanding the Digital Economy,* edited by Erik Brynjolfsson and B. Kahin, pp. 99–136. MIT Press.

Spector, Robert. 2000. *Amazon.com: Get Big Fast: Inside the Revolutionary Business Model That Changed the World.* New York: Harper Business.

Thomson, Maryann J. 1999. "Customers Feeding Frenzy: E-Retailers vie for $185 Billion." *The Industry Standard* (November 15) (www.thestandard.com/research/metrics/display/0,2799,10077,00.html).

7

PATRICIA M. DANZON
MICHAEL F. FURUKAWA

Health Care: Competition and Productivity

NATIONAL EXPENDITURE ON medical care reached $1.2 trillion, or almost 14 percent of gross domestic product (GDP) in 1999, up from 8.9 percent of GDP in 1980. By 2007 health care spending is projected to reach $2.04 trillion.[1] The potential economic impact of improved productivity in health care is therefore huge. Although medical technology has been the main contributor to this increase in health spending, advanced information technology (IT) has not been widely integrated into health care's basic administrative processes and business functions.[2] The Internet offers the potential for cost reduction and improved productivity in many of these functions. The main potential targets for savings are

—administrative cost related to insurance billing, medical records, and care coordination; together, these costs have been estimated at between 12 and 15 percent of total health care spending;[3]

—costs attributable to inappropriate care and "medical error" that result from physician uncertainty about best practices or from incomplete patient

---

1. HCFA (2000).

2. A survey by Fuchs (1996) found that 84 percent of health economists concur that the diffusion of new technology is the main driver of health care costs. Dorenfest (2000) found that IT investment in health care more than tripled during the 1990s, with annual expenditures for products and services rising from $6.5 billion in 1990 to a projected $20.4 billion in 2000.

3. OTA (1995), citing Lewin-VHI (1993).

records and poor care coordination; these costs have been estimated at 4 percent of total health expenditures;[4]

—"unnecessary" care, which has been estimated at 20 percent of the total, much of which is insurance-induced overuse that occurs because insured patients are not cost-conscious (moral hazard);[5] and

—costs associated with purchasing and the supply chain; estimated savings from moving to business-to-business (B2B) e-commerce are less than 1 percent of total health care spending.[6]

Even if these estimates are exaggerated, include some duplication, and reflect some costs that could not be totally eliminated, there is still clearly potential for significant savings that could release resources for spending on new clinical technologies or on other goods and services.

In addition to these direct, potentially measurable savings, productivity improvements in health care delivery could yield indirect benefits to the rest of the economy, through better population health, lower patient time costs, and lower public budget expenditures. Health improvement is the ultimate output of the medical services sector, but that output is not captured by standard GDP measures. Nonetheless, better employee health could increase labor productivity throughout the economy by reducing work loss caused by disability and illness. Recent estimates show 13.6 percent of the total population—and 22 percent of the 45–65 year age group—suffers from chronic medical conditions that limit activity.[7] That estimate does not include acute conditions or time out to care for sick family members. Moreover, because tax-financed public spending accounts for 45 percent of total health expenditures, primarily for the Medicare and Medicaid programs, any factor that controls these costs could reduce tax burdens and hence indirectly benefit the rest of the economy.

The application of the Internet to health care, commonly referred to as "e-health," is a diverse and complex undertaking.[8] Health care uses some of the same Internet business models, such as B2B e-commerce, used in other industries, although the fragmented structure of the industry may slow the

---

4. Thomas and others (1999).

5. Chassin (1998) concludes that at least 20 percent of all health care delivered in the United States is unnecessary and can be safely eliminated.

6. Based on EHCR (1996).

7. Kramarow and others (1999, table 59, p. 220).

8. For an overview of the Internet and health care, see Computer Science and Telecommunications Board and National Research Council (2000), Mittman and Cain (1999), and Nicholson (1999).

realization of potential savings. Other Internet opportunities are more specific to health care, particularly those that address costs related to imperfect
or asymmetric information and to insurance and third-party payment, two
factors that underlie the high costs of administration, medical error, and
unnecessary care.

This paper outlines the structure of the health care sector and its distinguishing features as a foundation for understanding the potential impact of
IT and the Internet. It then describes Internet activities in health care,
broadly categorized by the four "Cs": connectivity, content, commerce,
and care. Effects of these activities on competition and on measured and
unmeasured productivity are suggested. The concluding section summarizes findings.

Industry Background

The diversity of medical care, its fragmentation, and the overlay of third-
party payment create the potential for Internet-based savings—but also
obstruct their realization.

Industry Structure

Table 7-1 shows the breakdown of personal consumption expenditure
(PCE) in the National Income and Product Accounts (NIPA) and the
National Health Accounts from the Health Care Financing Administration
(HCFA). Hospitals and physicians dominate the provider side, accounting
for more than one-third and one-fifth, respectively, of PCE. Other
providers include home health, nursing homes, ambulatory surgery centers, dentists and other professionals, with a steady shift of care from inpatient hospitals to these diverse outpatient settings over the last two decades.
The supply side includes pharmaceuticals, medical devices, equipment,
and supplies, which are sold to providers and retail pharmacies.

Each of these sectors remains highly fragmented (table 7-2, column 1),
despite significant consolidation in the 1990s through the formation of
hospital systems, physician practice management groups, and integrated
delivery networks (IDNs) that link one or more hospitals with a network
of physicians, home health services, and possibly other services. It was
hoped that this consolidation could take advantage of new IT opportunities to realize economies of scale and efficiency savings in coordinating

Table 7-1. *NIPA Medical Care Expenditures, 1992, 1994, 1996–98*

Billions of dollars, unless otherwise indicated

Expenditure	1992	1994	1996	1997	1998
Selected NIPA health care expenditures, total	763.1	858.1	948.1	991.9	n.a.
Personal consumption expenditures	741.5	838.1	932.3	977.6	1032.3
Drug preparations, sundries[a]	75.9	85.8	100.3	108.1	116.8
Ophthalmic products, orthopedic equipment[b]	13.0	15.0	17.6	19.4	21.2
Physicians	167.3	181.0	199.1	206.9	219.6
Dentists	37.6	42.9	48.4	52.0	54.8
Other professional medical services[c]	85.2	103.6	119.7	125.1	131.8
Hospitals and nursing homes	319.2	353.9	390.8	408.5	428.4
Hospitals	269.0	299.9	327.6	341.9	357.1
Nonprofit hospitals	183.5	200.8	213.5	221.3	230.6
Proprietary hospitals	30.3	32.4	38.7	41.6	43.3
Government hospitals	55.2	66.6	75.4	79.0	83.2
Nursing homes	50.2	54.1	63.2	66.7	71.3
Health insurance	43.3	55.8	56.6	57.6	59.8
Medical and hospitalization insurance	37.6	44.4	45.3	46.9	49.7
Income loss insurance	2.1	1.6	1.0	1.2	1.4
Workers compensation	3.6	9.8	10.3	9.6	8.7

Government consumption expenditures and gross investment[d]	21.6	20.0	15.8	14.3	n.a.
Federal	14.3	16.7	17.5	17.2	n.a.
Veterans medical care	14.3	16.7	17.5	17.2	n.a.
State and local hospitals	7.3	3.3	–1.8	–2.9	n.a.
Addenda:					
Gross domestic product	6,318.9	7,054.3	7,813.2	8,300.8	8,759.9
Selected NIPA health expenditures as percent of GDP	12.1	12.2	12.1	11.9	n.a.
National health accounts[e]	785.6	889.1	976.5	1,019.0	n.a.
Personal health care	740.7	834.0	924.0	969.0	n.a.
Administration and net cost of private insurance	44.9	55.1	52.5	50.0	n.a.
National health accounts expenditures as percent of GDP	12.4	12.6	12.5	12.3	n.a.

Source: McCully (1999).

n.a. Not available.

a. Includes prescription and nonprescription drugs and medical sundries. Excludes drug preparations and related products dispensed by physicians, hospitals, and other medical services.

b. Includes eyeglasses, contact lenses, and prosthetic and orthopedic appliances.

c. Consists of osteopathic physicians, chiropractors, private duty nurses, chiropodists, podiatrists, optometrists (excluding optical goods), home health care, and medical laboratories.

d. Previously published estimates. Government consumption expenditures and gross investment by type and function consistent with the 1999 comprehensive revision have not yet been published.

e. Health Care Financing Administration. Figures exclude public health expenditures, research, and construction.

Table 7-2. *Number of Health Care Providers and Implementation Costs for HIPAA Administrative Simplification Rules, 2002–11*

Type of health care provider	Number of health care providers (2002 est.)	Average cost	EDI (percent)	Total cost (millions of dollars)	Savings (millions of dollars)
Federal hospitals	266	250,000	88	92	...
Nonfederal hospitals <100 beds	2,639	100,000	88	364	...
Nonfederal hospitals 100+ beds	2,780	250,000	88	960	...
Nursing facility <100 beds	9,606	10,000	90	134	...
Nursing facility 100+ beds	8,833	20,000	90	247	...
Home health agency	8,900	10,000	90	184	...
Hospice	2,027	10,000	90	28	...
Residential mental health/retardation/ substance abuse facilities	22,339	10,000	10	134	...
Outpatient care centers	24,034	10,000	75	300	...
Pharmacy	43,900	4,000	96	256	...
Medical labs	9,500	4,000	85	51	...
Dental labs	7,900	1,500	50	12	...
DME	112,200	1,500	50	168	...
Physicians solo and groups less than 3	193,000	1,500	50	290	...
Physicians' groups 3+ with computers	20,000	4,000	90	112	...
Physicians' groups 3+ no automation	1,000	0	0	0	...
Osteopaths	13,600	1,500	10	12	...
Dentists	120,000	1,500	30	144	...
Podiatrists	9,100	1,500	5	8	...
Chiropractors	32,000	1,500	5	26	...
Optometrists	18,800	1,500	5	16	...
Other professionals	33,400	1,500	5	28	...
Total (undiscounted)	...	...	...	3,566	20,200
Total (discounted)	...	...	...	3,300	14,100

Source: Federal Register, August 17, 2000, Table 2.

care. But the reality has fallen short, and many IDNs are integrated only in name and some business systems, with little online sharing of clinical information and patient records. Within specific hospitals, individual departments (general medicine, emergency room, intensive care, and others) remain poorly coordinated. Existing IT systems (known as legacy systems) are often incompatible and still based on mainframes rather than client-server platforms. The resulting lack of real-time, integrated patient records and poorly coordinated care have been identified as major contributors to medical errors.[9] According to a survey published in June 2000, health care organizations said their top IT priorities for the next two years are electronic medical records, integration, and improved connectivity with physicians.[10]

Financing

Health insurance is an integral part of the health care sector and has a pervasive influence on the cost and structure of the medical services industry. Although insurance is in theory intended to protect against unexpected, catastrophic expense, in practice insurance pays for more than 80 percent of personal health care, including much that is routine and predictable. Administration and net cost of private insurance are estimated at 5.1 percent of personal health care (see table 7-1). The expansion of private insurance has been driven by the tax subsidy to health insurance, whereby employer contributions are tax-exempt income to employees, implying a subsidy to insured medical care (including administrative costs) at the employee's marginal tax rate, which averages more than 30 percent. Given this subsidy, it is not surprising that employees choose plans with comprehensive coverage. The resulting insurance and medical norms become the standard for public programs.

Insurance adds an extra payment transaction for each service, because medical providers typically collect a co-payment from the patient and bill the patient's insurer for the remaining cost of the service—a transaction that may entail eligibility verification, preservice authorization, and postservice benefit denial. A potentially much larger cost of insurance results from the "moral hazard" effect, that is, the tendency for insured patients and providers to overutilize services because someone else is paying the

9. Kohn, Corrigan, and Donaldson (1999).
10. HIMSS-IBM Leadership Survey (2000).

bill, and from the potential for excessive prices because insurance makes demand less elastic. Estimates of unnecessary care differ, depending on whether the definition is economic (meaning that marginal benefit is less than social marginal cost) or is based on a notion of medical appropriateness, but given the incentives, the number is surely large.

The moral hazard effects of insurance mean that administrative expense is not necessarily a pure deadweight loss to be minimized. Many administrative functions are designed not only to pay providers, but also to control moral hazard and monitor the quality of care.[11] The managed care revolution reflects a shift away from the traditional patient-targeted approach of controlling costs through co-payments and toward provider-targeted incentives and controls, such as capitation payments, utilization review, and selective contracting. These managed care strategies add administrative cost, but that is usually offset by lower costs of care, attributable to lower prices or fewer expensive services, and less financial risk for patients. Thus administrative inputs produce several joint products—billing and reimbursement, moral hazard control, and care. The Internet, by improving information and data exchange, could therefore offer savings not only through lower administrative costs, as conventionally measured, but also through better monitoring and improved clinical care, which may be much harder to measure.

The private health insurance market is extremely fragmented (table 7-3, column 1), reflecting local differences in medical care infrastructure and regulatory structure and proliferation of health plans as they compete to find better trade-offs between cost control and freedom of choice. Insurance regulation is a state function, under the McCarran Ferguson Act of 1945. States have adopted a range of different regulations to address solvency, set minimum benefits, and, in some cases, regulate premiums and underwriting. Partly to help multistate employers deal with divergent state regulations, the Employee Retirement Income and Security Act (ERISA) of 1974 established federal oversight of employer-sponsored health plans that are self-insured. Most large firms and a significant fraction of medium-size firms are now self-insured, but often use a third-party administrator to design and administer benefits.

Public spending is dominated by the Medicare program, which covers seniors, the permanently disabled, and those with end stage renal disease.

---

11. Danzon (1992).

Table 7-3. *Number of Health Plans and Implementation Costs of HIPAA Administrative Simplification Rules, 2002–11*

Type of health plan	Number of health plans	Average cost	EDI (percent)	Total cost (millions of dollars)	Savings (millions of dollars)
Large commercials	250	1,000,000	90	350	...
Small commercials	400	500,000	50	200	...
Blue Cross/Blue Shield	400	1,000,000	100	98	...
Third-party administrators	400	500,000	50	375	...
HMO/PPO	400	250,000	60–85	487	...
Self-administered	400	50,000	25	1,875	...
Other employer health plans	400	100	0	127	...
Total (undiscounted)	...	...	...	3,512	16,600
Total (discounted)	...	...	...	3,300	11,600

Source: Federal Register, August 17, 2000, Table 1.

Traditional Medicare, a federal program run by the HCFA, has a uniform reimbursement structure nationwide, although it is administered by local intermediaries. In addition, the Medicare+Choice program offers seniors the option of selecting an approved private plan as an alternative to traditional Medicare. The number of plan offerings in Medicare+Choice fluctuates, depending on reimbursement levels. Medicaid is a federal-state program covering eligible low-income women and children, other needy groups, and long-term care. State autonomy, subject to federal constraints, has resulted in considerable diversity in structure and benefits. Many states contract with local private plans to administer benefits to Medicaid enrollees. Other public health care programs include the Veterans' Administration, the Indian Health Service, and many smaller state programs.

The diversity of the health insurance industry resulting from this private initiative and public regulation reflects a very competitive insurance marketplace, with continual innovation as plans compete on cost and quality. But it also makes for administrative complexity, as physicians and hospitals deal with multiple plans that differ in benefits covered and in billing and reimbursement protocols. But because plans must contract with providers and attract enrollees, they should internalize the "hassle costs" that they impose. Thus it is not clear that this diversity is excessive, except to the extent that the tax subsidy to health insurance subsidizes administrative expense as well as medical services. In any case, the Internet offers the potential to reduce measured administrative costs, plus unmeasured time costs of providers and patients; better controls on excess utilization and more appropriate care may be additional benefits. As discussed in more detail later, the Health Insurance Portability and Accountability Act (HIPAA) of 1996 authorized the federal government to establish federal standards for electronic transactions and security, which are intended to accelerate realization of these savings.

Characteristics of Health Care

Certain basic characteristics of health care contribute to the structure of the industry, its present inefficiencies, and the potential productivity gains from the Internet.

Imperfect Information

Imperfect information underlies the structure and many of the problems in health care.[12] Illness is stochastic, and uncertainty may confound both diagnosis and optimal treatment of patients. Rapid change in medical technology may exacerbate information asymmetries among both patients and providers. Because health states and outcomes are imperfectly observable, adverse selection and moral hazard can create further inefficiencies. The integration and communication aspects of the Internet hold much promise for mitigating the problems caused by imperfect and asymmetric information.

CONSUMERS. When illness strikes, consumers have traditionally had little information about potential diagnoses or appropriate providers and treatments and hence have relied on physicians as agents to advise on appropriate treatment as well as to implement care. The complexity of medical services means that information is costly, and search may impose a barrier to access for consumers. Physicians often face conflicting incentives in their role as advisor and supplier, leading to concerns about quality of care and charges of "supplier-induced demand." Asymmetric information between physicians and their patients (and third-party payers) underlies the requirements for professional licensure and other regulations on who can practice medicine, traditions of strong professional norms, and

12. Arrow (1963).

not-for-profit status of hospitals.[13] Others have argued that these regulations serve as barriers to entry that restrict competition and raise costs. Regardless of the origin of these institutions, the outcome is that physicians direct a much larger fraction of health spending than is reflected in their own income, which is only 20 percent of the total. The Internet offers an unprecedented source of free information for consumers on diseases and treatment options, products, provider report cards, and alternative medicine, information that is already contributing to a more consumer-driven health care system.

PHYSICIANS. In a world of perfect information, physicians, patients, and payers would understand symptoms, know the best course of treatment, and be able to evaluate the quality of care actually delivered. In reality, the rate of change of medical technologies outpaces the ability of technology assessment to evaluate them and the ability of many providers to keep up. Evidence-based medicine is in its infancy, and medical consensus on best practices is lacking. Numerous studies have documented large variation in treatment patterns for the same condition across geographic areas, which cannot be fully explained by patient demographics or insurance coverage. Physician uncertainty about best practices is the most plausible explanation for these practice variations, which have significant associated cost variation that is not correlated with outcomes. These variations impose a significant welfare loss, which is separate from and in addition to the insurance-induced loss attributable to moral hazard.[14] Physician-oriented Internet portals seek to address this information challenge, offering physicians such services as online access to medical information, decision support systems, and online continuing medical education.

Medical specialization and the fragmentation of care delivery are further consequences of the technological complexity of medical care. General practitioners (GPs) typically act as gatekeepers who form a preliminary diagnosis and then order additional tests and refer patients to specialists. A single episode of treatment may thus entail visits to a GP and a specialist, tests read by a radiologist, drug prescriptions filled by a pharmacist, and possibly hospitalization and postoperative therapy. Each of these providers may operate as an independent, separately located business unit, each with a separate medical record on each patient. Coordinating care and transmitting information across the continuum of care currently depends

13. Arrow (1963).
14. See Phelps (1992) on welfare loss.

largely on phone, fax, or mail. That entails not only the costs of the administrative staff required to handle the paperwork, but also the potentially much larger costs of duplicative or inappropriate care that results from incomplete patient records at the point of treatment.

The 1990s wave of mergers, acquisitions, and consolidation of various health care providers into integrated delivery systems was premised in part on the value of sharing information among multiple organizations across a continuum of care. Communicating across disparate entities—within a single organization or between trading partners—necessitated connectivity across an enterprise and potentially throughout a community or region. The promised benefits included lower cost, higher quality, better measurement of quality, and lower costs of transacting with payers. In practice these promised benefits were at most partially realized, and integration of information systems remains largely unfulfilled. Existing legacy systems have been costly failures but remain a barrier to integration and to Internet adoption, as many executives and boards are skeptical about further investments in information technology. Other priorities that have preempted the limited human and financial capital available to hospitals include compliance with changing regulations, and surviving under declining reimbursement after severe cuts in the 1997 Balanced Budget Act. Moreover, the Y2K problem—ensuring that computers could deal with the transition from 1999 to 2000—was literally a life-or-death issue for health care institutions.

The 1990s also spawned a renewed vision of idealized community health information networks (CHINs). Some of these failed; some, such as the Wisconsin Health Information Network, became operational through vendor sponsorship; and others remain works in progress.[15] Although the Internet may facilitate some goals of the CHIN movement, it seems plausible that the important components will be the proprietary networks and systems, linked to medical records that will remain private.

PAYERS. Payers, like patients, traditionally depend on physicians to determine appropriate care. This obviously limits their ability to monitor and challenge unnecessary expenditures that benefit the patient and the physician but that are not cost justified. The Internet offers significant improvement in at least two ways. First, online connections between providers and payers can offer real-time information on coverage limits and practice guidelines to the provider at the point of care. Modifying the course of treatment or choice of drug before it is delivered is potentially far more

15. Starr (1997).

cost effective than the current after-the-fact review process, in which denial of reimbursement for services already rendered or scripts already written is a major waste of time and aggravation to physicians and patients. In the longer run, better systems for tracking treatments, costs, and outcomes can provide the basis for data-driven, evidence-based practice protocols or norms of care for specific conditions. So-called outcomes studies are an infant but burgeoning industry, financed by government and private payers, because evidence-based studies offer the necessary foundation for eliminating inappropriate and unnecessary care. The feasibility of these studies depends heavily on IT, of which the Internet is one critical component.

More generally, improved information about the quality of care and outcomes is key to the efficient functioning of markets for health plans and medical care, as for other goods and services. As patients select health plans and providers and plans contract with providers, they need to be able to evaluate the quality of care, controlling for other factors that affect observed outcomes, such as the severity of the patient's underlying disease. The measurement of risk-adjusted outcomes and of provider care quality and the dissemination of this information become more possible with the advances of IT in general and the Internet in particular.

Regulation

Medical providers, suppliers, and insurers are heavily regulated by state and federal agencies. States regulate licensure and practice of professionals and insurance, which has contributed to diversity in health plans and treatment norms. The federal government has played a significant role in setting standards for reimbursement through the Medicare program, and some private plans have followed these standards. The 1996 HIPAA also implies a significantly greater role for the federal government in setting national standards for medical information. The Food and Drug Administration (FDA) must approve pharmaceuticals and medical devices for safety and efficacy before they can be marketed, and these products must comply with good manufacturing practices. The huge costs of the very paper-intensive drug approval process may be reduced through electronic filings. Regulatory compliance costs are a major contributor to administrative costs. The Internet may reduce the costs of complying with some of these regulatory requirements. At the same time, the increased regulatory demands to assure privacy and security of electronic communications may mean that, on balance, the Internet may add to the regulatory burden, at least in the near term.

Privacy

Medical information is extremely sensitive, and patients have legitimate fears that it will be misused, leading to discrimination in employment and in buying insurance. Concern about assuring privacy of personal records is a greater barrier to web-enabling transactions in medical care than in other industries. Indeed, several other countries with nationalized health care systems and hence no diversity of payment systems have even less coordination of medical records than there is in the United States, because they have regarded the use of unique patient identifiers as a threat to patient privacy. Even if the technology problem is solved by encryption and authentication technologies, the risk of human error or intentional misuse remains. Privacy concerns could undermine the widespread adoption of application service provider (ASP) models for medical records and claims processing. These ASP models offer much lower cost and financial risk for providers but have a greater potential for loss of control and increased security risk.

Competition and Market Power

Price competition in health care has increased in recent years but remains problematic as long as information about quality is imperfect and price is used as a signal of quality. Patents are granted for research-based pharmaceuticals and specialty medical devices with the express intention of limiting competition from perfect copies. Nevertheless, the Internet should improve consumers' and payers' information about provider quality (through report cards, for example) and about price dispersion and hence stimulate price competition. Increased price competition seems most likely for the types of medical products that are amenable to B2B exchanges and online auctions, as discussed later.

E-Health Initiatives

E-Health initiatives have been categorized as the "four Cs" of connectivity, content, commerce, and care. In practice, of course, spillovers and joint products make this an arbitrary division; for example, improved connectivity or content can improve care. Moreover, the most successful business models, at least among those that target physicians, are likely to offer con-

tent, connectivity, care support, and commerce in a single integrated interface, in order to provide maximum convenience and ease of operation to
the physician customer. Nevertheless, to understand the various opportunities for savings and the associated strategies of e-health businesses, we
consider the four Cs separately.

Connectivity

Estimates of administrative cost as a percent of total health spending range
widely. The NIPA estimate of administration cost is 5 percent of PCE, but
this estimate omits costs incurred in physicians' offices, hospitals, and other
providers. More generalizable studies estimate 12 to 15 percent, which is in
the range of reasonable estimates.[16] Wide variation in estimates of current
costs and potential savings is not surprising given joint production of
administrative and clinical functions by clerical personnel. Patient time
spent submitting claims is not included in any of the estimates, leading to
a downward bias in estimates of real administrative costs of the health care
system; however, patient time spent in care is also omitted from PCE, so
this bias may not affect the percentage spent on administration.

The connectivity ideal would link providers, payers, and patients in a
seamless system that could in theory reduce clerical staff and paperwork,
reduce physician and patient time spent on administration, and reduce the
incidence of inappropriate and unnecessary care. The components of the
ideal system include online access to
    —electronic medical records (EMR)
    —clinical decision support and payer guidelines, if any
    —prescribing, test ordering, and results reporting
    —real-time verification of reimbursement eligibility
    —claims processing
    —appointment scheduling and referrals
    —patient education and interaction
    —compliance monitoring
In practice, achieving these features in a fully integrated system is some
years away. Significant advances are under way, however, in the separate
components of claims processing, practice management, and medical
records.

---

16. OTA (1995), citing Lewin VHI (1993); Office of the Inspector General (2000) estimates average administrative expenses of 15 percent for managed care organizations.

CLAIMS PROCESSING. The greatest opportunity for cost savings through the Internet may be through processing transactions between providers and insurers, thus reducing billing and reimbursement costs. Many different formats for electronic health claims are currently in use in the United States, and each provider typically submits claims to multiple plans that use different formats. Specialized data clearinghouses have emerged as intermediaries to offer electronic data interchange services that transmit claims from providers to payers in a standardized format over proprietary networks, thereby realizing some savings from consolidation, reduction in personnel and processing time, and reduced error associated with paper claims.[17] EDI (electronic data interchange) providers claim to reduce costs per claim from \$10–\$15 using paper to \$2–\$4 per EDI claim.[18] Web-based connectivity providers charge under \$1 a claim, but there may be an additional monthly charge. Moreover, to the extent that these sites generate revenues from advertising and sponsorship, they may offer these services at less than their full marginal cost.

Most hospitals and insurers have managed to achieve some degree of computerization, but most physician offices and smaller health care entities remain mired in paper-based systems (see table 7-2). Although 62 percent of all claims are processed electronically, only 40 percent of physicians' claims are processed this way, compared with close to 90 percent or more for hospitals and pharmacies. Previous attempts to improve connectivity and coordination of care have had only limited success. Now the Internet provides a missing link, offering connectivity at a lower cost and vastly improved functionality, including greater potential for networking and for sharing more complex data, including eligibility verification and clinical information that has not moved to EDI. Moreover, the Internet permits new ways of outsourcing IT, including remote hosting of software applications by application service providers. The ASP model offers lower hardware and software acquisition costs, lower system maintenance costs, faster implementation time, easier upgrades, and faster deployment over geographic areas. Potential problems include some loss of managerial control

17. Forty percent of the 65 claims clearinghouses surveyed in 2000 received claims via the Internet, compared with 31 percent in 1999. Of those clearinghouses that did not use the Internet, 28 percent said they expected to by the end of 2000. About one-third of responding clearinghouses used the Internet to transmit claims, and 12 percent that did not do so at the time of the survey expected to by the end of 2000. Briggs (2000).

18. Rouse and Chalson (2000, p. 9). Percent of claims filed electronically is from Cohen (1996). See also table 7-2.

and risk of confidentiality. On balance, it seems likely that outsourcing to ASPs will accelerate the adoption of electronic claims processing, practice management, and ultimately other functions, particularly by physician practices and smaller institutions, which may be optimally scaled for care delivery but not for efficient IT implementation.[19] Two factors contributing to the slow uptake of these systems are lack of standardization and the potential for loss of medical privacy. In addition, physicians with existing practice management systems would need to integrate the web service with their existing computers, which would require costly software interfaces over and above the subscription fees.

To address these issues, the HIPAA requires the federal government, through the Department of Health and Human Services (DHHS), to adopt standards for financial and administrative transactions, and data elements for those transactions, including claims and encounter information, health plan enrollment, eligibility, premium payment, and referral certification and authorization. Standards are also to be set for unique identifiers for each individual, employer, health plan, and provider and for security standards to govern health care EDI. For each type of transaction, the standards specify the format, data elements required, and code sets where applicable. Health plans and providers are required to comply within twenty-four months (thirty-six months for small health plans) after the effective date of the final rules (October 2000 for electronic transactions). Providers are not required to use EDI, but if they do, they must comply with the standards. DHHS estimates aggregate HIPAA compliance costs for the administrative simplification rules at $3.5 billion to $4 billion, with additional costs for the privacy regulations (tables 7-2, 7-3).[20] HIPAA should accelerate the conversion to web-based systems, because nationwide standards should expand the potential scale of operations and hence facilitate the entry of online companies, which currently need to gain critical mass separately in each locality. Moreover, faced with the costs of making existing EDI systems HIPAA-compliant, providers may find investment in Internet technologies a lower-cost alternative.

The DHHS estimates the total net savings from the electronic claims regulations at $29.9 billion for the ten-year period ending in 2011, of which

19. Gartner Group, of Stamford, Connecticut, estimates that by 2005 approximately 20 percent of all patients will be using a medical record that resides in an ASP service. See Alan Joch, "EMR the Web Way," eMD Online (www.edotmd.com.s00/cover/htm [Summer 2000]).
20. Industry estimates of compliance costs are as high as $25 billion.

$13.1 billion is predicted to accrue to health plans and $16.7 billion to providers. The discounted present value of these savings is estimated at $19.1 billion, using a 7 percent discount rate. This is the estimated impact of standardization as a result of HIPAA, not the full impact of the switch to electronic claims processing, or the switch from EDI to web-based claims processing. In particular, it assumes that only 11.2 percent of the growth in electronic claims in the ten-year period is attributable to HIPAA. Thus the potential total net savings from switching to web-based claims processing could be nine times larger, or almost $270 billion, undiscounted, over the ten-year period, assuming a similar rate of net savings for the 88.8 percent of switching that is not attributed to HIPAA.[21] The DHHS cost estimates are based on 1999 estimates of the percent of claims that are billed electronically, by provider type, as shown in table 7-2. The estimated savings per claim processed electronically is $1 for health plans, $1.49 for physicians, $0.86 for hospitals, and $0.83 for others.[22] These estimates are based on 1993 data and seem conservative compared with current per-claim charges of Internet companies. Moreover, web-enabling claims processing could yield spillover benefits that encourage adoption of other online technologies. Additional impacts from administrative simplification are also not included. Nor do these estimates of net savings include Medicare and Medicaid, which account for more than 30 percent of total health expenditures.[23] At the same time, these estimates do not reflect possible costs from introducing uniform systems that deter innovation in health plan management. Rigidity in measurement systems may induce rigidity in management systems and slow innovation in insurance design. But if the long-run savings from moving to web-based claims processing is only 10 percent of current administrative expense, that would still be almost 1–2 percent of total health expenditures ($0.1 \times 0.15 = 0.015$). This estimate could be too high or too low, depending on whether the estimated total administrative cost of 12–15 percent of PCE is too high or too low, and on how much of the total administrative cost is represented by claims handling, as opposed to other administrative functions that may be less amenable to moving online, and on the systemwide savings from using the web.

21. This estimate also assumes that the cost savings per percent of automation are constant, whereas in practice there may be increasing or decreasing returns to scale that raise or lower the net savings.

22. Workgroup for Electronic Data Interchange (1993).

23. Early estimates by HCFA projected that the Medicare Transaction System, a new single automated system for processing claims, could save $100 million annually (GAO 1994).

Additional but unmeasured potential savings could be realized from web-based provider-payer links through real-time, online eligibility verification, referral authorization, and claims adjudication (verification from the payer that it will pay for a particular drug or service). Currently, these reimbursement decisions are typically made after the physician has provided the service, prescribed the drug, or made the referral. For example, for a significant fraction of drug prescriptions, the pharmacist calls the physician's office to ask whether an alternative drug can be substituted because the prescribed drug is nonpreferred (has a higher co-payment) on the patient's formulary. Even more costly are the cases where the patient receives expensive services, only to learn that they will not be reimbursed, leading to reclaiming and possibly litigation. Point-of-service eligibility verification could thus save time for providers, patients, pharmacists, and payers and result in better care and less aggravation for all parties.

PRACTICE MANAGEMENT. The management of physician practices has become more complex, with proliferating numbers of plans and payers and the consolidation of physicians into group practices and physician networks. The make-or-buy options for proprietary systems entail high upfront and maintenance costs and high risks. Management services organizations have developed to offer outsourced practice management but have had limited success. The Internet has enabled the development of ASPs, which charge a monthly fee in return for web-based access to remotely hosted practice management applications to handle administrative, financial, and clinical tasks; medical content and product procurement for supplies are possible further extensions of the ASP model. Because the ASP model reduces the need for expensive hardware and software and the staff to maintain it, it reduces the risks associated with large capital investments and facilitates upgrades. This in turn may lead to the automation of some office functions, such as online appointment scheduling and document imaging and storage and hence to some savings in clerical staff or substitution of more skilled information systems staff.

It remains to be seen whether a few national players or various regional players will capture the savings from moving claims processing and other associated business functions online. In addition to the start-up Internet-based companies, the traditional EDI companies are moving their systems online or allying with the Internet companies. For example, WebMD acquired the electronic health transaction firm Envoy Corp., which processes about 1 billion claims a year, mostly over private networks. WebMD plans to switch these claims to the Internet. To increase its physician subscriber base, WebMD has also acquired Medical Manager Corp. and CareInsite, to offer an integrated web portal that interfaces with doctors' existing software systems and can handle interactions with health plans, such as patient-eligibility checks and referrals to specialists. Countering these Internet upstarts, several insurer/health plans (Foundation Health Systems Inc., PacifiCare Health Systems Inc., WellPoint Health Networks Inc., Cigna Corp., and Oxford Health Plans Inc.), which together cover about 30 million people, are collaborating on a unified strategy for Internet-based claims handling, called MedUnite, presumably to avoid the transactions fees charged by the intermediaries. Although collaboration by incumbents might be viewed as a move to deter new entrants, physicians are unlikely to want to get their other services from health plans, hence opportunities for full-service intermediaries are likely to remain. Moreover, since health plans must compete for employer and employee customers and for providers to participate in their networks, competitive pressures should create incentives for adoption of the most efficient alternative or mix of options.

MEDICAL RECORDS. The holy grail of connectivity is the transformation of the current paper-based medical record into an electronic medical record that is accessible to all necessary providers and possibly to the patient. Each provider currently dictates or writes a separate medical record; hence linking these records should eliminate duplicative paperwork, duplicative treatments, and medical errors. A few large hospital systems have implemented proprietary EMRs, but costly failures abound.

Web-enabling the EMR expands the potential users and uses, and several Internet companies have entered this space. For example, MedicaLogic Inc. initially sold only client-server electronic medical records software accessible on private networks (a Windows-based application, Logician). In September 1999 it introduced an Internet-based version, which it leases to physicians on a monthly basis. The clinical and financial advantages of electronic medical records are large and incontrovertible.[24] Nevertheless, the EMR has been slow to catch on for several reasons. Privacy of the medical records remains a concern. Physician inertia is another obstacle, for reasons of cost, limited benefits as long as the network is limited, and process costs associated with changing the way they practice. It may be that, since the costs of installing the legacy paper-based systems are sunk, the marginal

24. Dick, Steen, and Detmer (1997).

operating costs are relatively low, particularly if the personnel who handle the charts also schedule appointments, do the billing, and deal with patients. Even in the longer run, the potential for reduction in clerical staff may be limited unless multiple office functions are simultaneously converted to electronic systems. Moreover, since many physicians are linked into IDNs or networks with other physicians, these systems choices are made at the network rather than the individual physician level.

A necessary step for moving toward large-scale adoption of EMRs with full potential savings is to make data entry easy for physicians. Surveys repeatedly show that physicians will use computerized technologies only if it saves them time. This rules out systems that require the physician to sit at a terminal during a patient encounter, which is less convenient than the current practice of dictating notes during or after the patient encounter or annotating the paper record. The dictated notes may already be transmitted to specialized transcription services, in which case web-enabling the resulting records should be simple. One of these transcription companies, Total eMed, was acquired by MedicaLogic, presumably to encourage adoption of the electronic record by physicians who have already accepted dictating. In addition, MedicaLogic bought Medscape, one of the leading physician content portals, which had some 480,000 physicians registered to use its online services such as access to peer-reviewed journals.[25] Like other leading physician portals, the strategy is to offer physicians a full product line in one package and to encourage physicians who are attracted by one component of the package to try the other components.

Another useful step toward realizing the potential savings from web-enabling medical records is the development of wireless and handheld devices that give physicians access to key information during the patient encounter. Several Internet companies (such as AllScripts and iScribe) already offer software combined with a handheld device to enhance drug prescribing. Using the handheld device, the physician can check the patient's prescription history, insurance coverage, and formulary status of specific drugs and then generate a printed prescription. Under some systems the physician might be able to submit the prescription electronically to a pharmacy of the patient's choice. Most pharmacists are already electronically linked to payers for reimbursement processing. By eliminating the time-wasters for physicians of phone calls from pharmacists or patients, online prescribing devices may be

25. Telephone conversation with Rick Turoczy, manager, Corporate Marketing, MedicaLogic, January 12, 2001.

more rapidly adopted by physicians than the complete EMR. One estimate is that 9 percent of prescription dollars will be prescribed using these devices by 2004.[26] The three largest pharmacy benefit management companies recently announced a joint venture (called "Rxhub") to develop an electronic exchange to facilitate online prescribing.[27]

Potential savings from online prescribing devices include time saved for physicians, patients, and pharmacists, and reductions in inappropriate prescribing with its associated costs. A recent study reported that the use of a real-time, integrated clinical information system in a major hospital led to challenging and subsequently changing 386 orders a day, an 81 percent decline in medical errors (such as the wrong drug or wrong dose), in addition to a reduction in unnecessary lab tests, a shorter average length of stay, and lower mortality rates.[28] The percent of hospital staff and physicians with access to the Internet is increasing rapidly, creating the necessary customer base for ASP-hosted applications.

Content

Content portals, which offer free access to clinical information for providers and patients, can be viewed as a market response to the problems of imperfect information and costly search, which is the root cause of many inefficiencies in health care. The effects of this information explosion are probably large but are hard to predict, much less to quantify. Since medical content is usually provided free to the user, its value to the user is not reflected in the expenditure-based NIPA accounts. Content sites are financed largely by site sponsorship and advertising revenues, which appear as expenses in the accounts of sponsoring firms, such as pharmaceutical companies. One implication of the heavy reliance on advertising is that the products of the sponsoring companies are somewhat misrepresented in the national accounts: in this case the drug company provides not only drugs and drug advertising, but also general medical information to patients and physicians. Of course, the problem of unmeasured e-content services is not unique to health care. Because of obvious measurement problems, the Census Bureau is not planning to attempt to measure the output of free e-commerce services.[29] Even if an Internet site's revenues were captured by

26. Boehm (1999); Rind and others (1997).

27. Ann Carms, "Trio of Big Pharmacy-Benefit Managers Announce Plans for Electronic Exchange," *Wall Street Journal,* February 23, 2001, p. B11.

28. Bates and others (1998).

29. Fraumeni, Lawson, and Ehemann (1999).

Census surveys, they would likely be attributed to e-commerce rather than to health care.

PHYSICIAN PORTALS. The Internet significantly reduces the time and money costs physicians face to keep up with new medical technologies and new evidence on the effectiveness of new and old technologies. Several sites provide online access to a wide range of medical journals, practice guide-lines, and protocols from respected sources; online programs for continu-ing medical education; and business training for practice management. Decision support tools are available to facilitate the interpretation of symp-toms, diagnosis, and selection of treatment options. Despite some resis-tance to "cookbook medicine," these tools are likely to be increasingly used if they are available on handheld devices for use in real-time treatment decisions.

These online information tools should increase physicians' productivity in producing real health, assuming that better information leads to more accurate diagnoses, better treatment choices, and improved implementa-tion. Rough estimates of the potential savings from improved physician information might be derived from estimates of the welfare loss from vari-ations in medical practices.[30] Physician productivity, however, measured by visits per hour or per week, could increase or decrease. Fees per visit are unlikely to fall, assuming that quality is improved. Moreover any potential time savings for physicians may be offset by increased demands from patients, in response to consumer content sites.

CONSUMER INFORMATION PORTALS. Some 24.8 million U.S. adults, or 43 percent of Internet users, used the Internet for health information in 1999, and this group is growing rapidly, served by more than one thousand Internet sites dedicated to healthcare.[31] Consumer information portals offer free information on wellness and disease, treatment options and providers, chat rooms and illness support groups, and programs for life-style management.[32]

There are serious concerns that this "information" is often incomplete, misleading, or wrong; the heavy reliance of many of these sites on adver-tising and sponsorship revenues also raises questions of bias. Several pres-tigious providers and professional associations, including the Mayo Clinic

30. Phelps (1992).

31. Rouse and Chalson (2000), citing CyberDialogue, reports several thousand health Internet sites; other estimates are lower. Definition is obviously an issue, as well as turnover and consolidation.

32. A Pew poll found that web surfers use the web more frequently to seek medical information than any other kind of information. "Web Users Search for Medical Advice Most Often," *Wall Street Journal*, November 27, 2000, p. B14.

and Johns Hopkins University, have entered this space, capitalizing on their reputations to signal credibility and quality. One nonprofit foundation, Health On the Net, has a system of voluntary certification (HONcode) to signify compliance with standards for reliability of information, for distinguishing content from advertising, and for ensuring customer privacy. The other route to establishing "brand-name" recognition (and at the same time gain viewers and hence advertising revenues) is through media alliances (such as WebMD with CNN; Medscape with CBS; drkoop.com with AOL). The net effect of opening the floodgates of free medical information will surely be that consumers will become better informed about their medical conditions, possible treatment options, and their choice of providers.

Better consumer information could increase both measured and real productivity of the health care sector in several ways. First, informed consumers should be more productive participants in the care process, with more appropriate initiation of care, better choice of providers, better compliance with treatment regimens, and better understanding of the role of life-style modifications. Second, using disease and product-specific information, suppliers are able to target their product advertising to consumers with relevant health needs, thereby improving advertising efficiency. Pharmaceutical companies also use these mechanisms to target patient recruitment for clinical trials.

Third, increased patient information could increase or decrease the productivity of physicians. On one hand, a more informed consumer can better control a physician who is an imperfect agent. On the other hand, a patient who is misinformed but who wants to be a partner in the decision process may actually increase the physician time required per visit. This additional time spent in discussion does not generally result in additional reimbursement under current fee schedules and may be one reason why some physicians do not welcome the more "informed" patient. Some portals offer physicians their own physician-specific web pages that can be used for selecting the information sources that they recommend to their patients, so that physicians can at least try to steer the patient searching for information in directions that will increase rather than reduce the productivity of the encounter. Sharing of the patient record, scheduling, and reporting test results are other options.

Better-informed consumers may stimulate better price and quality competition. Payers and regulators have initiated systems for generating report cards on provider quality, but the Internet makes them readily accessible to patients, which in turn should increase providers' incentives to meet quality standards drawn up by the National Committee for Quality Assurance. HealthGrades.com offers direct consumer rating of physicians, hospitals, and health plans. Virtual communities and discussion groups (such as HealthGate.com) also facilitate informal sharing of "reputation" information about providers. Lower consumer search costs could in theory reduce the price of physician services.[33] More competition on quality is another possible effect.

The effect of the information explosion on total health care expenditures is uncertain. Increased consumer awareness of symptoms and ability to recognize treatable diseases could in theory lead to substitution of self-care, prevention, or nontraditional treatment options. However, advertisers will continue to sponsor content sites only if the combined effect of the information plus the advertising increases demand for their products. Internet advertising of health care products has been predicted to grow rapidly. Jupiter Communications projects growth will rise from $100 million in 1999 to more than $700 million in 2004. Since half of the Internet health care advertising is for pharmaceutical products, this estimate suggests an increase from $50 million in 1999 to $350 million for pharmaceuticals in 2004. Skila Health Report estimates that online pharmaceutical product marketing of only $11 million in 1998 (just over 1 percent of total pharmaceutical direct-to-consumer spending) would grow to $890 million in 2002.[34] If use of online medical content indirectly increases the demand for drugs, this may generate additional physician visits to get the necessary prescriptions. Although the Internet is still a small fraction of direct-to-consumer advertising, its share is projected to grow, relative to TV and paper ads, because of its lower cost and better targeting capabilities.

In the long run, improved consumer access to self-education health resources must surely improve real health care productivity, through improved self-care and more productive interactions between patients and physicians, and because less asymmetric information will reduce the potential for inappropriate and unnecessary care and possibly reduce prices, adjusted for quality. Nevertheless, overall expenditure on health services seems likely to increase, particularly for advertised products. There may be concerns that the "digital divide" will exacerbate inequities in access to

---

33. Pauly and Satterthwaite (1981) find some empirical evidence of this.
34. These estimates appear in Rouse and Chalson (2000, pp. 16, 18).

quality health care for those without connections to the web. Conversely, the Internet may serve as an equalizer. The uninsured may have relatively better access to the free information that is offered over the Internet than they have to the information that requires a visit to the doctor, for which they would pay a higher out-of-pocket cost than would those who have health insurance.

Commerce

E-commerce promises significant potential savings in the purchase of supplies used in the health care industry, although estimates of those savings vary considerably. Savings generated by business-to-consumer e-commerce, such as the purchase of prescriptions or insurance over the Internet, are likely to be much more limited.

B2B COMMERCE. Business-to-business e-commerce offers significant potential savings in supply chain costs to institutional purchasers, including hospitals, integrated delivery networks, physician offices, ambulatory surgery centers and clinics, and long-term care facilities. A large hospital may buy 100,000 items in a year, including medical-surgical supplies, radiology and laboratory supplies, medical devices (such as stents and implants), nonretail pharmaceuticals, and capital equipment, as well as standard items such as food, office supplies, and cleaning and laundry supplies and services. Structurally, the medical products supply sector is fairly concentrated: the five largest manufacturers serve 90 percent of the world's hospitals and provide 70 percent of an average hospital's purchases, but there are a large number of smaller firms and potential entrants.[35]

With more than 5,000 hospitals and 400,000 physicians, plus home health, long-term care, and other providers, the customer base is highly fragmented. This fragmentation has been partly overcome through group purchasing organizations (GPOs) in the hospital, nursing home, and other sectors. These GPOs consolidate buying power to negotiate discounted prices from manufacturers in return for shifting market share to their products and to negotiate product delivery from distributors.[36] Distribution of medical supplies and pharmaceuticals is also concentrated, with a four-

35. Margaret Ann Cross, "Supply Giants Make an Internet Splash," *Internet Health Care Magazine,* May/June 2000, p.10.

36. The GPO power to shift share is limited, however, because GPOs lack enforcement power over their members, who continue to purchase significant fractions of their business off contract.

firm concentration ratio of roughly 75 percent. This reflects significant consolidation in recent years to take advantage of economies of scale in inventory management, EDI processing, and distribution and in offering customers a full product line. Specialty medical equipment and devices are often delivered directly by the manufacturer because personal relationships with the physician customers are important.

Estimates of expenditures on health care supplies range from $100 billion to $200 billion a year, depending on what is included. A widely cited study called Efficient Health Care Response (EHCR), based on 1995 data, estimated supply chain costs at 10 percent of personal health expenditures, or $83 billion in 1995, including costs borne by manufacturers (33 percent), distributors (26 percent) and providers (41 percent).[37] Based on this study, total expenditures are projected at $200 billion, of which $85 billion is medical and surgical supplies, $13 billion is nonretail pharmaceuticals, and $102 billion is office, food, and cleaning supplies and services.[38]

Estimates of the fraction of total costs accounted for by process, rather than product, costs range from just over one-fourth to one-half. The EHCR study reports process costs at $23 billion, or 28 percent of the total, including order management (37 percent), inventory management (25 percent), transportation (24 percent), and physical distribution (14 percent).[39] A more recent survey reports that for some IDN members, supply expenditures (excluding office, food, and cleaning) account for 10–15 percent of their total budget, of which 30–50 percent are medical-surgical supply costs,15–23 percent are pharmacy costs, and 11–24 percent are equipment costs. If processing costs are included, total supply chain costs increase to 25–30 percent of total budget, which suggests that processing is at least 50 percent of the total supply chain cost.[40] Clerical and other personnel often perform multiple functions in addition to supplies processing; hence identifying the marginal cost of supply processing may be difficult, leading to over- or underestimates. It is also likely that this cost of supplies processing is included in the estimate of total administrative cost at 15 percent of health spending.

37. EHCR (1996).
38. Marhula and Shannon (2000, p. 33). Applying the 10 percent to 1999 PCE yields roughly $100 billion for supply chain costs.
39. EHCR (1996).
40. Burns and others (2000, pp. 5–6).

A commonly used basis for estimating the savings from B2B e-commerce is still the EHCR estimate that 49 percent of the $23 billion processing cost (or $11 billion) could be eliminated. More than half of this estimated cost saving came from efficient product movement, and the remainder was from information sharing and order management. Updating these figures by applying the same percentages to 1999 PCE would yield an estimated gross savings of $14 billion before deducting costs of implementation of electronic processing.

Simply updating the EHCR estimate to 2000 levels is unlikely, however, to provide a reliable projection for potential B2B savings going forward. The estimate was based on a comparison of best practices to actual practice in 1995, before the development of web-based processes. Since then, both actual and best possible practices have changed, and the future potential savings could be larger or smaller than 49 percent of current costs. The fact that some savings have already been realized through consolidation of manufacturers, distributors, and providers and that proprietary EDI networks as well as some Internet business have been widely adopted all suggest a smaller potential savings going forward. The five distributors, who collectively process $80 billion annually, or 70 percent of the medical products used by hospitals, physicians, and nursing homes, handled 90 percent of this processing electronically, using proprietary EDI or the Internet.[41] But another survey estimated only $2 billion in commerce-related online business transactions in 1999.[42] These discrepancies may reflect the facts that purchasers have a much lower rate of online order processing than do intermediaries and that much of the intermediary EDI is probably still proprietary rather than Internet-based.

By one estimate, a phone or fax order costs $0.63 a line to enter, an EDI order costs $0.03 a line, and the Internet reduces this to $0.01 or less. Thus web-enabling existing EDI systems may yield only modest additional savings to distributors. But these estimates ignore the potential systemwide savings attributable to network and price reduction effects from Internet-based transactions. In addition, the Internet should accelerate the conversion to electronic purchasing by providers, which still largely use paper, phone, and fax for order entry. For hospitals, ordering is poorly coordinated not only between the largely autonomous departments, but also with

41. Burns and others (2000).
42. Boehm (1999). It is unclear whether this survey includes only Internet activity or also proprietary EDI.

inventory management, and inventories are often excessive. In a recent survey of chief information officers of hospitals and integrated systems, only one reported already ordering supplies online, 31 percent of the 213 respondents said that they planned to begin online ordering in 2000, and another 12 percent predicted that they would move to online supply ordering within two years.[43] Online ordering presumably occurs even less in smaller institutions and in physician offices, where supplies account for only 11 percent of practice expense.[44] Given the advances in web-based technologies but the lag in adoption, it is possible that the gap between actual practice and current best practice is even greater than in 1995. If that is the case, then the potential savings from B2B e-commerce looking forward from 2000 could be greater than the 1995 estimate of 49 percent of processing costs. Some analysts, however, estimate only 25 percent savings from use of B2B by hospitals.[45]

The pace of competitive entry in the e-health B2B space suggests that many see potential opportunities. New online product procurement companies, such as Neoforma.com and Medibuy.com, offer connectivity and an ASP model to link buyers to a large pool of vendors, using either catalogue or auction models, which should offer savings in processing costs and in lower prices. Online ordering should reduce paper, fax, phone, and personnel costs; automated inventory tracking and replenishment systems avoid waste or inadequate inventory levels and off-contract ordering; and invoice disputes should decrease. Some companies focus on specific product lines or market opportunities; for example, one component may provide an exchange for medical supplies between providers and wholesalers, while another component links manufacturers and wholesalers.

Although analysts estimate significant potential savings from online ordering, the fact that providers have not rushed at the opportunity suggests that significant obstacles remain. These include the decentralized administrative structure of hospitals; incompatible legacy systems in the different components of IDNs; and reluctance to invest in the systems and

43. Howard J. Anderson, "CIOs Forecast a Boom in Internet Activity," *Internet Health Care Magazine,* May/June 2000. Of the 65 percent of hospitals with websites, the most common offerings were information about the organization, a directory of physicians and e-mail; 40 percent offer patient education material, 26 percent physician referral transactions, and less than 15 percent offered physician access to records, drug interaction guides, physician ordering of tests and reporting of results. Only 2 percent offered appointment scheduling or patient access to records.

44. Boehm (1999).

45. Burns and others (2000, p. 18).

process reengineering at a time when many have difficulty covering operating costs in the wake of federal cuts in reimbursement levels, the growth of managed care, and the need to comply with HIPAA. But several factors should facilitate adoption of web-based systems. First, the flat or declining pricing environment facing hospitals and other providers implies strong pressure to reduce costs. Second, the growth of ASP options permits outsourcing of the IT responsibility, an attractive option for providers because subscription pricing transfers fixed costs and risk from the purchaser to the ASP supplier. Because fewer privacy concerns are involved in purchasing supplies than in sharing clinical records, ASP models may be adopted first for these B2B functions. Third, the development of standards and the activities of the GPO, distributor, and vendor exchanges should reduce the costs and increase the returns to making the necessary investments. Small scale and low capitalization is likely to slow the switch to online ordering for smaller hospitals, nursing homes, and physician offices unless online purchasing of basic supplies becomes simply one component of standard practice management software.

The price reduction potential from B2B in health care differs across the range of products. Prices for basic supplies and disposables, such as rubber gloves, bandages, and some generic pharmaceuticals, are reportedly already at competitive levels. Online catalogs and auctions may permit some price reductions by facilitating further price comparisons, expanding the possible sources of supply, and eliminating supply mismatches. Leading GPOs and their e-commerce affiliates (including Premier/Medibuy, Novation/Neoforma, Consorta, and HealthTrust Purchasing Group) have recently formed the Coalition for Healthcare Standards to develop common standards, including universal product numbers, for ordering medical, surgical, and other nonpharmaceutical products on Internet exchanges. As this push for transparent catalogue pricing proceeds, one unresolved question is whether actual transactions prices will also converge. Traditionally, manufacturers give discounts ("chargebacks") to large GPOs that are able to move market share toward their products. Essentially, this discount system permits manufacturers to segment the market and charge different prices based on buyer demand elasticity, as reflected in ability to move share.[46] Such price differences benefit large purchasers as well as the

---

46. For analogous price differences for pharmaceuticals sold for the outpatient sector, see Danzon (1998).

manufacturers, so they may see less advantage in an open exchange system in which prices are at some intermediate level without discounts. If so, large hospital systems may do better by ordering directly from manufacturers, bypassing the GPOs, whose intermediation value is reduced once the web reduces the costs of comparison shopping and order entry. In contrast to the GPOs, the distributors seem more likely to survive, since they perform essential logistics and inventory management functions.

High-end specialty medical devices often have larger margins over marginal cost, reflecting product differentiation, patents, and the costs of research and development. An important obstacle to pure price competition for these products is the role of specialist physicians in selecting the products that they use based not only on price, but also on quality and follow-up service, including having the technician-salesperson present in the operating room when the device is inserted. Because the product life-cycle for many of these devices is shortened by the rapid introduction of new improved generations, price pressure from B2B may be significant for products of older vintage. Similar considerations apply to used capital equipment, for which online auctions may create a significant global marketplace.

The battle is on for the control of the Internet-based health care supply chain, and the long run structure remains uncertain. A number of start-up B2B firms (such as Medibuy, Neoforma, and Broadlane) offer online catalogs and electronic invoices and purchase orders, thereby threatening the traditional turf of the GPOs. Not surprisingly, the major GPOs or their parent hospitals have taken over or formed alliances with these B2B firms, with the GPOs gaining access to the online technology while the B2B firms gain access to the GPO's customer base. For example, two major hospital chains, Columbia/HCA and Premier, are allied with Medibuy, which acquired empactHealth; Tenet, another large hospital chain, partnered through its GPO BuyPower with online supplier Chemdex to form Broadlane Inc.; and Novation, a large nonprofit GPO, awarded an exclusive e-commerce contract to Neoforma in return for a large ownership stake in Neoforma.

In response to this activity of purchasers—who threaten to intensify price comparisons while charging vendors 5–8 percent fees for processing orders—the leading supply and device manufacturers (J&J, GE, Baxter, Medtronic, and Abbott) in March 2000 announced plans for a "Global Health Care Exchange." The exchange, which is to be open to any company that makes hospital products, will serve as a single site where purchasers can execute and track their transactions. The exchange will not set prices or conduct auctions. Pricing and purchase terms must be settled with the manufacturer separately.

The leading distributors (Amerisource, Cardinal Health, FisherScientific, McKesson/HBOC, and Owens&Minor) have countered with an online industry consortium (HealthNexis) for purchasing drugs, supplies, and laboratory products, in competition with GPO and supplier exchanges. The distributors aim in particular to establish standard product information and simplify the rebate program, in addition to offering online catalogs, order entry, and processing. Competition among these initiatives, combined with standardization, should accelerate the adoption of online purchasing, at least by the larger institutions. Full adoption of a web-based supply chain by the smaller institutions is likely to take several years.

The resulting savings in clerical and inventory costs and possibly some supply price reductions could in theory reduce service fees charged by hospitals, physicians, and other institutional providers, particularly for those services with a significant supply content. In practice, however, the savings as a percent of the total costs is small, so the potential price reduction is probably small. Moreover, any savings may be offset by increased adoption of other new medical technologies, depending on incentives for price competition as opposed to competition on the basis of technology or quality. In that case, real health productivity may increase, but productivity as measured in the national accounts may remain unchanged or fall. To the extent that online purchasing results in disintermediation, with manufacturers shipping directly to the end-user rather than through distributors, shipping costs may appear as income to transportation companies such as Federal Express or UPS rather than as income to health care distributors.

B2C COMMERCE. Business-to-consumer (B2C) e-commerce is concentrated in prescription and over-the-counter pharmaceuticals, medical supplies, health and beauty aids, vitamins, and supplements. One estimate put total B2C at $440 million in 1999 (7 percent of total online health transactions), and projected it would grow to $22 billion in 2004.[47] Other estimates of current B2C commerce are much lower, at $81 million.[48] Estimates of online prescription drug sales in 1999 range from $6 million to $40 million. The federal government has proposed a plan to regulate

---

47. Boehm (1999).
48. Rouse and Chalson (2000, p. 21).

online pharmacies more closely, but it has not yet been implemented; so far, the only control on online sales is a voluntary certification program operated by the National Association of Boards of Pharmacy. The concerns include illegal online prescriptions issued without appropriate medical exam; substandard and counterfeit products; and (from a supplier perspective) imported products at prices that undercut U.S. price levels.

Although there were at least thirty online drugstores, the stand-alone online drugstore is arguably a flawed business model if it is focused solely on the legal supply of prescription drugs. Consumers cannot legally purchase prescription drugs without a physician's prescription, and if the consumer has insurance coverage, the transaction must somehow trigger reimbursement from the payer to the pharmacist. (Over-the-counter drugs, which do not require a prescription and are typically not reimbursed are a small but growing share of total pharmaceutical expenditures.) Not surprisingly, the leading online pharmacies have either been acquired by or aligned with the bricks-and-mortar pharmacies, which deliver the drugs, and with pharmacy benefit managers (PBMs), which represent the payers, negotiate discounted prices, and reimburse the pharmacy. For example, the drug store chain CVS purchased Soma.com, an online pharmacy, and aligned with the PBM Merck-Medco. Another PBM, Express Scripts, purchased part of the online PlanetRx, which is aligned with distributor McKesson. Ultimately, multiparty agreements seem more likely, assuming that online pharmacies will want to give consumers access to their PBM and their neighborhood pharmacy, whichever that may be.

The savings from online prescriptions are limited until physician prescriptions can be transmitted directly online to the pharmacy, eliminating the need for the patient to take a paper script to the pharmacy. Exceptions are chronic medications (34 percent) and refill prescriptions (estimated at 50 percent of all prescriptions, presumably including chronic medications).[49] Many PBMs already handle these drugs through mail order, however, which permits the PBM to save the pharmacy dispensing fee, to substitute a lower-cost drug where possible, and to reduce the time costs for the patient. Online pharmacies thus offer little in addition to existing mail order services, at least until the physician prescription is transmitted directly online to the pharmacy. Online prescribing combined with online pharmacies will offer significant savings in physician and patient time, plus reduced medical error. For purposes of national accounts, consumer time

49. Rouse and Chalson (2000, p. 20).

savings will not be captured; rather, they may show up as increased expenditures on overnight and other delivery companies, as in the case of mail order.

Given these obstacles to buying prescription drugs directly over the Internet, it is not surprising that a major share of sales of online pharmacies are vitamins, nutraceuticals, over-the-counter drugs, and health and beauty aids, for which prescriptions and reimbursement are not an issue.[50] Online pharmacies, like other consumer portals, are likely to derive their revenue partly from advertisers such as pharmaceutical companies, which may find this a cost-effective medium for targeting specific patient subgroups and for recruiting patients for clinical trials.

ONLINE INSURANCE PURCHASING. The potential savings from online purchase of health insurance are probably small. Although web-based insurance distribution has potential to reduce costs relative to traditional agency distribution, significant scale economies have already been realized for most health insurance because of employer sponsorship. Roughly 80 percent of private health insurance is obtained through employment, which significantly reduces the costs related to selling and enrollment and eliminates costs related to medical underwriting, at least for medium and large groups. Employers may reap some savings from using the web to comparison shop for health insurance products and from moving their employee benefit functions online, using the web to give employees information about health insurance options and to streamline the open enrollment process. The potential for online purchasing of individual insurance is limited to those who do not receive health insurance through their employer and to supplementary and disability policies.

The potential savings from e-health insurance would be larger if employers follow through on threats to drop their group plans or convert them to defined contribution plans, in which they make a fixed contribution to each eligible employee but leave the employee considerable autonomy in choosing how that contribution is spent. Some start-up companies are developing products that offer alternative networks of physicians to employees with these plans. Another potential use for e-health insurance is the Medicare+Choice program, which offers seniors the choice of private health plans as an alternative to the traditional Medicare plan. Similarly, if

---

50. There are online pharmacies that sell drugs either without a prescription or with the prescription available after the consumer responds to a few questions online. This phenomenon is likely to be confined to so-called "life-style" drugs, such as Viagra (for erectile dysfunction) or products for baldness, weight reduction, and the like, which are less likely to be covered by insurance.

a Medicare prescription drug benefit is added in a form that offers choice to seniors, the web could be a useful vehicle for disseminating information on plan options and handling enrollment.

Currently available business models illustrate these alternatives, including defined contribution plans with community healthcare exchanges (MyHealthBank.com); cafeteria-style health plans allowing the beneficiary to build his or her own provider panel within an employer-budget constraint (Vivius.com); online brokers of health plans to employers with online auction for managed care organizations to bid for employer contracts (Sageo.com); online medical savings accounts (HealtheCare.com); and high-deductible catastrophic coverage for individuals (eHealthInsurance.com)

One issue facing insurance providers in any medium is the risk of adverse selection. Online distribution lacks the personal interview and even the phone conversation, which insurers may use to obtain health risk information. Nevertheless, online enrollment may achieve more positive selection than insurance that is sold over the phone, if high risk individuals are reluctant to report their conditions over the Internet, or if those who use the Internet are on average better educated and have higher income, factors that tend to be positively correlated with health. Online insurers may also choose not to operate in states that require guaranteed issue and community rating (that is, the insurer must take all applicants at standard rates).

Care: E-Medicine

The Internet offers several new production possibilities for health care, although regulations constrain the practice of medicine online.

The online provision of care by physicians to patients seems likely to be limited to various uses of clinical messaging (e-mail) such as online health questionnaires, requests for a prescription refill, a specialist referral, or feedback for follow-up purposes. Although surveys vary widely, one reports that only 10 percent of physicians say they use e-mail to interact with patients.[51] E-mail is more likely to substitute for phone calls than for visits, however, not only because of the importance of the physical exam, but also because of liability risks. Moreover, payers may be reluctant to reimburse for e-mail "visits" if these are more prone to patient moral hazard and

---

51. (www.medem.com/Corporate/press/corporate_medeminthenews_press023.cfm); Westberg and Miller (1999).

harder to monitor for appropriateness, and physicians may be concerned about responding to unnecessary e-mail visits, once travel time is eliminated as a cost to the patient. Some health plans offer interactive gatekeeper or call centers that handle simple questions. This could increase physician productivity, by reserving the physician/patient encounter to address more serious questions.

Patient participation in health production may be enhanced through online monitoring and post-treatment disease education and management, and through self-care. Some health plans encourage patients to complete online risk assessments, track their own health status in a personal database, and interact with the plan to monitor compliance, for example, with drug regimens. More generally, the Internet should reduce the cost and improve the effectiveness of disease management programs that are operated by health plans, pharmaceutical companies, hospital systems, and others. These programs target patients with chronic conditions such as diabetes and asthma, who account for a large and growing fraction of total health spending. Patient compliance with basic regimens, such as glucose monitoring, can avert costly acute episodes.

Care-related savings from use of online medical records and online prescribing have already been discussed. More generally—and even harder to measure—the Internet may accelerate the diffusion of new technologies such as new surgical techniques, by increasing awareness of and education in using the new techniques. Since new technology is the main driver of rising health care spending, this acceleration could stimulate spending growth, to the extent that lack of knowledge is the binding constraint on diffusion. This impact will be less if the binding constraints are more often lack of third-party reimbursement or the insufficient scale of smaller hospitals and physician offices to support capital expenditures in the technology.

Internet-based telemedicine may increase access to both physician visits and some specialty care in remote locations, prisons, and in other situations where patients and providers cannot easily meet face to face.[52] Centers of excellence in highly specialized fields may expand their market reach through the Internet. An example is teleradiology, which offers remote reading of diagnostic tests. In general, however, the much-touted boom of telemedicine seems to have fallen flat, and health care delivery remains a predominantly local industry.

52. See Darkins and Cary (2000) for an overview on telemedicine; also Mandl, Kohane, and Brandt (1998).

Online clinical decision support using expert systems has already been discussed. Online access to clinical data repositories for measuring and monitoring outcomes not only serves to inform consumers, as discussed earlier, but also provides a knowledge base and incentives for providers to benchmark and improve quality of care. Several states have mandated the collection of hospital discharge data through health data organizations for provider report cards and population-based outcomes research.[53] Hospitals and insurers create data warehouses to profile physician-specific practice patterns, identify performance improvement opportunities, and define clinical pathways.

The Internet facilitates such data collection and dissemination. Other obstacles to dissemination remain, however, including conflict over data ownership and incentives for institutions to use IT and knowledge management as a strategic weapon to gain competitive advantage. There may be a conflict between the need for proprietary intellectual property rights, in order to encourage innovation, and the "public good" interest in the widest possible dissemination of information, for example, on outcomes and best practices. Greater knowledge that improves real health productivity from given resources will not be reflected in national accounts, whereas data collection and mining costs may show up in the costs of hospitals, physicians, or employee benefits managers.

The Internet and the Pharmaceutical Industry

Pharmaceuticals account for about 10 percent of health expenditures and have been the most rapidly growing component in recent years. The growth has been driven primarily by increased insurance coverage, leading to more prescriptions and patient switching from older, less costly drugs to newer, more effective, or more convenient products that are often more expensive. The impact of the Internet on the pharmaceutical industry—particularly on its research and marketing practices—is somewhat different than for service-oriented medical providers and is therefore discussed here briefly.

The cost of bringing a new drug to market has been estimated at more than $500 million, including the costs of failures and interest costs over the twelve or so years of the research and development (R&D) process. Drug discovery has been revolutionized in recent years, moving from a random search for active compounds toward rational drug design, based on

53. Donaldson, Lohr, and Bulger (1994).

genomics and microbiology and using technology intensive tools such as combinatorial chemistry, high throughput screening, and robotics. The most costly part of R&D is development, which includes refining the formulation and dosage of a promising drug candidate, then testing in human clinical trials to demonstrate safety and efficacy, subject to approval by the Food and Drug Administration (FDA) in the United States and similar regulatory bodies around the world. These trials are often global and on average take more than six years and tens or hundreds of millions of dollars, plus forgone interest on the funds invested and loss of patent life attributable to delay in launch.[54]

The Internet may reduce these high costs of drug R&D in several ways. The new tools of drug discovery are extremely data intensive, and the Internet facilitates the efficient management and manipulation of data. Enrolling patients and physician investigators for trials through disease-specific websites could cut several months off the typical time required. Even bigger savings could be realized if data collection during trials could be moved online, with electronic submission initially from clinical investigators worldwide to the host company, and then from the company to the FDA, yielding savings in clerical time, paperwork, and data error. B2B procurement of supplies for drug manufacturing and other operations should save administrative costs and possibly reduce some supply prices though online bidding, similar to B2B in other industries.

Pharmaceutical marketing has traditionally focused on "detailing" of individual physicians by trained representatives. This is an enormously costly and time-consuming way of getting information and samples to physicians. Many physicians limit the encounter to one or two minutes per representative, and some health plans do not permit such detailing. Online physician detailing and symposiums could potentially reduce the drug company's costs of detailing; for the physician, time costs may be the same but scheduling of the online detail could be more convenient. Since regulations on direct-to-consumer (DTC) advertising were relaxed in 1997, DTC advertising has expanded rapidly through all media forms. As already noted, online DTC advertising on disease-specific websites lowers advertising costs to pharmaceutical companies while allowing them to target patients more effectively.

These uses of the Internet to increase efficiency in R&D and marketing should in principle reduce the cost of developing and marketing a given drug. This tendency for cost reduction per drug may be offset by changes

---

54. Pharmaceutical Research and Manufacturers Association (2000).

in the type and cost of drugs produced; for example, genomics and bio-informatics make possible the development of drugs that were inconceivable under traditional discovery methods, leading to higher failure rates and costs, at least initially. Similarly, Internet-based marketing may be used as a complement rather than a substitute for other forms of marketing, leading to higher total sales for a given drug. If so, real health of patients should increase, but total expenditure on drugs is also likely to increase.

The Economic Impact of E-Health on Competition

The effect of Internet initiatives on competition in health care can be related to each of the four Cs. At a minimum, the start-up Internet firms put competitive pressure on incumbents in several areas. More broadly, Internet and other information technology strategies may offer new ways for providers, suppliers, and payers to compete on price and quality.

The start-up Internet firms that use the ASP model to offer claims processing to physicians and hospitals may not yet be a significant competitive threat to incumbent EDI providers, but that could change as more health care providers and payers sign up and network effects take hold. HIPAA-based standardization may be a significant impetus to this trend. Established EDI providers are responding to the new source of competition by developing their own web-enabled systems. Whoever the winning players are, it seems likely that ultimately the winning products will be those that offer the physician's office a full product line in a single package that includes claims processing; some electronic medical records; access to web-based content and decision support; online prescribing, scheduling, and referrals; interactions with patients through e-mail; and interactions with other network participants. Winning systems are also likely to be open to adding on new, specialized products as they are developed. Because proprietary EDI systems have less flexibility in adding new and more complex products, web-based products are likely to dominate. The one possible exception to this is the electronic medical record. For this clinical information, privacy is a greater concern and the web-based ASP model is more vulnerable than proprietary systems. But given the cost savings and convenience of a single product suite, it seems likely that the medical record will ultimately be included in the web-based product portfolio for physicians' offices, once the other components are widely available and in use. Widespread adoption of the single product suite ASP model may be several years away, but if it is widely adopted, the overall systemwide savings could be billions of dollars a year from reduced administrative cost; less medical error and unnecessary care; and more productive physicians, office personnel, and patients. Of course, the savings to the health care system could be less, to the extent that the vendors of these services capture part of the savings through their pricing strategies. But these markets seem highly contestable, so competitive entry should reduce prices to competitive levels and possibly lower, if advertising remains an important source of site revenues.

The Internet may stimulate competition between providers, as report cards and chat rooms disseminate information about perceived quality. Some physicians may also compete by offering Internet services, such as e-mail and online appointment scheduling, or by offering websites with patient-targeted content that they are willing to discuss during visits. In general, there may be both quality competition and price competition, with net effects uncertain.

Large hospitals and IDNs may be able to support the fixed costs of proprietary systems. If these can be used to improve care quality, through reduced medical and prescription error and better clinical protocols, they can significantly reduce costs and gain at least a medium-term competitive advantage on both cost and quality, relative to competitors that have inferior information management systems. Indeed, now that the potential savings from reducing inpatient days have been largely exhausted, achieving significant cost reductions will require changing practice styles to eliminate waste, error, and suboptimal practices. These potential savings in clinical costs are likely to yield sustainable competitive advantage; by contrast, savings in administrative costs from moving to web-based claims processing or B2B procurement could yield large, ongoing cost savings, but these are accessible to all competitors and thus will not give a sustainable competitive advantage to any single firm.

The start-up B2B firms that offer online catalog and auction models for supply sourcing are posing a significant competitive threat to the GPOs. The B2B firms offer hospitals and other institutions the opportunity to move to web-based supplies procurement, thereby cutting their processing costs in addition to possibly getting lower prices than the GPOs can negotiate. Thus in the long run GPO functions seem likely to be absorbed by web-based marketplaces or exchanges, whether run by the GPOs or by start-up Internet competitors.

The use of online catalog and auction models will stimulate competition in the medical supply sector, with the greatest effects likely for product lines where quality differences are small and price competition predominates and can intensify; lesser effects are likely for the highly specialized devices. Similarly for pharmaceuticals, online catalogs and auctions may stimulate even more price competition for multisource, off-patent products with several generic producers. For on-patent, single-source drugs, aggressive price competition is more likely in therapeutic classes with multiple compounds with the same mode of action and very similar effect profiles than in therapeutic classes where each compound has significantly different effects or side-effects.

The Economic Effect of E-Health on Productivity

The production function of health H embeds the production functions of the various medical services, $M_1 \ldots M_n$, which use as inputs specialized labor L, capital K, and information I; inputs of patient time T and nutrition and life-style N, both of which depend on the patient's knowledge base I_p; and other social and environmental factors E and genetic makeup G:

$$(7\text{-}1) \qquad H = h \left[M_1(L_1, K_1, I_1); M_2 \ldots M_n(L_n, K_n, I_n); T(I_p); N(I_p); E; G \right].$$

Since the true output H is intangible, measurement focuses on observable medical services. Medical care expenditure is not defined in the NIPA. The PCE accounts do measure purchases of medical goods and services by individuals, including services financed by private or public insurers, and premiums less benefits and dividends for medical and hospitalization insurance, including workers' compensation. The other components of GDP—gross private domestic investment, exports, and government consumption and investment—include other components of spending related to medical care, but these are not always identified separately. The share of GDP accounted for by these NIPA medical expenditures has been 0.3–0.5 percentage points less than the HCFA's estimate of total personal health care.[55]

Real output and productivity are generally obtained by the double deflation method, which separately deflates output and input expenditures by their respective price indexes. Measures of productivity are therefore only as accurate as the price indexes used to derive them. The medical care

55. McCully (1999).

components of the consumer price index (CPI) were used to deflate health expenditures until recently. But the medical CPI is a measure of prices paid by consumers and does not include prices paid by third-party payers, which now account for roughly 80 percent of total expenditures, more for hospitals and physician services and less for other medical services. Moreover, the CPI traditionally priced individual medical service inputs, such as a hospital room, rather than some quality-constant measure of output of health. Between 1985 and 1995, while the overall CPI rose 3.6 percent a year, the medical components rose 6.5 percent, in part because with this measurement methodology, the CPI measured all quality-related price increases as excess health inflation.

In the 1990s producer price indexes (PPIs) were substituted for CPI components for hospitals (1993), physicians (1994), nursing homes (1995) and home health (1997). PPIs are superior in that they include care financed by third-party payments and are based on more appropriate output measures for some services. For example, the PPI for hospital services uses a probability sample of medical conditions, based on diagnosis-related groups, and then tracks the change in the cost of treating each condition.[56] In the 1990s measured medical price inflation slowed, from nearly 6 percent a year, from 1991 to 1993, to near 4 percent in 1994 and 1995, and to just over 2 percent from 1996 through 1998. Although it is tempting to attribute this apparent price deceleration to productivity growth spurred by information technology, the deceleration more likely reflects the shift to PPIs from CPIs.[57] The PPIs also reflect the lower prices paid by managed care plans and their gain in market share relative to traditional indemnity insurance.

The Bureau of Economic Analysis (BEA) data show the health services sector employs 6.9 percent of the labor force and has relatively low labor productivity: $45,000 in health care compared with $57,000 in all services and $59,000 in manufacturing (1992 data).[58] Moreover, average labor productivity growth in health was –2.2 percent for the years 1987–97, which implies a slowdown of –2.8 percent, compared with a 0.6 percent average annual growth rate estimated for the years 1960–73. The story for multifactor productivity is similar, based on a BEA estimate of the net stock of

56. Catron and Murphy (1996); Berndt and others (1998).

57. McCully (1999) reports that from 1994 to 1996, the PPI for hospitals increased at 3.2 percent a year, compared with 5.1 for the comparable CPI; from 1995 to 1998 the PPI for physicians' services increased 2.0 percent a year, compared with 3.5 percent for the CPI.

58. Triplett and Bosworth (2000).

plant and equipment as a proxy for an index of capital inputs. But these estimates of health care productivity growth may be seriously downward biased by the upward bias in health care price indexes.

At least two dimensions of e-health activity are likely to increase real health productivity. First, the vast increase in free medical information that is available online to patients and physicians should increase productivity of resource use throughout the health care industry, as patients play a more informed role and physicians make better informed diagnoses and treatment choices. This could result in an increase or decrease in total expenditure, with differences across services. In particular, use of pharmaceuticals is likely to increase due to online advertising, which is a major source of funding for e-health sites. Some of this increased use may be appropriate, as patients learn more about their symptoms and availability of drugs to treat them; some of the increased use may be less appropriate but demanded because of insurance. This tendency for insurance to stimulate overuse (moral hazard) is no different for Internet-induced care than for services the patient learns of through other media.

Second, although content sites give physicians better access to general medical information and online decision support, electronic medical records will ultimately make the patient-specific information more readily available and hence reduce errors as well as duplicative and inappropriate care. This should reduce inappropriate use of medical resources and hence reduce measured expenditures. Real health productivity should increase, but this increase will not be reflected in the national accounts, except to the extent that a healthier work force is more productive generally.

Conclusions

Undoubtedly the Internet will ultimately have a major impact on the health care sector, improving information available to consumers and providers and reducing the large share of total expenditures that is currently spent on administrative costs and on unnecessary and inappropriate care. But achieving these savings is several years away. The recent decline in market valuations of e-health firms probably reflects more realistic estimates of the time and costs involved in realizing the potential. Major hurdles must still be overcome, including rolling out and implementing HIPAA standards for electronic claims, medical records, and privacy; combining the various components of the ideal physician office suite into a simple and cost-effective package; and making the new technologies sufficiently attractive to encourage adoption by physicians and hospitals.

Estimates of savings or effects on competition and productivity attributable to the Internet are highly speculative because the ultimate technologies and the rate of uptake are still uncertain, and effects on prices are uncertain. Moreover, health care delivery is likely to remain highly fragmented, which means that diversity in practices may remain. Nevertheless, with all these caveats, the ultimate potential savings are probably equal to at least one or two percentage points of total health spending. This may not show up as lower total spending because of offsetting pressures to increase utilization, including more rapid adoption of newer and more expensive medical technologies and increased use of drugs and other products. Even if the net effect is for little decrease or even an increase in the rate of growth of health spending, real productivity in the health care sector is likely to increase. But these improvements in real health will not be captured in the national health accounts.

References

Arrow, Kenneth. 1963. "Uncertainty and the Welfare Economics of Medical Care." *American Economic Review* 53 (5): 941–73.

Baldwin, Gary. 2000. "Can MedicaLogic make Net Gain?" *Health Data Management* (April): 50–58.

Bates, David W., and others. 1998. "Effect of Computerized Physician Order Entry and a Team Intervention on Prevention of Serious Medication Errors." *Journal of the American Medical Association* 280 (15): 1311–16.

Berndt, Ernst R., and others. 1998. "Price Indexes for Medical Care Goods and Services: An Overview of Measurement Costs." NBER Working Paper 6817. National Bureau of Economic Research, Cambridge, Mass.

Boehm, Elizabeth W. 1999. *Sizing Healthcare eCommerce* (www.forrester.com/ER/ Research).

Briggs, Bill. 2000. "Early Feast for Clearinghouses?" *Health Data Management* (August): 76–80.

Burns, Lawton R., and others. 2000. "Strategic Management of the Health Care Supply Chain." Unpublished paper, Wharton School, University of Pennsylvania. September.

Catron, Brian, and Bonnie Murphy. 1996. "Hospital Price Inflation: What Does the New PPI Tell Us?" *Monthly Labor Review* 120 (7): 24–31.

Chassin, Mark R. 1998. "The Role of Government in Health Care Quality." Paper presented at a forum sponsored by the National Institute for Health Care Management, Research and Educational Foundation, Washington, D.C. July 17.

Cohen, Linda, ed. 1996. *Health Data Directory.* Chicago: Faulkner & Gray.

Computer Science and Telecommunications Board and National Research Council. 2000. *Networking Health: Prescriptions for the Internet,* Committee on Enhancing the Internet for Health Applications. Washington D.C.: National Academy Press.

Danzon, Patricia M. 1992. "Hidden Overhead Costs: Is Canada's System Really Less Expensive?" *Health Affairs* 11 (1): 21–43.

———. 1998. "Welfare Implications of Price Differences for Pharmaceuticals in the US and the EU." *International Journal of the Economics of Business* 4 (3): 301–21.

Darkins, Adam William, and Margaret Ann Cary. 2000. *Telemedicine and Telehealth: Principles, Policies, Performance, and Pitfalls.* New York: Springer.

Dick, Richard S., Elaine B. Steen, and Don E. Detmer. 1997. *The Computer-Based Patient Record: An Essential Technology for Health Care,* rev. ed. Washington: National Academy Press.

Donaldson, Molla S., Kathleen N. Lohr, and Roger J. Bulger. 1994. *Health Data in the Information Age: Use, Disclosure, and Privacy.* Washington: National Academy Press.

Dorenfest, Sheldon. 2000. "The Decade of the '90s." *Health Informatics* 17 (August): 64–67.

EHCR (Efficient Healthcare Consumer Response). 1996. "EHCR: Improving the Efficiency of the Healthcare Supply Chain." CSC Consulting.

Fraumeni, Barbara M., Ann M. Lawson, and G. Christian Ehemann. 1999. "The National Accounts in a Changing Economy: How BEA Measures e-Commerce." Paper presented at Brookings Workshop on Measuring e-Commerce. Washington, D.C.

Fuchs, Victor R. 1996. "Economics, Values, and Health Care Reform." *American Economic Review* 86 (1): 1–24.

GAO (U.S. General Accounting Office). 1994. *Medicare: New Claims Processing System Benefits and Acquisition Risks.* GAO/HEHS/AIMD-94-79.

HCFA (Health Care Financing Administration). 2000. "National Health Expenditure Projections" (www.hcfa.gov/stats).

Health Care Information and Management Systems Society (HIMSS). 2000. "Eleventh Annual HIMSS-IBM Leadership Survey." Chicago.

Kohn, Linda, Janet Corrigan, and Molla S. Donaldson, eds. 1999. *To Err Is Human: Building a Safer Health System.* Washington: National Academy Press.

Kramarow, E., and others. 1999. *Health United States 1999, with Health and Aging Chartbook.* Hyattsville, Md.: National Center for Health Statistics.

Mandl, Kenneth D., Isaac S. Kohane, and Allan M. Brandt. 1998. "Electronic Patient-Physician Communication: Problems and Promise." *Annals of Internal Medicine* 129 (6): 495–500.

Marhula, Daren C., and Edward G. Shannon. 2000. "eHealth B2B Overview: Distributing in an Internet World: What Will It B2B?" New York: U.S. Bancorp Piper Jaffrey Equity Research, February.

McCully, Clinton. 1999. "The Treatment of Medical Expenditures in the National Income and Product Accounts." Workshop on Measuring Health Care, Brookings Institution, December 1999.

Mittman, Robert, and Mary Cain. 1999. *The Future of the Internet in Health Care: Five-Year Forecast.* Report to the California HealthCare Foundation, Oakland, Calif. (www/ehealth.chcf.org)

Nicholson, Louis, ed. 1999. *The Internet and Healthcare*, second edition. Chicago: Health Administration Press.

Office of the Inspector General, Department of Health and Human Services. 2000. *Administrative Costs Reflected on the Adjusted Community Rate Proposals Are Inconsistent among Managed Care Organizations.* A-14-98-00210.

OTA (Office of Technology Assessment), U.S. Congress. 1995. *Bringing Health Care Online: The Role of Information Technologies.* OTA-TCT-624.

Pauly, Mark V., and Mark A. Satterthwaite. 1981. "The Pricing of Primary Care Physicians' Services: A Test of the Role of Consumer Information." *Bell Journal of Economics* 12 (2): 488–506.

Pharmaceutical Research and Manufacturers Association. 2000. "Pharmaceutical Industry Profile 2000." Washington.

Phelps, Charles E. 1992. "Diffusion of Information in Medical Care." *Journal of Economic Perspectives* 6 (Summer): 23–42.

Rind, David M., and others. 1997. "Maintaining the Confidentiality of Medical Records Shared over the Internet and World Wide Web." *Annals of Internal Medicine* 127: 138–41.

Rouse, Robert, and Jeffery S. Chalson. April 2000. *The Evolution of eHealth.* New York: Lehman Brothers.

Starr, Paul. 1997. "Smart Technology, Stunted Policy: Developing Health Information Networks." *Health Affairs* 16 (May/June): 91–105.

Thomas, Eric J., and others. 1999. "Costs of Medical Injuries in Utah and Colorado." *Inquiry* 36 (Fall): 255–264.

Triplett, Jack E., and Barry P. Bosworth. 2000. "Productivity in the Service Sector." Working paper. Brookings.

Westberg E. E., and R. A. Miller. 1999. "The Basis for Using the Internet to Support the Information Needs of Primary Care." *Journal of the American Medical Informatics Association* 6 (1): 6–25.

Workgroup for Electronic Data Interchange. 1993. *Report to Secretary of U.S. Department of Health and Human Services.* Reston, Va.

8

JANE E. FOUNTAIN
with
CARLOS A. OSORIO-URZUA

Public Sector: Early Stage of a Deep Transformation

AMERICAN GOVERNMENT IS in the early stages of deep transformation as a result of the Internet and a host of related developments in information and communications technologies. Rapid growth of web-based applications in the government sector promises significant cost savings through structural changes in the production and delivery of government information and services. Deeper organizational and institutional restructuring in government is likely to generate further efficiency gains. But cost savings that result from institutional and organizational transformation are more difficult to calculate because savings due to technology cannot be disaggregated from those due to structural modification. Furthermore, it is in the nature of a revolution that some future developments remain unpredictable as entirely new and unanticipated innovations and interactions emerge.

The authors gratefully acknowledge the support of the Brookings Institution and the Internet Policy Institute. Christopher Avery, Robert Bedell, Claudia Boldman, Dick Griffin, Kathleen Hirning, Robert Jenkins, Robert Litan, Mark Musell, Alice Rivlin, Steven Steinbrecher, David Temoshok, and many others too numerous to name here offered valuable data, assistance, and comments on earlier versions of this chapter. Michael Collins coded selected attributes of state government websites and provided other valuable research assistance. Responsibility for any errors or misinterpretation of data rests with the authors.

This chapter parses the transformation of the government sector into early-stage innovations in boundary-spanning functions that produce efficiency gains in information provision and service delivery and later-stage, deeper, transformation of internal government agency and cross-agency structures and processes. It also distinguishes between the quantifiable cost savings to government of web-based service delivery systems versus the less readily quantifiable benefits to corporate and private citizens that come from doing business with government over the net. Annualized cost savings to the government sector of as much as $12 billion provide a rough but conservative estimate of near-term efficiency gains. Yet serious structural, institutional, and political obstacles may cause the actual savings to fall short of purely economic estimations. Challenges for government include lack of funding for information infrastructure development, uncertainty about the rate of penetration of Internet use in society, privacy and security concerns, bureaucratic politics, insufficient technical expertise in government, and unresolved practical and normative issues regarding the appropriate roles of the public and private sectors in the development and management of digital government.

Government, more than any other sector in the economy, is characterized by information processing coupled with relational and operational complexity. The sector is the largest purchaser of goods and services and comprises arguably the largest and most arcane set of organizations and relationships within the U.S. economy. Its monopoly position further complicates comparison with other sectors. Moreover, government is the only sector required to enforce laws and regulations and to deliver information and services to 100 percent of the nation's population and firms. Finally, the normative dimensions of these relationships further differentiate government strategy, decisionmaking, and behavior from those features in other economic sectors.

In government operations, as in any other sector, the value chain generates relationships that, from a systemic point of view, can be classified in three ways: relationships between the government and its suppliers; those between government and individual citizens and businesses; and those that lie within and among the government's subsystems.[1] In this chapter, these categories are defined as government-to-business (G2B) to denote procurement activities, government-to-citizens (G2C) to refer to transactions

---

1. In this chapter the sharing or exchange of information or resources among public agencies is considered to be a G2G relationship.

between government and individuals or corporations, and government-to-government (G2G) to delineate interagency or intergovernmental linkages.

This chapter examines the current use and impact of the Internet on government as well as developments anticipated during the next decade. It summarizes key impacts of information technology (IT) on government structure, capacity, and operations; examines leading uses of the Internet at several levels of government, noting not only cost savings but transformation of service delivery and internal structure; and presents a set of estimates for Internet penetration and cost savings in the G2C and G2B categories. The chapter then details the importance of managerial, political, and organizational arrangements for the development of e-government. The report concludes by raising emergent and critical policy issues that will become more pressing during the next decade.

The Impact of Information and Communication Technologies

The economic impact of the Internet on government is potentially enormous yet poorly understood. Major economic effects may be classified into three categories: lower transaction costs; gains in efficiency as a result of increasing positive network externalities; and new strategic and operational possibilities enabled by the Internet. The organizational use of electronic mail alone is reported by Ferris Research to generate an average annual savings of $9,000 per typical office worker, or productivity gains of 15 percent.[2] The report focused on the quantifiable benefits of substituting e-mail for drafting and producing letters, sorting and answering paper-based mail, preparing and faxing documents, filing paper, and trying to reach people by telephone. The study found that an office worker saves, on average, 381 hours a year by using e-mail. Loss of productive time due to e-mail was estimated to be 115 hours a worker. Nie and Erbring report that "90 percent of all Internet users claim to be e-mailers."[3] Given the labor intensiveness of preparing paper-based correspondence and memos, the estimated productivity gain seems reasonable.

Some of the most dramatic examples of reductions in transaction costs, the first category, are found in the differences in cost between web-based

2. Leslie Schroeder, "Ferris Research Shows That Company Policies on Email Use Can Measurably Improve Staff Productivity." Ferris Research Press Release, January 18, 2000 (www.ferris.com/pub/FR-109.html).

3. Nie and Erbring (2000, p. 5).

Table 8-1. *Cost of Processing Bills, on Paper and Online*

Cost	Traditional	Online
To biller	$1.65–$2.70	$0.60–$1.00
To customer	$0.42	$0
To bank	$0.15–$0.20	$0.05–$0.10

Source: Secretariat on Electronic Commerce (1998, table 6, p. A4-36).

and traditional methods of bill payment and document submission. Caveats with respect to estimates of savings are important. Projected savings vary widely in terms of the estimates themselves as well as the variables used for analysis. For example, few analysts consider the costs of infrastructure development, integration of cross-boundary transactions with other internal processes, or upgrades when estimating savings, omissions that lead to upward bias in results. Firms that sell web-based transaction services typically generate and publicize cost savings figures. Detached, rigorous analysis of generalizable samples of transactions remains rare. According to EzGov.com, a major producer and vendor of e-government software and services, online bill payment is 67.2 to 95.6 percent more efficient than paper-based operations.[4] The U.S. Department of Commerce, however, estimates that the cost to the government of processing a payment would be reduced from $1.65–$2.70 for traditional processing to $0.60–$1.00 for web-based processing (table 8-1).[5] Hundreds of millions of paper-based transactions are conducted, in the form of bill payments or document submissions, that involve public agencies to which similar types of efficiencies can be applied.

In addition to transaction costs savings, positive network externalities associated with Internet penetration increase the estimated savings from the use of e-mail. In other words, the larger the network of e-mail users, the greater the benefits of using e-mail because e-mail may be substituted for other forms of communication to a greater extent than would be possible if the network of users was smaller. Each additional person online generates a positive network benefit to those who are already online not only because

4. Data are from a figure titled "EZGov research: e-government cost savings," and from EZGov, "E-Government: Making Sense of a Revolution," an advertising supplement. Figure and supplement e-mailed to the authors by Nicole Corvette, EZGov.com, August 29, 2000.

5. Secretariat on Electronic Commerce (1998, table 6, p. A4-36).

of reductions in transaction costs, but also through the scalability of web-based communication.

One of the more dramatic current examples of the third category, new strategic opportunities, lies in potential efficiencies achieved by the use of multiple "exchanges." These exchanges significantly improve the efficiency of procurement for some types of goods and services through the creation of wider, deeper, and more transparent markets that allow government agencies both to reduce administrative costs and to obtain lower prices in markets.

Infrastructure is a limiting factor in the development of e-government. The speed at which information can be transferred affects the cost savings of transactions that are time sensitive. Transaction time affects reliability of transmissions as well as the feasibility of e-government use by the public. For example, the transfer of a ten megabyte file, roughly equal to the contents of six or seven floppy disks, varies from eight seconds to forty-six minutes depending upon the sophistication of the connection. The impact of information and communication technologies in terms of time and cost is significant for procedures and functions that require sharing information or validation of data. In principal, the Internet makes it possible to transfer enormous amounts of data in seconds, saving time and money. But the ability to realize these cost savings depends on the type of technology acquired by public agencies to connect to the Internet; their policies regarding information, data sharing, and transfer; and a number of emergent security and privacy issues. With regard to the latter, security is positively correlated with transmission speed.[6]

Funding for information infrastructure that enables efficiency gains, reliability, and required levels of security is currently a serious impediment to the development of electronic government. The results of a survey of county-level governments, for example, indicate that funding represents the chief obstacle to e-government.[7] Funding is likely to be more difficult to obtain in some county governments as well as in relatively poorer state, city, and town governments. Nearly half the state governments in the United States voted in referendums between 1978 and the mid-1980s to support tax and expenditure limitation measures, most of which remain in

6. Two recent reports from the U.S. General Accounting Office (2000 a, b) detail problems with security and privacy on federal government websites.

7. National Association of Counties. 2000. "E-Government Survey" at (www.naco.org/pubs/surveys/it/2000egov.pdf [August 27, 2000]).

effect and limit the ability of local governments to raise taxes.[8] Wealthier states and the federal government are expected, therefore, to develop information infrastructure first, with other governments following. Yet even at the state and federal levels, significant variation in infrastructure within state and federal agencies and across state governments will lead not only to heterogeneity of adoption and development, but also to lack of interoperability across units and levels. Thus, fragmentation in infrastructure limits efficiencies that flow from positive network externalities.

Infrastructure for e-government must provide security as well as transaction speed. Faster communication technologies would help solve security problems raised by web-based transactions but at a cost to governments. Governments have invested in security primarily through the use of secure web servers that protect data and information "on site." It is also necessary to ensure data security during transfer. At the county level of government, the results of a survey conducted by the National Association of Counties indicate that 85 percent of counties that responded to the survey provide at least one employee with access to personal computers. Only 50 percent of counties report that at least one employee has access to e-mail; 54 percent of counties report that none of their employees have access to the Internet. Among those counties with Internet access, 84 percent reported that they connect to the Internet using a dial-up modem, the slowest form of connection available. Note that the response rate of the survey was only 23 percent, with the majority of respondents from small counties in the midwestern, southern, and western United States.[9] Levels and types of connectivity may be proxies for the status of infrastructure to support e-government. In sum, any discussion of the cost savings of electronic government must account for the extent and cost of the national information infrastructure development necessary to support web-based transactions.

Government functions are information intensive. Thus, it is not surprising that public administration possesses one of the highest rates of computer use at work. As a result of the explosive growth of e-commerce since 1995, government expenditures for computers have been decreasing as a percentage of total U.S. expenditures for computers (figure 8-1). The

8. California was the first state to vote in a tax and expenditure measure, Proposition 13, in 1978. Massachusetts followed with a referendum to approve Proposition 2 1/2 in 1980. See Susskind and Fountain Serio (1983).

9. National Association of Counties. 2000. "2000 E-Government Survey" at (www.naco.org/pubs/surveys/it/2000egov.pdf [August 27, 2000]).

Figure 8-1. *U.S. Government Expenditures on Computers, 1987–99*

Chained billion dollars (1996)   As percent of U.S. expenditure in computers

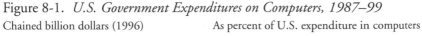
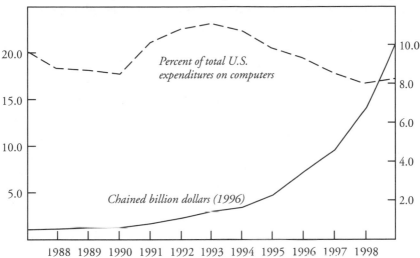

Source: Bureau of Economic Analysis, U.S. Department of Commerce (www.bea.doc.gov/bea/dn/comp_gdp.exe [June 29, 2000]).

number of public sector domains has increased at a rapid rate, beginning with about fifty domains in 1995 and approaching eight hundred in 1999. The growth rate from 1998 to 1999 alone was 38 percent. In contrast to the private sector, the number of web and file transfer protocol (FTP) servers in the federal government is high relative to the number of domains. In 1999 the federal government had twenty-six web servers, twenty-two secure web servers, and twenty-eight FTP servers per domain.[10] However, these figures for government growth contrast sharply with the growth of "dot.coms" in the private sector whose number grew by 280 percent during the same period.[11] Given the numbers of government servers, larger government units in the public sector already possess at least the minimum technological infrastructure needed to adopt Internet-based applications.

10. U.S. General Services Administration (1999).

11. Matthew Zook, Department of City and Regional Planning, University of California at Berkeley (www.socrates.berkeley.edu/~zook/domain_names/Domains/Coms_by_states.xls [February 27, 2001].

The cost savings of e-government also depend upon penetration, or growth, of Internet usage by the public. Specifically, savings will vary according to the rate and level of penetration of web-based transactions in the population and in private sector firms. It is not currently known how rapidly individual citizens will adopt e-government, which means that a key variable needed for the calculation of cost savings is unknown. For the foreseeable future, then, governments must maintain capacity for traditional operations and transactions. It is well documented that the adoption of the Internet varies greatly as a function of ethnicity, race, age, income level, and distance from major business, technological, and decisionmaking areas. These characteristics vary in part by geographic region. For example, slightly more than 50 percent of the adult populations in cities such as Washington, San Francisco, Austin, and Seattle/Tacoma currently use the Internet, whereas 30 percent or less of the populations in cities such as Pittsburgh, Tulsa, Birmingham, and Charleston/Huntington, West Virginia, are Internet users.[12] Disparities in rates of Internet use are likely to be correlated with socioeconomic variables in less densely populated areas as well.

An increasing number of public sector units at the federal, state, and local levels are incorporating or planning web-based government transactions. The focus in governments at all levels on G2C features reflects a desire to increase "customer service" that has been predominant since the mid-1980s. Although G2C features are of strategic importance, governments have done little to market web-based services to the public. Government marketing might alienate citizens without Internet access. It also risks creating demand that cannot yet be met. But this situation may be changing. The results of a survey of state information resource executives indicate that a number of state governments have begun to take measures to motivate their constituents to use e-government features.[13]

Federal, State, and Local Innovators in E-Government

Several governments currently deploy first generation web-based services that allow citizens, businesses, and other governments to transact with a

12. Cyberatlas.com, "Five U.S. Cities Reach 50 Percent Internet Penetration," *The Big Picture: Demographics,* October 18, 1999, p. 1 (www.cyberatlas.internet.com/big_picture/demographics/article/0,1323,5911_220481,00.html [February 23, 2001]).

13. National Association of State Information Resource Executives. 1999. "Information Security in State Government Information Technology" (www.nasire.org/publications/99IFR.pdf [May 30, 2001]).

government agency over the web.[14] The electronic government applications available at the federal, state, and local levels vary widely with respect to interactivity, complexity, and convenience. Current initiatives fall into two broadly defined categories. Whereas some agencies and governments have assumed lead roles in offering a large number of electronic government services to citizens and business, others have focused on creating a web-based environment designed to facilitate search and use of existing services and information. A small but growing number of governments attempt to do both and have created portals, or "one-stop shops," for interaction with government.

When governments provide electronic services online, they save money by generating less paperwork, decreasing time and effort expended by employees to process routine transactions, and lowering error rates. Governments may field fewer inquiries for routine information and instructions for completion of routine tasks. Citizens and business save on the costs of compliance including search costs, travel costs (including time waiting in line), repetitive entry of information, verification of task completion, and notification of errors during the transaction. Users benefit from reduced search costs involved with locating the correct agency or agencies for their task and from having to spend less time filling out forms with replicated information.

E-government "best practice" examples consistently strive to increase responsiveness to clients by eliminating process steps, redundancy, and confusion for the user. Washington State, for example, employs an enterprise strategy to coordinate the web-based activities of agencies, offices, and departments within its portal. State government portals are currently designed to target segments of the population that can be grouped demographically (such as senior citizens), geographically (such as residents of a particular region), or vocationally (such as state employees, other employees, employers, and businesses). Portals that target specific population segments contain interfaces to the online services of interest to those populations, regardless of agency. In the best cases, portal development would lead to reasonably well-integrated web design standards and back-end systems coordinated across agencies to facilitate completion of transactions on agency web servers. Some designers believe the user does not need to know before or even during a transaction which agency web server he or she must

14. Internet-based innovations in federal, state, and local government are presented in greater detail in Fountain (2001a).

access to accomplish a task, but rather need only know the web address of the government portal where the needed functions are located.

The portal model is designed to reduce or eliminate redundancy and confusion in transactions with government. However, these gateways to electronic government are ultimately dependent upon the existence, availability, and quality of information and transaction-based services within agencies. In other words, the limiting factor on portal quality is information and service quality at the agency level. The usefulness of a portal is directly dependent upon the number and quality of government services offered online. The corollary is also true: decreasing the cost of access to existing services through a well-designed portal increases the usefulness of the services. Ultimately, portals will reflect the autonomy and lack of integration of the agencies behind the virtual interface. The technical logic of government by portal demands that the integration and seamlessness presented on the web be reflected by structural changes that would transform business processes and relationships within and across agencies.

Lack of coherence in government web portals reflects inconsistent standards of security and privacy; differing levels of service, transparency, and documentation; and redundancy of information and data requirements. Solving the problems of agency-specific "stovepipe" applications has been slowed by bureaucratic politics, siloed oversight and budgetary systems, and security and privacy constraints. With respect to the latter, agency and program officials are rightly concerned about—and currently lack adequate safeguards for—storing and managing information from and about private citizens or businesses in centralized interagency databases.

Washington State has developed a "Digital Government Plan" that describes in depth a framework and vision for state electronic government in a five- to ten-year time frame. The plan includes guidelines for developing e-government applications and incentives for successful implementation of e-government services. The state has developed a set of standards including uniform web design guidelines and back-end protocols to guide process redesign at the agency level. Washington's comprehensive approach sets the state apart from the modal state government website or portal in which services online accrete according to the initiative and entrepreneurship of public managers. Executive level leadership in Washington State not only guides the development of web-based capacity, but also leads inexorably to greater rationalization and standardization across agencies and programs.

Following are examples of innovative web-based applications of e-government at the federal, state, and local levels of government. The examples were selected on the bases of a review of the current research and empirical data regarding e-government and of several rewards programs that identify lead actors in the development of web-based services. State-level findings are based on a comprehensive examination of all state government websites. Thus, these illustrations are outliers in the statistical sense and represent developments in government that may take decades to become central tendencies. Most writing on digital government underestimates how long it might take for the rest of the population to move online with Internet connections that would allow interactivity at a speed that would make digital government feasible. Moreover, problems of access and income are compounded by those of literacy.

Proponents of digital government also tend to discount the current inability of many local governments to offer web-based transactions to the public, given their lack of budget, infrastructure, and expertise. Nearly a decade passed between the development of the first web browser, Mosaic, and dramatic growth in e-commerce. Longer lags in the public sector are likely.

Federal E-Government Innovators

The federal government's efforts over the past decade to put government information on the web, prompted by the Paperwork Reduction Act of 1995 and other legislative mandates, have been energetic, with volumes of information now available to the public through government agency websites. Despite achievement on this front, however, efforts to develop online functionality and transaction-based services to complement the availability of information have lagged behind the private sector.

Recent initiatives have begun to change this state. Spurred in part by the impressive success of e-commerce in the private sector, the Clinton administration committed to placing key government services on the Internet. The National Performance Review (later renamed the National Partnership for Reinventing Government) was established in 1993 with the call of "putting customers first" and striving for a "customer-driven government that matches or exceeds the best service available in the private sector."[15]

15. Executive Order 12862, "Setting Customer Service Standards, September 11, 1993. See (www.customersurvey.gov).

One of the key metrics of a best practice e-government initiative is the degree to which it offers one-stop customer service, allowing all of a customer's business to be completed in a single instance. Two efforts within the Access America project, sponsored by the National Performance Review, focused on building one-stop shops for citizens: the www.students.gov and the www.seniors.gov portals.[16]

STUDENTS.GOV. Access America for Students is a portal site of government resources—including a collection of links to various government websites, forms, and programs—of interest to students. It provides a searchable database of links to relevant government or nongovernment sites with descriptions and ratings of each site. By registering on the site, students can participate in the "Grade-A-Site" feature and contribute to the site ratings themselves.

The portal layout familiar to most Internet users makes finding tools or information related to a specific topic relatively easy. The search engine also facilitates information acquisition. Additionally, all major interactive features of the site are grouped together on the home page under "Fast Links," which allow students to jump directly to the service they need. Application for federal student financial aid is more convenient, responsive, and error free on the web. A link exists to the Department of Education website that contains the Free Application for Federal Student Aid (FAFSA). A PIN (personal identification number), used as an electronic signature, is assigned to an individual upon registration. The online version of the FAFSA allows an applicant to save a partially completed application form to a hard drive or diskette and then continue the application process at a later time by reloading the saved file. The site also provides extensive documentation and help.

The economic payoff from this process is significant. Tens of thousands of students have applied for student financial aid online since its launch in June of 1997. Completing the FAFSA online is easier and less time consuming in part because the software automatically selects the appropriate questions and checks responses on submission for completeness and consistency, eliminating delays and rework caused by the 10 percent of paper applications returned because of errors or incompleteness.[17] Currently, one step in the FAFSA process still requires the applicant to mail in a signed

16. Bureaucratic and institutional challenges in the development of the first federal portal, the U.S. Business Advisor, are analyzed in Fountain (2001c).

17. Correspondence with Dick Griffin, National Performance Review, June 23, 2000.

paper document. Once the document is logged, an electronic FAFSA takes only seventy-two hours to process, in contrast to fourteen days (not including mail time) for the paper version of the process.[18] Beginning in 2001 digital signatures will allow the entire transaction to take place over the web.

The Department of Education also uses the web to integrate service provision in part by expanding the range of transactions for which an individual's PIN can be used to access account and personal information. Access to the department's Central Processing System (CPS) database, access to Title IV student aid (currently limited to Access America pilot schools), and Student Account Manager reports—web-based reports on student loan origination and aid disbursement to schools (also limited to Access America pilot schools)—are all currently supported. Great potential exists in this area. The department currently pays a contract fee of $12 per 800-access telephone call to consult student account information. Web-based queries to the CPS data system cost a few cents. With approximately 20 million student loan accounts in service, the cost savings of moving a large number of these transactions to the web are tremendous.[19]

SENIORS.GOV. Access America for Seniors, at www.seniors.gov, is a portal to resources on the web for senior citizens. The home page features news articles of interest to senior citizens. A special feature, "Seniors and Computing," provides links to help seniors learn to use technology in ways that can benefit them. Ten topical categories, organized similarly, each include a list of links to and detailed descriptions of federal and state government agencies, commercial firms, and nonprofit organizations with resources for seniors. For example, the "benefits" section of Access America for Seniors links to resources and information concerning Social Security, railroad retirement benefits, veterans benefits, food stamps, retirement benefits for federal employees, and health care, including Medicare, Medicaid, and the Veterans Health Administration. A drop-down list linking the user to the veterans' affairs agency of each state provides access to state and local level resources.

Seniors.gov also includes online services, downloadable government forms, and several online applications. The "Services" category links to and describes twenty e-government applications relevant to seniors. The "Retirement Planner" category also links to a number of online applications

18. Access America, "A01: Improve the Public's Access to Government Services," at (www. accessamerica.gov/docs/public2.html [June 2000]).

19. Telephone interview with David Temoshok, General Services Administration, June 23, 2000.

including retirement resources regarding financial, medical, life insurance, and housing topics. For example, the "Financial Planning" subcategory links to sites with dynamic cost calculators to help citizens develop financial projections based on user inputs and assumptions. The "Medical" subcategory allows users to compare Medicare and Medigap health care plans available in their geographic area on multiple criteria including costs and benefits covered and several other measures of quality. Cost savings to the public of these types of services are likely to be significant, although difficult to estimate in advance, and include reduced search costs and improvements in analytical tools available to the public.

SOCIAL SECURITY ADMINISTRATION. The Social Security Administration (SSA) website is not an interagency enterprise portal but a strong example of a large, vital government agency's leading efforts to develop superior e-government capacity and service. The SSA provides services to current and future recipients of Social Security benefits. Its customer service record has been favorably compared with the highest-rated service firms, including Disney and L.L. Bean, in "courtesy, responsiveness, and knowledge."[20] The agency is committed to a similar standard of service excellence on the web. The SSA offers an online retirement planner that employs user-supplied parameters and financial information to estimate future benefits payments. The SSA's most frequently demanded service, the "Social Security Statement Request," can be ordered online and received by mail in two to four weeks.[21] The entire business process for this service will be conducted online in the future with the benefit statement returned over the web in seconds after a request. Online administration will save SSA more than a dollar for each statement issued.[22]

INTERNAL REVENUE SERVICE. The Internal Revenue Service has developed an e-government strategy to allow citizens to file taxes online without the potentially huge costs of developing the service internally. The private market for offline tax return software is strong, and the IRS has allowed vendors to harness commercial products with online capabilities through the "e-file" program. Several commercial software packages, a few of which are entirely web-based, allow users to submit tax return informa-

20. Ken Apfel, "Social Security—World Class Customer Service," *Reinventing Government to Get Results Americans Care About,* at (www.npr.gov/library/announc/customer.html [June 2000]).

21. (www.ssa.gov/top10.html).

22. Associate Commissioner for Program Support, Social Security Administration, "Internet PEBES Request Services," January 22, 1997.

tion to the IRS electronically. For most users, a paper form with a signature stating that the user filed his return electronically must be mailed in; however, the IRS is piloting an authentication process to enable an entirely paperless return with a digital signature.[23] The IRS acknowledges acceptance of an electronic return within forty-eight hours.[24] Direct deposit of tax refunds into a user's bank account is available for electronic returns. The early results of the e-file program indicate an error rate for electronic returns of less than 1 percent, compared with 20 percent for traditional returns.

Innovation in E-Government at the State Level

State governments typically lead other levels of government in innovation. Often, reform begins at the state level and diffuses to federal and local governments. For this reason, Fountain undertook a comprehensive examination of state government websites to determine the types of services migrating to the web. Results indicate that electronic government services vary widely from state to state.[25] Several services are common to a number of states. A few states offer features that are unusual, innovative, and powerful. The mean number of electronic services offered by state governments in 2000 was 4.38, with a median of 4. A few states offer a significantly greater number of services. Although the number of services offered is not the only criterion for comparing the development of electronic government, the frequencies provide clear evidence of strong variance among states in number and type of services offered.

The most frequently offered service, state employment postings, is available on thirty-two state government websites, which also allow citizens to find and apply for state government jobs online. The second most common service, personal income tax e-filing, was found in twenty-four states that provide links to online filing applications. The prevalence of tax e-filing did not result simply because citizens demanded it, but because state governments can easily implement a low-cost, outsourced solution through the IRS e-file program. Other frequently occurring services allow members of the public to order vital records (birth, death, and marriage certificates) online (thirteen states), purchase fish and game licenses and

23. Internal Revenue Service, "Filing Season 2000 PIN Piloting Information for Taxpayers," (www.irs.ustreas.gov/prod/elec_svs/sig-txpyr.html).

24. Internal Revenue Service, "IRS E-File for Taxpayers Using a Personal Computer" (www.irs.ustreas.gov/prod/elec_svs/ol-txpyr.html).

25. Details of this study are presented in Fountain (2001a).

permits over the web (fifteen states), search state government sex offender registries (fourteen states), and renew motor vehicle registrations (seventeen states).[26] No other web-based application was found on more than 20 percent of state government websites.

A small number of innovative services, although present on only a few state sites, warrant attention and are noted in table 8-2. Access Washington (www.access.wa.gov) is currently the leading state government web portal. Georgia and a small number of other states offer a greater number of online services than does Washington. Georgia's state web strategy illustrates an innovative, but less integrated, approach to e-government than the strategy pursued by Washington. Other states have taken the lead in the design and customization of their sites. North Carolina and Virginia have advanced beyond a simple state portal model to create more powerful interfaces. No dominant state government templates have yet emerged. Selected key features presented in the table suggest the range, scope, and utility of first-stage, web-based government services.

Local Level E-Government Innovation

City, county, and town governments vary strongly in the socioeconomic characteristics of the citizenry, services offered, and nature of the interactions required. Electronic government, therefore, can be applied in a wide variety of ways with different impacts at the local level. City governments can ease the burden on busy agencies. Rural and county governments covering large geographical areas can decrease costs associated with geographic distribution that include not only travel time, but availability of transportation and the infeasibility of repeat visits to government offices.

Indianapolis, Indiana, is, according to many, the most impressive example of municipal government on the web and the recipient of several awards.[27] (Some of its innovative applications are listed in table 8-2.)

26. Vital records ordering is available primarily through vitalchek.com, a private third-party provider of online ordering for these types of records. Regarding fish and game licenses, North Dakota is unique in its implementation of this service by allowing licenses to be printed immediately from a web browser rather than delivered by mail. Motor vehicle registration renewal is one of several online services related to motor vehicles including driver license renewal or replacement, payment of citations, and order processing for personalized license plates. Motor vehicle registration renewal is one of the fastest growing services, with several states claiming to have the service "coming soon" on government websites.

27. Winner of the 1998 Global Information Infrastructure Government Category Award and cited by ZDNet Inter@ctive Week and the *New York Times* as one of the most powerful and useful munici-

Table 8-2. *Selected Innovations in E-Government Services*

Access Washington (www.access.wa.gov)	State government web portal offering: technology procurement for state and local agencies; fraud reporting system; business and excise tax filing; criminal records search; unedited coverage of state government deliberations and events; vital records ordering; unemployment insurance benefits filing.
Washington State Enterprise Budget and Allotment Support System (BASS)	Internal agency budget development and monitoring tools. Reduces response time for budget proposals by 50 percent.
State of Georgia	Georgia Net (www.ganet.org): renew professional licenses; www.permit.com: purchase hunting and fishing licenses and boat registrations; TeachGeorgia.org: teacher recruitment site for Georgia public schools; students pay state university tuition online by credit card.
North Carolina (www.ncgov.com)	Three separate Yahoo-integrated state portals for citizens, business, and state government employees.
Virginia (www.state.va.us)	Allows users to create a customized "My Virginia" homepage linking to government services and features selected by the user.
New York State (www.state.ny.us)	Offers 1,108 permits online for 187 types of business.
Maryland State (www.state.md.us)	More than 40 types of professional licenses may be renewed online.
City of Indianapolis (www.Indygov.org)	Integration across agencies at the website level, use of geographical information systems, wealth of information, ease of use, range of interactive features.
Contra Costa County, California (www.co.contra-costa.ca.us)	Use of geographic information systems for customized mapping using assessor's office property parcels and values; school, police, and fire station locations; risk of natural disaster; environmental hazards; and political districts. Use of visual information for identification and adoption of stray animals.

Source: Compiled by authors.

pal e-government sites, IndyGov offers a wealth of services to citizens. See www.indygov.org/winner.htm. ZDNet Inter@ctive Week, September 13, 1999; David M. Herszenhorn, "For the People, by the Computer," *New York Times,* September 30, 1999.

Perhaps the most powerful aspect of IndyGov is its nearly seamless integration of agency and department functions into a citywide portal. Like Access Washington, the portal will become more powerful and useful as new services become available online and older proprietary systems are integrated and web enabled. These positive network externalities drive agency restructuring required for further integration at the portal level.

County government encompasses a range of activities that differ from those at state and municipal levels. Contra Costa County, located in the San Francisco/San Jose region of California, is currently developing innovative visual digital tools for citizen use. Contra Costa is not a representative county example because of the high rate of Internet penetration and literacy among its residents. Seventy percent of households in the county are estimated to be online. Use of Geographic Information Systems (GIS) data allows residents to custom design maps and suggests the potential of broadband visual information and geographic information systems for e-government. Such examples indicate next-generation services that advance beyond online administrative and clerical processing of transactions.

The Economic Impact of E-Government

In the current turbulent environment, it is difficult to predict developments in information and communication technologies during the next five years or their migration to government. The following section estimates the magnitude of the economic impact that the current state of information and communication technologies would have on the American economy if they were widely diffused in government.[28] Thus, the following estimates hold technology constant, although they estimate future values for other variables including penetration of Internet use and implementation of current Internet-related technologies in government. Given the heterogeneity of state, county, municipal, and town governments, adoption of e-government is likely to remain highly varied during the next decade.

Diffusion of e-government will occur unit by unit. Yet no consensus exists regarding the precise number of government units in the country. The count varies based on definitions and measurement. Figures presented

28. For a detailed description of the assumptions and methodology used in the following section of the report, please contact the lead author.

here are based on U.S. Census Bureau data. According to the 1999 *U.S. Statistical Abstract,* there were 87,568 governmental units in 1997, including executive and independent federal agencies, state and local governments, and special and school districts. Disregarding special and school districts, the number of public units at the federal, state, and local levels is 39,159.[29]

A likely scenario of e-government adoption follows. The adoption rate of e-government features will differ among government units for the reasons described earlier. Services for individual citizens and businesses are expected to be implemented first as public organizations begin to experiment with e-government. We base this claim not only on existing evidence from all levels of government, but also on the lower unitary costs of coordination for G2C versus G2B or G2G operations. After gaining experience with G2C operations, government actors may use their knowledge to develop G2B web-based procurement.

In the scenario drawn here, which is by no means the only reasonable one, it is expected that G2B operations will begin in the largest individual government organizations—for example, the Defense Department and other large purchasing agencies—and then diffuse to smaller units. Alternatively, the adoption of web-based procurement could begin with moderate-value operations that involve highly sophisticated actors in markets where high savings are anticipated, followed by adoption in the highest-value operations and then wider diffusion across the public sector.[30] The potential efficiency gains from the first scenario lend it greater credibility than the more risk-averse second example.

Over a longer period of time, on the order of decades, efficiencies will accrue from the adoption—or, more properly, the implementation—of internally integrated G2G operations. Linkages and coordination will increase as new norms, processes, and structural arrangements are negotiated. External pressure from executives and legislatures will be necessary to drive bureaucratic transformation at this level. Currently, a small number of innovators, described elsewhere in detail by Fountain, have built portals that provide virtual, or web-based, integration across agencies.[31] However,

---

29. The breakdown is 65 federal units, 50 state units, and 39,044 local units. Of the local units, 3,043 are classified as county; 19,372, as municipal; and 16,629, as town. U.S. Census Bureau (1999, table 500, p. 309).

30. It is assumed that 20 percent of procurement operations represent 80 percent of the public sector's expenditures in government procurement.

31. Fountain (2001c).

the back-end integration vital to capturing the efficiencies of G2G operations has barely begun.

This type of integration faces formidable bureaucratic and political obstacles, but represents the next major wave of government reform as redundancies and overlap among programs and agencies become more transparent and less easily justified in an Internet-based environment. To grasp the slow adoption of e-government relative to some other sectors of the economy, it is important to understand that a presence on the web is only a first step in a long series of deep modifications in the structure of the state.[32] Thus, adoption curves for e-government are likely to show the steepest rise in adoption, or the most rapid implementation, for G2C activities during the next half decade or so, followed by a more moderate adoption function for G2B in procurement and then by the relatively slow adoption of G2G over at least two decades as institutional changes are negotiated. Estimated differences in adoption functions for G2C, G2B, and G2G activities are given in figure 8-2.[33]

G2C: Estimated Cost Savings of E-Government

Efficiency gains of G2C e-government are currently the result of reductions in the operational, administrative, and compliance costs of processing the payments and documents required of citizens and business to transact with governments. These transactions include tax and nontax payments as well as new orders for and renewal of permits, registrations, and licenses, and hundreds of other types of transactions ranging across policy domains and government levels.[34] According to the Bureau of Economic Analysis, the sum of federal, state, and local government receipts, excluding contributions for social insurance and—for state and local governments—federal grants-in-aid, was $2.138 trillion dollars in 1999 (table 8-3).[35] U.S. Census Bureau data indicate that property, individual, and corporate income taxes

32. These types of technology-based institutional changes are analyzed in detail in Fountain (2001c).

33. Adoption patterns and functions summarized in this chapter are presented and motivated in detail in Osorio-Urzua (2000).

34. The analysis does not include taxation of Internet operations. For an excellent first approach to this topic, see Hal R. Varian, "Taxation of Electronic Commerce," Internet Policy Institute, Washington (www.Internetpolicy.org/briefing/4_00_story.html. [April 2000]).

35. Bureau of Economic Analysis (2000b, tables B-82, B-83). The BEA data used in this report estimate 1999 corporate profit tax accruals based on historical values.

at the state and local level represent, on average, 56.5 percent of the tax revenue of those governments.

The number of transactions between government and constituents that are amenable to web-based processing is enormous. In order to indicate the scale of transactions in the government sector given lack of information regarding the total number and cost of transactions between government units and citizens or businesses, one might consider a selected subset of transactions. Nearly 443 million transactions to register or monitor births, elementary and secondary school enrollment, college enrollment, motor vehicle registration and inspection, voter registration, construction permits for new housing, and patent and trademark initial applications take place annually. (The annual volume by type of transaction is presented in table 8-4.) All of these transactions require clerical handling, and, in many cases, administrative processing as well, making them more complex in nature, and therefore more expensive, than online bill payment. With few data available that measure cost reduction per type of transaction, our estimates are necessarily broad and provisional. The estimates given below suggest the scale of e-government G2C activities in terms of potential savings as well as complexities of institutional change.

Cost savings to government fail to capture the efficiencies of web-based transactions for citizens and business. For instance, the cost of compliance with current tax law given present administrative processing represents a drag on the economy. The *Tax Complexity Fact Book*, published by the Joint Economic Committee states that the IRS and the Office of Management and Budget (OMB) "estimate that Americans will spend 6.1 billion hours (over 3 million person-years) filling out tax forms, keeping records, learning tax rules, making calculations, and other tax-related work in fiscal 2000. . . . A measure of the 'opportunity cost' of compliance time has been roughly estimated by the OMB at $26.50 per hour in 1996, or about $30 today. . . . Thus, federal tax compliance costs based on 6.1 billion hours of compliance time are about $183 billion per year."[36] In addition, the *Fact Book* cited a report by Joel Slemrod, which estimated that "tax compliance costs represent about 10 percent of income tax collected." According to the *Fact Book,* this figure is more conservative than those generated by the Tax Foundation and the U.S. General Accounting Office, which estimate compliance costs of 15 percent and 19 percent, respectively.

36. Joint Economic Committee (2000).

Figure 8-2. Differences between G2C, G2B, and G2G Adoption of E-Government Activities
Rate of adoption

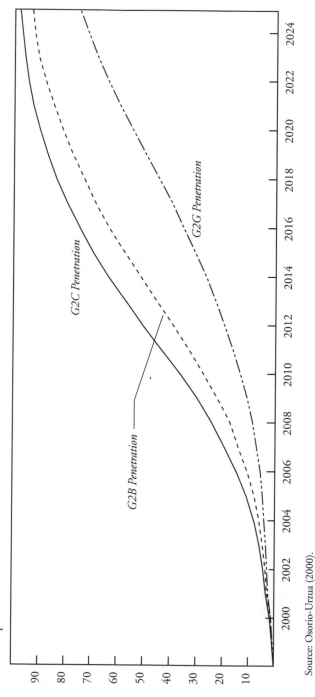

Source: Osorio-Urzua (2000).

Table 8-3. *Federal, State, and Local Government Receipts, 1999*
Billions of dollars

Government level	Personal tax and nontax	Corporate profits tax	Indirect business tax	Total
Federal	908.0	222.4	101.5	1,231.9
State and local	252.4	37.0	616.8	906.2
Total	1,160.4	259.4	718.3	2,138.1

Source: Bureau of Economic Analysis (2000b, Tables B-82, B-83).

With respect to tax processing costs for local governments, according to estimates produced by GovWorks, cited in *Business 2.0*, "local governments collect more than $200 billion in property taxes each year, with manual, paper-based processing costs of more than $1 billion," or 0.5 percent of those revenues.[37] The processing costs for income taxes are likely to be much higher given their greater complexity. Tax processing costs to government are likely to be highest for federal taxes, followed by processing of state taxes, which are relatively lower in complexity and cost, and then local property taxes.

Few estimates have been developed to suggest the aggregate potential cost savings in the G2C category. An analysis in the *Forrester Report* projects that the number of online submissions to government will reach almost 320 million by 2006. Moreover, the analysis predicts that revenue collected online by governments will increase from $5.1 billion a year in 2000 to $602.4 billion in 2006.[38] These figures indicate the potential size of e-government but fail to provide estimates of cost savings. Moreover, the analysis in the *Forrester Report* is based on a small, unrepresentative sample of fifteen governments. Thus, the numbers reported may be much higher or, if implementation were slowed, much lower. The increase in the size of e-government during the time period considered seems ambitious given our findings on the implementation, adoption, and institutional issues still to be resolved and and the pace that innovation is adopted.

Using the *Forrester* projections for adoption, a discount rate of 7 percent, and a highly conservative estimate of savings at 7 percent of revenues

37. Sean Donohue, "And Now, Ladies and Gentlemen, the Internet Will Streamline Government Bureaucracy," *Business 2.0*, EBusiness Section, June 27, 2000.

38. Sharrard and others (2000).

Table 8-4. *Volume of Selected Government Transactions by Type*
Thousands

Year	Births of registry	Motor vehicle registration and inspection	Patent application	Trademark application	Voter registration	School enrollment, entry operation	College enrollment, entry operation	Number of new housing units, construction permits
1998	3,803	210,881	239	230	2,137	…	…	1,441
1999 (estimated)	3,900	213,992	247	245	2,157	222	209	1,612
2000 (estimated)	3,914	217,103	255	260	2,176	224	210	1,652

Source: All data are from U.S. Census Bureau. Births (www.census.gov/population/projections/nation/detail/componen.a). Motor vehicle registration: U.S. Statistical Abstract, 1999 (table 1439); registration is counted twice to account for registration and inspection. Patent and trademark applications: U.S. Statistical Abstract, 1999 (table 893). Voter registration (www.census.gov/population/socdemo/voting/history/htab01.txt); 71.9 percent of the population was registered to vote. School and college enrollment (www.census.gov/population/socdemo/school/taba-1.txt). Construction permits (www.census.gov/const/C40/table1/table1a.txt).

(meant to offset partially the more ambitious adoption rate), the estimated annualized savings of G2C adoption of web-based tax processing alone would be $20.22 billion, or $2.83 billion a year for the period 2000–2006. These savings equal 0.031 percent of gross domestic product (GDP). (All numbers are in 1999 dollars.) They do not include hundreds of millions of other transactions moving to web-based processing. Working with the subset of 443 million transactions, described earlier, if each transaction costs, on average, $10 for government to process using paper-based methods and if on-line processing costs led to a 30 percent reduction in those costs, then moving this subset of government transactions to the web would save very roughly an additional $1.34 billion a year (443 million × $10 × 0.3).

G2B: Estimated Effects of E-Procurement in the Government Sector

On average the American government spends approximately $524 billion a year on procurement operations, or about 6.04 percent of GDP (in 1999 dollars).[39] Between 1995 and 1999, procurement expenditures totaled $2,621 trillion (table 8-5). Attention to the potential of G2B for cost savings in government is beginning to affect the way public organizations manage procurement operations. Electronic procurement yields three types of efficiency benefits: operational savings from using digital instead of traditional manual operations; higher efficiency of the procurement process itself; and improvements in the transparency of government procurement markets and their processes.

Although there are overlaps among these three categories of savings, each category offers distinct benefits. In some bidding processes, for example, full transparency before or during the process might endanger competition if signaling and reputation among incumbents in a process affects the influence of new entrants. Transparency usually increases efficiency but does not always do so. Operational, or transaction costs, savings are different from efficiencies in the procurement process itself that might allow enhanced competition over a broader market. Some, but not all, enhancements to competition are attributable to transparency. The benefits of e-procurement depend upon variables such as type of operation; the goods or services involved; the sophistication of the counterparts (suppliers and public agencies); and time (due to network externalities). Private firms such

39. Bureau of Economic Analysis (2000a, tables 307, 308). Numbers adjusted by the Consumer Price Index.

Table 8-5. *Government Procurement Expenditures*
Billions of 1999 dollars

Expenditure	1995	1996	1997	1998	1999
GDP	8,114	8,291	8,679	9,026	9,299
Government consumption					
expenditure and investment	1,492	1,509	1,543	1,569	1,628
Government procurement	482	498	518	539	584
Federal defense	172	174	169	166	177
Federal nondefense	39	42	45	48	56
State and local	271	283	304	324	351

Source: Bureau of Economic Analysis (2000a, tables 307, 308). Numbers adjusted by CPI.

as FreeMarkets.com and SupplierMarket.com report overall average savings of approximately 20 percent for web-based procurement activities. Goldman Sachs estimates product cost savings from electronic markets of 2 to 39 percent, depending upon the industry segment involved.[40] As of February 12, 2001, FreeMarkets.com claims to have generated $2.7 billion in savings to its customers from a total market volume of $14.0 billion.[41]

One scenario of the adoption of online procurement in government follows. The early adopters, attracted by potential cost savings, are likely to be bigger buyers, not only in number of operations but also in value. In a second stage of development, joint operations might be developed between state and local governments, obtaining higher efficiency rates. For example, Washington State focuses in its strategic e-government plan on interaction and integration between the state and local governments. Similarly, Massachusetts is actively pursuing a regional procurement consortium, called EMall. The state estimated unitary operational savings for one procurement operation as follows: the paper-based operation took 265 minutes at a cost of $110.37; processing using electronic data interchange (EDI) required 120 minutes and cost $49.98; web-based procurement using EMall required only 25 minutes and cost $10.25.[42] Low-cost operations are likely to continue being performed as usual. Thus, given gains in efficiency and purchasing power, high-value operations are estimated in

40. Goldman Sachs, "B2B: 2B or Not 2B?" Version 1.2: the Tech Conference Edition, Feb. 24, 2000, p. 4. New York.
41. www.freemarkets.com/enter_marketplace.asp (February 12, 2001).
42. Commonwealth of Massachusetts (1999, table 6, p. I-42).

this scenario to be adopted more rapidly. If such adoption is not the case, efficiency gains would be smaller.

Figures produced by Goldman Sachs analysts estimate "government spending to businesses," a category somewhat different from procurement operations given above, at $1.65 trillion in 1998, with only 0.3 percent of these transaction on the Internet in that year. They project that government spending to businesses will grow to $2.09 trillion, of which 4.5 percent will be online by 2004.[43] Using the Goldman Sachs growth projection, a 7 percent discount rate, and a 20 percent savings rate, a rough estimate of cost savings from G2B activities from 2000 to 2004 is $13.44 billion, or $2.69 billion annualized, which represents 0.03 percent of GDP. (All figures are in 1999 dollars.)

Adding these cost savings for G2B to those for G2C tax processing online yields estimated cost savings with a net present value of $59.78 billion from 2000 to 2004, or $11.96 billion annualized. These highly conservative estimated cost savings represent 0.13 percent of GDP. They do not include savings from G2C nontax transactions or several efficiencies gained from, for example, the use of geographic information systems. If those are added and if G2C savings are higher, the cost savings estimate could easily double or triple in size.

Government to Government: Convergence in the Public Sector

In addition to the savings reported for G2C and G2B channels, major efficiencies are anticipated from the development of G2G relationships. In fact, some of the more substantial savings are likely to fall into this category. These institutional developments, as noted previously, will take longer to negotiate, and the resultant savings are more difficult to measure because they derive from organizational and structural changes, the counterpart of structural changes in an industry sector, rather than from relatively simpler business process redesign along a short segment of the value chain. The adoption of e-government in its G2G dimension will be pulled forward by the success of G2C and G2B, but G2G integration implies institutional complexities and political challenges that are more difficult than those at the other two levels.

---

43. Goldman Sachs, "B2B: 2B or Not 2B?" Version 1.2: the Tech Conference Edition, Feb. 24, 2000, table 6, p. 10. New York.

The natural next step of G2C applications—and an innovation already taking place—is to graduate from websites oriented to type of service to portals oriented to "type of customer." Well-functioning portals, as discussed earlier, require back-end integration and significant cooperation, or social capital, within networks of agencies and programs.[44] Development of G2G capacity will require greater technological, managerial, and political readiness than is currently found in many agencies and governments. Current constraints on G2G development include the following: institutional stovepipes, or silos, reflected in oversight and budget processes that maintain incentives for autonomous operations; administrative independence of federal, state, and local governments, which implies that executives face contradictory political interests in their environments; and legal restrictions regarding information sharing for some key organizations (such as the Internal Revenue Service). Moreover, public concern remains high regarding privacy and security of citizen and firm data in forms that are integrated and manipulated across agencies and on the web.

Few data are available to estimate the economic impact of G2G, which is an additional obstacle to its development. Reliable information and accurate data are needed for both policy and decisionmaking processes. Major cost savings with respect to G2G initiatives will lie in avoiding duplication of information gathering, updating, and storage within networks of programs and agencies; reducing mailing and paper storage of information sent and received; and saving time and resources by more efficient service. It is highly likely that G2G integration and consolidation would lead to downsizing. Despite serious obstacles—and a truism in policy studies that interagency coordination is inordinately difficult—a surprising number of partnerships across agency boundaries indicates a growing readiness and ability to engage the benefits of G2G arrangements. In fact, cross-agency systems offer one of the most exciting and promising developments in government with the promise not only of cost savings, but also of the ability to solve otherwise intractable policy problems that fall inherently between the boundaries of agencies.

A recent federal experiment, the International Trade Data System, demonstrated the dramatic efficiency gains possible to government and business from greater integration of the sixty-three federal agencies with jurisdiction over some aspect of the trade administration process. A more integrated, streamlined trade system has become a necessary adjunct to

---

44. Fountain (1998).

just-in-time, global business processes. But this experiment, currently stalled, also demonstrates the vast political and bureaucratic struggles that lie on the horizon as governments attempt to restructure at deeper levels to gain efficiencies of e-government.[45]

Other economic effects of e-government have not yet been considered. As government actors begin to exploit G2G integration, the efficiencies that result are likely to produce reductions in assets owned and rented by public agencies. It may not be necessary for governments to maintain as many separate local offices of various agencies. The types of co-location and service integration projects that have been continuing in government for more than a decade, before the use of the Internet, will be catalyzed by the potential of the Internet for consolidation, rationalization, and integration.

Regardless of the extent to which e-government is developed and managed by public units or outsourced to third parties, labor force reductions are likely in the public sector given the current political and cultural antipathy toward government. Productivity estimates are difficult to calculate, in part, because deep downsizing in government during the past decade has put many units below adequate staffing levels. Thus, some of the productivity gains from e-government will be used to restore capacity in services and activities that require people rather than automation. For example, many regulatory agencies currently lack enough qualified employees to carry out inspection and enforcement functions. In other cases, programs have been understaffed in anticipation of expected productivity gains from information technologies. Thus, some productivity gains have already been anticipated and employee cuts made.

Finally, in a networked environment, policymakers must consider the significant political and financial risks associated with failures in some of the network's major nodes. Recent alarming events in financial networks readily convey the types of risks inherent in networked government.[46]

Measuring Readiness for E-Government

To analyze the economic impact of information and communications technologies in government, it is necessary to discuss, at least briefly, the

---

45. See Fountain (2001c) for a detailed case analysis of the International Trade Data System and its development.

46. For an analysis of networked computing and its risks, see Rochlin (1997).

elements of readiness for e-government development. Three different levels of readiness may be considered in the strategy of development for any e-government project. These dimensions are expressed in terms of the levels of technological, managerial, and political readiness of any public sector's subsystem target for an e-government project. These levels of readiness will influence the time and shape of efforts to introduce web-based services and transactions. Technological readiness is a necessary but not a sufficient precursor to e-government development. Management and political readiness influence whether a project will be undertaken at all and, if so, how it will be developed and managed. Here "readiness" represents a number of institutional variables.

Technological readiness should be understood as both internal and external. External readiness is defined as access to and quality of Internet use for constituencies. Internal readiness refers to the agency's technological infrastructure and the technical skills of its work force.[47] Government salary structures make it hard to compete for technically qualified workers, especially at the local level of government. Constituencies with different levels of expectations, sophistication, education, or income, among other variables, present different interests and drive different priorities for e-government projects. In addition, the quality of an agency's information and communication technology infrastructure and overall skill level are critical inputs to make-or-buy decisions.

Managerial readiness encompasses an agency's internal capacity, including the quality and sophistication of internal operations. This area of readiness may be understood broadly to include the efficiency and effectiveness of the supply chain, the characteristics of the agency's culture, its capacity to adapt to and manage change, and other features. Independent of technical readiness, an agency that is well managed is likely to have a higher probability of success implementing either internal or outsourced e-government solutions.

Political readiness points to the political feasibility of e-government projects. Political variables that affect readiness include perceptions and inter-

---

47. This model for e-government has been adapted from frameworks in the field of strategic analysis and, in the public sector, from Sebenius and Lax (1986) and Moore (1995). For a detailed description, see Osorio-Urzua (1999) and Information Technologies Group, Center for International Development at Harvard University, "Readiness for the Networked World: A Guide for Developing Countries" (www.readinessguide.org).

ests of public servants, potential labor cuts generated by e-government development, administrative turnover or changes in executive direction, the desire of political actors to be associated with e-government, budgetary resources and directions, orientation to long- versus short-term results, and public perception about an initiative. In this context, the effect of programs like the National Performance Review has been critical for generation of managerial and political readiness for e-government. Large-scale reform efforts at all levels of government during the past fifteen years have generated conceptual, managerial, and technological arrangements in which e-government has become feasible. These reform movements have contributed to a political and managerial environment focused on public sector effectiveness, responsiveness to constituents, modernization and greater rationalization of government operations, and the use of information technology to modernize and enhance government.

The failure rate of government information technology projects has been estimated by Todd Ramsey, IBM's worldwide head of government services, at approximately 85 percent in the sense that the projects take longer to implement, have higher costs, and deliver less than expected.[48] The major reason for this failure rate derives, in part, from lack of alignment among technological, managerial, and political variables in the government sector. It also derives from the need to produce and deliver services, in the absence of a pricing structure, to the entire population rather than to a carefully selected and "educated" market segment.[49] What is less widely reported, however, is that major information technology projects in the private sector typically run over budget and schedule as well, in large part because of the complexities involved in integrating new technologies with existing organizational systems and processes.

Thus, the efficiency criterion provides only a minimal basis for evaluation of the desirability and feasibility of electronic government. Serious, unresolved, barely analyzed issues regarding the ownership, security, and privacy of citizen and business data; Internet penetration in the population; interest groups; differing capacities among public agencies; and private support for government versus downsizing of the public sector, among others, will continue to affect the development and shape—and, hence, the efficiency gains—of e-government.

48. "Government and the Internet," *The Economist*, June 24, 2000.
49. Fountain (2001b).

Conclusions

To reiterate the opening of this chapter, American government is in the early stages of deep transformation as a result of the Internet and a host of related developments in information and communication technologies. Examples of significant cost savings are growing in number as institutional changes continue in the production and delivery of government information and services. Deeper organizational and institutional restructuring of government is likely to be negotiated more slowly than the adoption of web-based applications that function largely at the boundary of agencies. But this restructuring has the potential to generate further cost savings to government.

In this chapter we distinguished between early-stage innovations in boundary-spanning functions producing efficiency gains in information provision and service delivery and later-stage, deeper transformation of internal government agency and cross-agency structures and processes, predicting that the latter are likely to play out over the next twenty years rather than at Internet speed. We also focused on the quantifiable cost savings to government of web-based service delivery systems rather than on the more difficult-to-quantify benefits to corporate and private citizens from interacting with government over the net. Annualized cost savings to the government sector of as much as $12 billion are not unreasonable to expect. It would not be surprising if the savings were significantly higher given the volume of transactions and the administrative and information-processing intensity of government. Yet several obstacles, noted in this chapter, are likely to affect efficiency gains and unproblematic development of digital government. Under the general term, "readiness," we included lack of funding for information infrastructure development, privacy and security challenges, bureaucratic politics, insufficient technical expertise in government, and unresolved normative challenges regarding the appropriate role of the private sector in the development and management of digital government. With respect to the final challenge, the current pricing structures for private development of e-government provide substantial profits to the private sector and have been insufficiently analyzed and scrutinized by governments.

Fundamental, normative questions of governance and state structure are raised by e-government. Will e-government empower democratization and decentralization? If it does, what then are the effects on demand for infrastructure, information, services, and interactivity? These types of questions, at the boundary between abstract theory and concrete institutional structure and process, have been virtually ignored in treatments of electronic government. Yet they are vitally important.

A critical set of policy questions bears on the nature of public-private partnerships and their appropriate role in the design, development, management, control, and, in some respects, the ownership of e-government. Related to concerns regarding privacy and security are a new set of questions regarding the ownership, control, use, and manipulation of what has traditionally been government data. A recent Supreme Court case enjoined government from selling some types of government data to private firms. The current legal structure is inadequate as a framework for e-government. Studies of privatization do not take into account the environment and risks posed by the Internet. Governments must be careful, in their zeal to modernize, not to unwittingly betray the public interest. It will remain the province of public servants and elected officials to forge long-term policies that guard the interests of citizens, even when those policies seem inefficient or lacking in strategic power.

Private sector firms have aggressively targeted government as a lucrative, enormous market to be tapped for the sale of e-solutions. Economic incentives in the private sector lead rapidly to the generation of quick, often useful solutions and applications that should not be ignored by governments. But information architecture, both hardware and software, is more than a technical tool; it is a form of governance. The outsourcing of architecture is, in effect, the outsourcing of policy decisions. Economic and competitive processes that drive product development and marketing in the information technology industry must not substitute for—or be confused with—the far-reaching obligations of policymaking.

References

Bureau of Economic Analysis. 2000a. "Government Expenditures and Gross Investment by Type (1959–1999)." U.S. Department of Commerce (www.bea.doc.gov/bea/dn/seltabs.exe [July 10, 2000]).
———. 2000b. *National Accounts Data.* U.S. Department of Commerce.
Commonwealth of Massachusetts. Office of the Comptroller, Operational Services Division, Information Technology Division. 1999. "Pilot Project Evaluation: A Multi-State Cooperative Procurement System on the Internet." Boston. October.
Fountain, Jane E. 1998. "Social Capital: A Key Enabler of Innovation." In *Investing in Innovation: Creating a Research and Innovation Policy That Works*, edited by L. M. Branscomb and J. H. Keller. MIT Press.

————. 1999. "The Virtual State? Toward a Theory of Federal Bureaucracy in the 21st Century." In *Democracy.com?: Governance in a Networked World,* edited by Elaine Ciulla Kamarck and Joseph S. Nye Jr. Hollis, N.H.: Hollis Press.

————. 2001a. "Digital Government: A View from the States." Working paper, John F. Kennedy School of Government, Harvard University, Cambridge, Mass.

————. 2001b. "Paradoxes of Public Sector Customer Service." *Governance* 14 (1).

————. 2001c. *Building the Virtual State: Information Technology and Institutional Change.* Brookings.

Joint Economic Committee. U.S. Congress. 2000. "Tax Complexity Fact Book." April.

Lessig, Lawrence. 1999. *Code and Other Laws of Cyberspace.* Basic Books.

Moore, Mark. 1995. *Creating Public Value.* Harvard University Press.

Nie, Norman H., and Lutz Erbring. 2000. "Internet and Society: A Preliminary Report." Stanford Institute for the Quantitative Study of Society. Stanford University. February 17 (www.stanford.edu/group/siqss/Press_Release/Preliminary_Report.pdf [February 16, 2001]).

Osorio-Urzua, Carlos A. 1999. "Alignment of Readiness Factors." John F. Kennedy School of Government, Harvard University, Cambridge, Mass.

————. 2000. "Patterns of Adoption of E-Government." John F. Kennedy School of Government, Harvard University, Cambridge, Mass. May.

Rochlin, Gene. 1997. *Trapped in the Net: The Unanticipated Consequences of Computerization.* Princeton University Press.

Sebenius, James, and David Lax. 1986. *The Manager as Negotiator.* Free Press.

Secretariat on Electronic Commerce. 1998. "The Emerging Digital Economy." U.S. Department of Commerce (www.ecommerce.gov/EmergingDig.pdf [August 14, 2000]).

Sharrard, Jeremy, and others. 2000. *Sizing US eGovernment.* Forrester Report. Cambridge, Mass.: Forrester Research (August).

Susskind, Lawrence E., and Jane Fountain Serio, eds. 1983. *Proposition 2 1/2: Its Impact on Massachusetts.* Cambridge, Mass.: Oelgeschlager, Gunn, and Hain.

U.S. Census Bureau. 1999. "Statistical Abstract of the United States," section 9, State and Local Government Finances and Employment.

U.S. General Accounting Office. 2000a. "Information Security: Serious and Widespread Weaknesses Persist at Federal Agencies." GAO/AIMD-00-295. September.

————. 2000b. "Internet Privacy: Comparison of Federal Agency Practices with FTC's Fair Information Principles." GAO-01-113T. October.

U.S. General Services Administration. 1999. "Governmentwide Registration Services: Domain Manager's Annual Report, FY 1999."

9

AUSTAN GOOLSBEE

Higher Education: Promises for Future Delivery

ALTHOUGH THE EDUCATIONAL sector is not a business in the conventional sense, there has been tremendous interest in the role of the Internet and of electronic commerce as they relate to educational spending. This interest has taken two forms: the supply of education online through for-profit Internet start-ups and the demand for Internet technology and access on the part of nonprofit public schools.

Educational spending in the United States was projected to total about $772 billion in 2000, making it the second largest industry in the country, at about 9 percent of GDP.[1] Although most of this spending was for non-profit and government-run educational institutions, there has been a marked trend toward for-profit education in the past two decades, and an increasing amount of distance education.

The sometimes awkward relationship between the Internet and education has grown rapidly in both the supply and the demand directions. This chapter examines these two sides of the Internet education market, focusing on what has happened thus far and where it may be going. Its overall

I wish to thank Robert Litan and members of the Brookings conference on the Internet economy for helpful comments, and the Alfred P. Sloan Foundation, the National Science Foundation, the American Bar Foundation, and the Robert P. Reuss/Centel Fellowship at the University of Chicago for financial support.

1. Urdan and Weggen (2000), p. 5.

theme is that the growth of the educational Internet has been rapid throughout the educational system, but that due to the nature of the product, the impact on educational productivity is likely to be fairly modest over the next several years, except in certain niche areas, such as information technology (IT) training and executive education.

After presenting a brief overview of the benefits and the costs to learning online compared with conventional instruction, I examine the for-profit supply side of education on the Internet and discuss the likely productivity effects in three segments: general distance education, corporate training, and executive and business education. I then examine the demand side of educational Internet technology in the school system, documenting the rapid spread of Internet access in schools but also its lack of integration into the curriculum.

Costs and Benefits of Online Education

A brief evaluation of the pros and cons of the Internet as a medium for education makes it easier to understand which segments are amenable to online education, as well as the types problems that can occur.[2]

The most obvious benefit from Internet education and training is the convenience. Students do not need to travel and can take the classes according to their own schedules—so-called asynchronous learning—substantially reducing the opportunity cost of education and offering an appealing approach to introverted students or students not confident in their spoken language skills. A second major benefit is that if done properly, Internet education is completely scalable, with very low marginal cost. Education providers can potentially reach large audiences cheaply. Third, the Internet and computer training in general is very good for teaching automated tasks, when it might be expensive to pay teachers to cover repetitive lessons over and over again. Albeit with considerable investment in course development, it is possible to create problem- or simulation-based content that can teach very effectively.

The most obvious downside of Internet education is that at present it has very low bandwidth, even when compared with other forms of distance learning, such as video or CD-ROM, and certainly much less than

2. This analysis is akin to that of C. J. DeSantis, "What Are the Pros and Cons of e-Learning?" (www.elearners.com/elearning/q2b.asp [September 5, 2000]).

live instruction. This should give pause to anyone planning to start an online educational venture by putting lectures on the web. Second, although the marginal replication cost of Internet education content is low, it can be very costly and time consuming to create, thus limiting the profitability of customized instruction. If a school does not invest in the enhanced form of performance- or simulation-based learning but instead puts its regular reading materials online or puts up streaming video of lectures, content retention is substantially worse than in conventional education. Third, although proponents claim that the Internet can enhance interaction between students, in practice, such interaction is minimal.[3] Subjects based primarily on discussion and interaction are not well suited to online instruction at this time.

Fourth, identity can pose problems, since with existing technology it is difficult to prevent cheating, dropping out, or other negative outcomes when the student is at a distance. Finally, a large segment of the U.S. population does not have a computer and has no Internet access, limiting the inherent market for Internet education. Moreover, appealing directly to customers online has proven an expensive proposition, and many customers have shown reluctance to pay for products online.

Given these costs and benefits, one can suggest which segments of the education sector are most amenable to Internet education.[4] The Internet is likely to have its most successful impact on education in areas, for example, where students are employed, and so value time flexibility; where content does not need to be highly customized; where personal instruction would involve travel; and where students are computer literate.

The Supply Side: Internet Education Ventures in Various Segments

Throughout the twentieth century, when the returns to schooling have risen, the demand for education has typically risen significantly.[5] The 1980s and 1990s were no exception. The skilled worker wage premium grew dramatically, and this fueled a rise in all types of education, and especially for distance and for-profit educational providers who cater to older

3. This claim is put forward by Urdan and Weggen (2000), p. 10. For empirical evidence to the contrary, see Dalton and others (2000).

4. In similar vein, De Figueiredo (2000) determines which online products will be successful.

5. See Goldin (1999) for a discussion of the history of schooling in the United States.

Table 9-1. *Postsecondary Schools by Profit Status*
Percent

Profit status	All postsecondary	Four year	Two year	Less than two years
For-profit	48	8	34	86
Nonprofit	15	22	21	7
Public	36	70	45	7

Source: Close and Hum (2000).

students and to students who require more job-oriented instruction. Employers, recognizing the value of higher skilled employees, have driven spending on corporate training to all-time highs. The shift toward higher educational demands on the job is clear.[6]

Total spending on education and training in the United States in 2000 is estimated at $772 billion, of which $40 billion is for child care, $386 billion for K–12, $268 for postsecondary education, $12 billion for continuing education, and $66 billion for corporate training.[7] The largest category is K–12 spending, but this is unlikely to shift toward the Internet in any serious way over the next five years. The same is true for child care spending. This leaves the postsecondary education, continuing education, and corporate training markets as the leading targets for Internet education start-ups.

Over the next ten years, the number of people seeking postsecondary education is expected to rise by almost 2 million, many of whom will be looking at for-profit and distance education.[8] Table 9-1 shows that for-profit companies already account for a large share of postsecondary institutions: almost half overall, with the highest rates being in the two-year and continuing education (less than two years) segments.[9] Further, even the number of nonprofits that provide distance education is growing. A study by the National Center for Education Statistics (NCES) suggests that in 1998, about one-third of two- and four-year postsecondary institutions offered some kind of distance education.[10]

6. Using Bureau of Labor Statistics data, Wit Capital Group (1999) claims that the share of unskilled workers in the U.S. economy fell from 45 percent in 1991 to only 15 percent today.

7. Urdan and Weggen (2000).

8. Close and Hum (2000), p. 13.

9. Close and Hum (2000).

10. National Center for Education Statistics (1999).

General Distance Education

The greatest activity relating to online education has been in distance education versions of the basic two- and four-year college experience. The NCES report on distance learning in 1998 indicates that there were 1,680 colleges and universities with distance education programs, and an additional 990 planned to start such a program in the next three years. There were 1.66 million students enrolled in all distance education programs, 1.08 million of whom were in undergraduate courses. This represented a 120 percent increase in enrollments since the previous NCES report, for 1996.[11] The International Data Corporation (IDC) forecasts that the number of distance education students will rise by more than 1 million from 1999 to 2002.[12] Although it is growing quickly, it is worth noting that this is still only about 0.05 percent of the total student body in the United States.[13]

Simultaneous with, and probably contributing to, this increase in distance education has been a major shift toward using the Internet in distance instruction. The share of distance education institutions that use the Internet for some aspect of their courses had risen from 14 percent in 1995 to 58 percent in 1998.[14] The Internet appears to give these programs the ability to reach wider audiences.

One issue that all the Internet education start-ups must confront, however, is the limited pedagogical success of several other media used in distance education in recent years: videotape, television, and CD-ROM. Each of these was touted as a new way to deliver content to the educational consumer—a star teacher lecturing on videotape, for example, was thought to be superior to a mediocre teacher lecturing in person. Their success, however, has only been moderate; distance education is still a small segment of the overall market. The Internet has even lower bandwidth than these technologies, so its ability to supplant other methods may be limited. Indeed, although the NCES survey found that 58 percent of distance education courses used the Internet, it found that half also rely on videotapes and more than half use videoconferencing. And while 82 percent of them say they intend to increase the amount of Internet instruction, 61 percent say they also intend to increase the amount of videoconferencing.[15] In this

11. NCES (1997, 1999).
12. Laurie Carr, "College Off-Campus," *Industry Standard*, September 13, 2000, p. 118.
13. Urdan and Weggen (2000).
14. NCES (1999).
15. NCES (1999).

sense, the Internet may be viewed as just another input into a typical distance learning course.

In fact, shifting to general distance education online presents some major difficulties. First, it is quite expensive to create problem- and simulation-based classes, so most insititutions have just been using the Internet to post reading materials, problem sets, and the like from existing courses. Yet there is evidence that reading retention from online material is about 30 percent lower than from books.[16]

Second, the difficulty of identifying students online inherently limits the ability of Internet education programs to move up the quality ladder. For the most part, the successful distance education firms are lower market educational or hybrid institutions, for example, the University of Northern Colorado, the University of Phoenix, Capella University, and Kaplan University. It will be difficult for an Internet-based program to achieve the kind of prestige held by institutions such as Yale and Harvard until one can be sure of who is turning in the work.

In addition, the dark side of the identity question is that the types of students getting education at for-profit institutions are noticeably higher risks than traditional students, which threatens the accreditation process and various types of federal funding—both of which are affected by high student loan default rates and high dropout rates—for these schools. Richard Close and Robert Hum show that among postsecondary schools, the student loan default rate at for-profit institutions is almost double the national average. Their discussion also indicates that students at these for-profit schools sue over placement and education issues with disturbingly high frequency.[17]

Third, it is not easy to create the community aspect of a standard college environment online. Fathom.com, an alliance of the Smithsonian, the New York Public Library, the British Library, and the London School of Economics, is trying to do just that, but the low bandwidth of the Internet and the inability of students to get together limit the chances of success.[18]

Finally, even as the Internet is increasingly being used for distance education, it is worth considering whether it will have much effect on educational productivity. According to most analyses (though many were conducted before the Internet existed), distance education is at best equally

16. Dalton and others (2000).
17. Close and Hum (2000).
18. See Vincent Kiernan, "A For-Profit Web Venture Seeks to Replicate the University Experience Online," *Chronicle of Higher Education,* April 14, 2000.

effective as instructor-based education, and many clearly feel that it is worse.[19] In most cases, there is little cost advantage, other than in relation to travel, to taking a distance education course. The NCES data for 1998 indicate that 77 percent of the institutions with distance education programs charged the same tuition for those courses as for their conventional classes, 6 percent charged more, and only 3 percent charged less.[20] Thus for general distance education, the use of the Internet probably costs about the same for tuition (slightly less counting travel), but it provides content that is somewhat inferior to conventional instruction. The total effect on productivity probably is not very large. At best, Internet education may dominate the distance education segment of the market, but it will likely have significant problems cutting into the market for conventional instruction.

Business Education

Postgraduate business education is one of the segments most in demand in the current educational environment and it presents some distinct differences from the problems of general distance learning discussed above. First the buyer is typically the student's employer, which limits the customer acquisition costs and financial defaults. It also makes it easier to establish a reputation for quality—an institution can say, "Our courses have been used by IBM, Microsoft," and so on. Most of the students are busy, want to avoid taking time off from work, and currently have to travel to get similar education from a traditional program. Frequently the demand for this type of education is to learn some basic knowledge area, such as accounting, rather than to get a degree. The NCES data for 1998 show that 55 percent of institutions offering any distance education offer business courses.[21] This amounted to almost 20 percent of all two- and four-year postsecondary institutions in the country, so the current market seems ripe for an Internet approach.

Several Internet start-ups have targeted this segment: some are run by offline business schools, some are pure-play Internet firms that form alliances for content, and some are online firms that create their own content. Pensare and UNEXT.com, for example, have each contracted with leading business schools to help provide content and then create learning

---

19. See Phipps, Wellman, and Merisotis (1998).
20. NCES (1999). Fourteen percent had varying tuition rates.
21. NCES (1999).

environments based on that content.[22] Both companies employ instructors to facilitate discussion and try to encourage "community" among students on the site. UNEXT also intends to offer degree programs through its Cardean University brand. The two companies have signed up customers from major companies such as IBM, Fujitsu, and Unisys, though most of their courses are still in testing stages. Multinational firms provide a particularly good market for such products, since they often have English-speaking students stationed far from offline business schools.

The cost of taking an online course from Pensare is estimated to be around $300 to $600 per student, with volume-based discounts available.[23] At this price, the courses are likely to cost less than half as much as a comparable unit at an executive education center. *Forbes* estimates the cost of a UNEXT course at 80 percent of a comparable instructor-led M.B.A. class.[24] There do seem to be cost savings in this area, independent of travel expenses.

These programs aim to create content that is explicitly problem- and simulation-based rather than merely based on video lectures and online readings. This is likely to greatly improve the quality of these courses compared with standard distance education, and in some areas it may even be better than conventional methods. One study of simulation-based Internet education on accounting at Harvard Business School finds that training times were reduced by 50 percent and scores significantly improved relative to conventional instruction.[25] If this is so, the Internet stands to be a major productivity enhancement to the executive education market. However, it can cost more than $1 million to create one of these courses.[26] The simulation- or problem-based approach is easier in fields that lend themselves to quantitative problems, such as finance and accounting, than in softer subjects, such as organizational behavior or ethics.

One interesting competitor to these online executive programs is the new Global Executive Program at Duke University's Fuqua School of

22. Pensare has allied with Harvard Business School publishing, the Fuqua School of Business at Duke University, the Wharton School at the University of Pennsylvania, and the Annenberg Center at the University of Southern California. UNEXT has allied with Stanford University, Columbia University, the University of Chicago, the London School of Economics, and Carnegie-Mellon University.

23. Urdan and Weggen (2000).

24. "Higher Education," *Forbes.com Best of the Web,* September 11, 2000, pp. 307–11.

25. Dalton and others (2000).

26. Arlyn Tobias Gajilan, "An Education Revolution," *Fortune Small Business,* November 29, 2000.

Business. This hybrid program is taught by the same faculty as the regular M.B.A. program, but many of the classes are conducted online. In addition to the online requirements, however, students must spend some time in residence, and the tuition is higher than for a traditional M.B.A. This residence requirement gives the Duke program the potential to create community and raise its perceived quality, but it also prevents the model from being scalable. It will be interesting to see if the Fuqua School will have sufficient incentive to develop the expensive simulation- and problem-based learning environments needed for good online instruction when it cannot resell that content to tens of thousands of students at low marginal cost. It seems likely it will be difficult for hybrid classroom-Internet models to become widespread for this reason.

Corporate IT Training

Another clear market for Internet education is computer-related training for corporations. Spending on corporate training exceeded $62 billion in 1999, and IT training accounted for about 50 percent of that total.[27] In terms of Internet education, this area has many of the same advantages as executive education, with the further benefit that the workers and the subject matter are, by definition, closely related to computer technology. Some have gone so far as to argue that IT workers are *more* comfortable with computer-based training than they are with human teachers.

There is a fair amount of anecdotal evidence about the use of Internet-based IT training at high-technology firms such as Cisco Systems and Sun Microsystems. The data suggest, however, that in 1999 Internet-delivered training represented only about 8 percent of corporate IT training, while instructor-led training still accounted for more than 70 percent, even of computer training.[28] Data on effectiveness are difficult to come by, but fragmentary evidence suggests that IT training online may represent a productivity improvement. John Dalton and others (2000) report that in interviews with training managers at major companies, two-thirds of respondents say that the main benefit from online training is cost savings, albeit largely through reduced travel costs. Trace Urdan and Cornelia

27. Corporate training spending is from *Training Magazine* (1999); IT training, from Urdan and Weggen (2000).

28. Internet data are from Urdan and Weggen (2000); instructor data, from *Training Magazine* (1999).

Weggen claim savings of 50 to 70 percent for Internet-based training compared with instructor-led training.[29] Outside the IT area, though, Internet training is unlikely to be as successful. Training managers report dropout rates from online programs as high as 80 percent.[30] These courses are apparently much less effective, perhaps because the nature of the content cannot be easily adapted to an online format.

One firm that has succeeded in the corporate IT training marketplace is DigitalThink. Its model is to provide fully web-delivered computer training for between $195 and $450 for four- to fifteen-hour courses. These prices are significantly lower than for a typical instructor-led course. DigitalThink has more than 200 courses on subjects such as C++ programming, MS Office applications, and the like. Since 1997 it has delivered 150,000 training courses to customers including Cisco Systems, Motorola, Intel, and many other companies.

Urdan and Weggen estimate that spending on online corporate training will rise from about $550 million in 1998 to about $11 billion in 2003.[31] This would be an extremely successful spread, but it is unlikely to have a dramatic effect on the overall productivity of training courses, since online training would still be only about 10 to 15 percent of the corporate training bill. Such growth in online corporate training would probably involve quite productive improvements to IT training, perhaps even coming to dominate that segment. But the total impact of the Internet on the quality of training outside of the IT area may continue to be quite small.

The Internet in Public Schools

Although rather far removed from the high-flying world of Internet education start-ups, thousands of public and private schools around the country are clamoring to increase the amount of Internet and computer technology in the classroom. The demand side of the Internet education market has become a major political issue in the last five years, with President Clinton and both candidates in the presidential election of 2000 pledging their support for various initiatives to increase the use of technology in the schools. Much of this push has been in the context of the so-

---

29. Dalton and others (2000); Urdan and Weggen (2000).
30. Dalton and others (2000).
31. Urdan and Weggen (2000).

called digital divide between information "haves" and "have-nots," which often seems to break along income and racial lines.[32]

In 1994 President Clinton called for all public schools to be wired by 2000 and proposed a series of measures to help make that happen. The most important federal initiative has been the Universal E-Rate program, passed under the Telecommunications Act of 1996 and operated through the Federal Communications Commission. This program established subsidies of 20 to 90 percent for school and library access to the Internet—with the largest reserved for low-income schools—funded by a regulatory charge on long-distance telephone service.[33] Spending on this subsidy has totaled more than $2 billion per year. Compared with total computer spending (including hardware, software, training, networking, service) in public schools of $3.3 billion in 1999, the Universal E-Rate program has clearly been very large.[34] It is worth considering its impact on schools.

Effectiveness

It is generally not understood by the public how far this program has gone toward wiring schools. The shares of public schools and of instructional rooms with Internet access, based on data compiled by the National Center for Education Statistics, are reported in tables 9-2 and 9-3, respectively. In 1994, about one-third of public schools had Internet access and only 3 percent of public school instructional rooms had such access. By 1999, 95 percent of public schools had Internet access and the share of instructional rooms with access had increased more than twenty times, to 63 percent. Moreover, these data show that even among schools where over half the students are eligible for free or subsidized school lunches (that is, low-income locations), more than 90 percent have Internet access, although the very poorest schools have a noticeably smaller share of instructional rooms with Internet access. In this sense, then, it might be said that the wiring of schools is almost complete.

Given that success, however, it is worth considering how this spending on technology affects educational outcomes. Measured as an enhancement to the productivity of the educational system, the Internet may have only

---

32. See Walsh, Gazala, and Ham (2000).

33. This funding arrangement has not been without controversy. For a critique of the deadweight costs of the tax involved, see Hausman (1998).

34. David Lake, "Surfing at School," *Industry Standard,* September 12, 2000, p. 117.

Table 9-2. *Share of Public Schools with Internet Access*
Percent

Type of school	1994	1996	1998	1999
All public schools	35	65	89	95
Elementary	30	61	88	94
Secondary	49	77	94	98
Share of students eligible for free or reduced-price lunch				
0–10 percent	40	78	87	94
11–30 percent	39	72	94	96
31–49 percent	33	62	94	98
50–70 percent	31	53	88	96
71–100 percent	19	53	80	90

Source: National Center for Education Statistics (2000a).

subtle impacts. It is probably unrealistic to expect that giving an otherwise poor school Internet access will make the instruction significantly better, especially if the Internet is not integrated into the curriculum. Although almost two-thirds of teachers have used computers or the Internet for classroom instruction, less than half of these go beyond the simplest computer applications and actually use computers or the Internet for drills, projects,

Table 9-3. *Share of Public School Instructional Rooms with Internet Access*
Percent

Type of school	1994	1996	1998	1999
All public schools	3	14	51	63
Elementary	3	13	51	62
Secondary	4	16	52	67
Share of students eligible for free or reduced-price lunch				
0–10 percent	4	18	62	74
11–30 percent	4	18	53	71
31–49 percent	2	12	61	68
50–70 percent	4	12	40	62
71–100 percent	2	5	39	39

Source: NCES (2000a).

or multimedia presentations, for example.[35] And given the costs of installing and maintaining a school technology plan, it will be interesting to see whether schools maintain their Internet connections once the E-Rate program ends.[36]

There is also some question about the qualifications of teachers to instruct children in the use of computers. In a Department of Education survey of teachers, only one-third reported that they were well prepared or very well prepared to use computers and the Internet.[37] The share is notably lower among those with ten or more years of teaching experience. According to another recent study, most teachers are "novice or completely inexperienced."[38] In many schools, and especially in high schools, it is hard to imagine that the teachers know more about the Internet than the students already know themselves.

The next wave of investment in Internet education will need to be in the area of training teachers and incorporating technology into the curriculum. These investments may have larger educational payoffs but may be slow to spread. Without such training, the investments in Internet access are unlikely to pay major dividends in school productivity.

It would be easy to design experiments to assess the impact of Internet and computer access on test scores or academic performance. In fact, the Department of Education's technology planning handbook emphasizes that evaluation should be an important part of a technology plan, although in most places it is an afterthought.[39] Even without experiments, simply making such evaluation data available to researchers would allow for econometric tests. There has been little direct work on the impact of computer investments in the 1980s and 1990s on school performance, however, and any such analysis of the impact of the Internet may remain a pipe dream.

Given that school spending generally has little apparent impact on school outcomes, at first pass it may be hard to imagine spending on the Internet doing much better.[40] But it might, especially if it increases something as

35. See the data in NCES (2000b).
36. M. Hawkes (1998) has estimated, using 1995 data, that a school technology plan—computers and the Internet—would cost between $180 and $501 per student to install and would require ongoing spending of $40 to $105 per student to maintain.
37. NCES (2000b).
38. Blair Clarkson, "Ready or Not? Not," *Industry Standard,* September 12, 2000.
39. McNabb and others (1999).
40. See Hanushek (1996).

fundamental as a student's motivation to come to school. This is also not to say that the productivity effect is zero. Certainly, the Internet has given students access to some resources that they might otherwise not have had. There are now numerous online libraries, for example, which include millions of books that small school libraries could not carry. For a student wanting to read such materials, access to the Internet at school could be a boon, although how many actually use these resources is unknown.

Another small productivity enhancement is represented by state and federal clearinghouses of information, such as the Educational Resources Information Center (ERIC). This network catalogs, summarizes, and provides access to education information, through features such as AskERIC, an electronic question answering service for teachers; sixteen subject-specific clearinghouses; and the National Parent Information Network, which offers information to parents of school children. The database and ERIC document collections are housed in about 3,000 locations worldwide, including most major public and university library systems. ERIC also produces a variety of publications and provides user assistance. The capabilities may be several years ahead of consumer usage, but there are some potential benefits.

The Internet could also conceivably enhance productivity in back office functions for educational institutions, including the handling of student records, transfers of transcripts, and the like. As in the case of medical records, privacy issues may prevent a comprehensive conversion at the moment, but there are technologies that may develop on this front in the coming years that enable schools to exploit this approach more thoroughly.[41]

Conclusion

The educational sector is massive, regulated, and bureaucratic. In recent years there has been an explosion of interest in for-profit online educational ventures, as well as in the use of the Internet in public schools around the country. While there has been a great deal of activity, the impact of the Internet on educational productivity is likely to remain modest for the next several years, except in areas particularly amenable to the

41. See Zittrain (2000).

Internet, for example, in executive education and in corporate IT training. There is still a long way to go before the Internet can replace the typical college or junior college experience.

On the demand side, the spread of Internet access to public schools in the past five years has been quite dramatic, and access is now close to 100 percent. This is true in both rural and urban areas and is quite an accomplishment. The Internet's impact on school performance is likely to be modest, however, because teachers are generally not prepared to teach students Internet or computer skills, and the Internet has not been integrated well into the curriculum. It would be interesting to learn whether investment in information technology in poor-quality schools has a higher rate of return (in educational terms) than do other types of school spending.

On both the for-profit supply side and the public school demand side, one gets the sense that the forecasts might be very different fifteen years from now than they will be five years from now. In the near future, the Internet appears destined to be used increasingly in education, but not to have the potentially major impact that it could have in other sectors of the economy. Looking to the longer-term, the impact could be substantially greater, albeit much harder to quantify. The most promising development might be the diffusion of best-practice simulation-type training from private industry down into either vocational or standard classrooms. Further, given sufficient training or software development, teachers might be able to access learning programs designed specially for certain subsets of students who have difficulties in the typical classroom or whose interests are more specialized than a small rural school can accommodate. At that point, it is likely that the productivity gains to the Internet will spread throughout the education sector and raise educational productivity in general, rather than just in certain niches. That is the challenge that education poses for the Internet in the next twenty years.

References

Close, Rich, and Rob Hum. 2000. "Proprietary Higher Education: Intellectual Capital for the Knowledge Economy." SunTrust Equitable Securities (January).

Dalton, John P., and others. 2000. "Online Training Needs a New Course." Cambridge, Mass.: Forrester Research (August).

De Figueiredo, John. 2000. "Finding Sustainable Profitability in Electronic Commerce." *Sloan Management Review* 41 (4): 41–52.

Goldin, Claudia. 1999. "A Brief History of Education in the United States." Historical Working Paper H0119. Cambridge, Mass.: National Bureau of Economic Research.

Hanushek, Eric. 1996. "School Resources and Student Performance." In *Does Money Matter? The Effect of School Resources on Student Achievement and Adult Success,* edited by Gary Burtless. Brookings.

Hausman, Jerry. 1998. "Taxation by Telecommunications Regulation." In *Tax Policy and the Economy*, vol. 12, edited by James Poterba. MIT Press.

Hawkes, M. 1998. "Funding a Technology Network in Your School." *Schools in the Middle* (National Association of Secondary School Principals) 7 (5): 24–28.

"Industry Report, 1999." 1999. *Training Magazine* 36 (10): 37.

McNabb, M., and others. 1999. "Technology Connections for School Improvement: A Planner's Handbook." U. S. Department of Education, North Central Regional Educational Laboratory.

National Center for Education Statistics. 1997. "Distance Education in Higher Education Institutions." NCES 98-062. U.S. Department of Education, Office of Research and Improvement.

———. 1999. "Distance Education at Postsecondary Education Institutions: 1997–1998." NCES 2000-013. U.S. Department of Education, Office of Research and Improvement (December).

———. 2000a. "Internet Access in U.S. Public Schools and Classrooms: 1994–1999." NCES 2000-086. U.S. Department of Education, Office of Research and Improvement (February).

———. 2000b. "Teacher Use of Computers and the Internet in Public Schools." NCES 2000-090. U.S. Department of Education, Office of Research and Improvement (April).

Phipps, R., J. Wellman, and J. Merisotis. 1998. "Assuring Quality in Distance Learning: A Preliminary Review." Report for the Council of Higher Education Accreditation. Washington: Institutue for Higher Education Policy.

Urdan, Trace, and Cornelia Weggen. 2000. "Corporate E-Learning: Exploring a New Frontier." W. R. Hambrecht and Co. (March).

Walsh, Ekaterina, with Michael Gazala and Christine Ham. 2000. "The Truth about the Digital Divide." Research brief. Cambridge, Mass.: Forrester Research (April 11).

Wit Capital Group. 1999. "E-Knowledge—New Ways to Build the New Economy." Research report. New York (August 11).

Zittrain, Jonathan. 2000. "What the Publisher Can Teach the Patient: Property and Privacy in an Era of Trusted Systems." *Stanford Law Review* 52 (5): 1201–50.

Brookings Task Force
on the Internet

Co-organizers
Robert E. Litan
   Brookings Institution
Alice M. Rivlin
   Brookings Institution

Members
Joseph P. Bailey
University of Maryland

Enrique Canessa
University of Michigan

Eric K. Clemons
University of Pennsylvania

Patricia M. Danzon
University of Pennsylvania

Charles H. Fine
*Massachusetts Institute
   of Technology*

Jane E. Fountain
Harvard University

Michael F. Furukawa
University of Pennsylvania

Austan Goolsbee
University of Chicago

Lorin M. Hitt
University of Pennsylvania

Andrew McAfee
Harvard Business School

Will Mitchell
University of Michigan

Anuradha Nagarajan
University of Michigan

Carlos A. Osorio-Urzua
Harvard University

Daniel M. G. Raff
University of Pennsylvania

C. C. White III
University of Michigan

Index